Exhibits in Libraries

Exhibits in Libraries

A Practical Guide

MARY E. BROWN *and*
REBECCA POWER

McFarland & Company, Inc., Publishers
Jefferson, North Carolina, and London

LIBRARY OF CONGRESS CATALOGUING-IN-PUBLICATION DATA

Brown, Mary E. (Mary Esther)
Exhibits in libraries : a practical guide / Mary E. Brown and Rebecca Power.
p.   cm.
Includes bibliographical references and index.

ISBN 0-7864-2352-8 (softcover : 50# alkaline paper)

1. Library exhibits — Handbooks, manuals, etc.   I. Power, Rebecca, 1975–
II. Title.
Z717.B84   2006   021.7 — dc22   2005018508

British Library cataloguing data are available

On the cover: Two kids in the Science in the Stacks exhibit
(*photograph by Jon Gilbert Fox;* see page 203)

Manufactured in the United States of America

McFarland & Company, Inc., Publishers
Box 611, Jefferson, North Carolina 28640
www.mcfarlandpub.com

In memory of my father

mehb

To Joan Waltermire and Bob Raiselis

rp

Contents

Preface

MARY E. BROWN

We began our collaboration on this book with a grant proposal. But the work began before that. It began one afternoon in late spring 2003, when I sat with two colleagues (Harvey Feinberg, professor of history at Southern Connecticut State University, and Dorothy Woodson, curator of the African collection at Yale University Libraries) in Yorkside Pizza behind Yale's Sterling Memorial Library discussing the relationship between librarianship and curatorial studies and the need for librarians to be trained to curate cultural heritage. I took a number of ideas from that lunch into a conversation with colleague Jane Moore McGinn, associate professor of library science at Southern Connecticut State University, and began researching and writing. Just about the time I realized the initial ideas were not yet viable, the résumé of an entering master of library science student crossed my desk. From the ideas that took form from the lunch meeting with Harvey and Dorothy arose a modified idea, securely held together with the experience and expertise of Rebecca Power, who has been more of a colleague if not a mentor through this yearlong project. This book is the culmination of that work, which has been supported through a graduate school graduate assistantship awarded to Rebecca.

Our work began with focused interviews with museum directors. We wanted to know what are the minimum general skills necessary for an individual without museum training to mount a simple and effective exhibition. We soon realized that the questions we were asking were not exactly right and that we needed to broaden the audience to whom we asked the questions. Relying on Rebecca's knowledge and experience, we developed a more structured questionnaire for museum and library staffs, the results of which are reported in Chapter 1.

Our conclusions, after considering the literature, interviews, and survey results, were that a comprehensive how-to text and a workshop course were needed. We decided

1

to set about writing this book to cover, to some degree, both; Rebecca wrote the sections covering the exhibit process and I wrote the sections that cover exhibition theory, education theory, and the status of exhibits in libraries. Together we constructed a suggested syllabus for a workshop, course or a self-study alternative.

In the introduction we have provided a sense of the place and importance of exhibitions in libraries and the status of training in exhibition theory and techniques for librarians. We hope to foster an excitement about the potential for exhibitions to extend to a greater number of patrons, and access to the knowledge held in library collections.

In the section on exhibition theory we begin with a brief history of exhibitions and the relationship of exhibitions to libraries and museums. We then move on to the reasons for an exhibit, the mechanism of collecting objects, and a plan for collecting for and preparing exhibits. We conclude this section with some comments on the physical and cognitive load of exhibits on exhibitgoers.

In the section on learning theory we review overarching theories that can apply to all exhibit visitors and then focus on theories that focus on developmental level or age. After discussing learning in children and in adults, we discuss learning in a family unit.

In the section on the status of exhibits in libraries we look at the websites of major libraries in all 50 states and the District of Columbia for information that can be found on exhibits in the library. Through analysis of this information, we determine the visibility and extent of exhibits in libraries. Finally we look at professional competencies for librarians to establish the responsibility for exhibitions within librarianship.

Most of the book covers the process of creating an exhibit. Two sections are provided: The first is the basic ten-step exhibit process designed for beginners. The second is the comprehensive exhibit process and covers, step-by-step, everything a librarian or staff member might need to consider. The comprehensive process is divided into four parts, or stages, of exhibits: the beginning idea and preliminaries; development and design; fabrication; and installation to de-installation. Each part uses a structured format that addresses: taking stock of the situation; exhibit concerns; administration concerns, including funding, insurance, contracts, and security; programming; and public relations, including opening events. Part I, walks the reader through identifying goals and theme, possible locations and basic setup, budgeting, staff, and time considerations. Part II, covers writing the exhibit labels, prototyping the exhibit, and finishing the design and layout. Part III, includes identifying and purchasing materials, label fabrication, and preparing for installation. Part IV covers the installation process (including feeding volunteers), exhibit maintenance, evaluation and documentation of the exhibit, preparing for and de-installing the exhibit and storing reusable materials.

In the final sections we focus on special considerations of traveling exhibits and hands-on exhibits and discuss defining an exhibit program within the library. We include a short discussion on cataloguing library exhibits and provide three examples of the exhibit planning process. Finally, we present representative syllabi for an in-service workshop and a college course on exhibits in libraries as well as a self-study guide. The self-study guide includes suggestions for setting up and evaluating mentoring experiences in exhibit making. The continuing education guide includes a precourse needs assessment survey. A survey can be used to assess level of satisfaction, learning, individual benefit, and institutional benefit gained from study (self-study, continuing education, or graduate course) based on this book. Throughout we have included checklists, timelines and other resources to assist the librarian or staff member in mounting exhibits.

We hope this resource helps to strengthen the notion of exhibits as an essential component of a library's program of service. We also hope this resource makes library exhibit planning more efficient, effective, and enjoyable; and that our work enables more walls, display cases, tables, and rooms in libraries, whether academic, public, special, or school libraries, to be filled with exhibits that increase access to knowledge and understanding.

I wish to thank Sandra C. Holley, dean of the School of Graduate Studies at Southern Connecticut State University, whose leadership made possible the funding that supported, in part, Rebecca's work on this book. I thank my husband, Donald M. Brown, for his ongoing support of my many projects and for his ongoing editorial guidance.

meb · New Haven, Connecticut

REBECCA POWER

I can't thank Mary Brown enough for letting me assist in her research, an opportunity that grew into so much more: the co-authoring of this book and plenty of advice, laughs, and mutual procrastination. She has been a true mentor. I would also like to thank dean Sandra Holley for her support of the graduate school graduate assistants at Southern Connecticut State University.

The staff of the Montshire Museum of Science in Norwich, Vermont, has been a great help in the writing of this book. In particular I would like to thank Joan Waltermire and Bob Raiselis for their advice, editing, and all they have taught me. Thanks to Amy Vanderkooi for lending her hands to the project and Kevin Coburn for his help with photos.

A number of other museums and libraries have helped during this project. I greatly appreciate the generosity of Gloria Dosen of the East Chicago Public Library and Margaret Clark of the Kansas City Public Library in sharing their time and exhibit experience with me. Thanks also to Marjorie Power of the Barre Historical Society and Karen Lane of the Aldrich Public Library of Barre, Vermont, for their inspiration.

Without Heidi Schwartz, Jen Fowler, Kate and Casey Prestwood, and Elaine Allen I might not have made it through the first half of this book, and without Jeff, Kathy, Nathan, and Myra Parsonnet and Jonathan Lehr I might not have made it through the second half. Not to mention Marjorie Power, my mom, and Michael Power, my dad, without whom I would not have made it to either. Thank you.

rp · Montpelier, Vermont

1

Exhibits from Beginnings to Libraries

The word "exhibitions" conjures up memories and fantasies of World's Fairs, art museums, zoos, 4-H and county fairs, backyard shows, trade fairs, circuses, and sideshows. While we tend to associate exhibitions with more formal and adult pursuits, the activities of choosing, arranging and sharing items through display is also appealing to children. Planning for an exhibition can begin minutes or years in advance with budgets of millions of dollars or an inventory of a few trading cards or a collection of curios. Whether installed for the afternoon in the back yard or over acres of land for a week or years, exhibitions bring out in their visitors curiosity, wonder, a desire to explore, and delight in learning.

Recently we happened to observe a five- and a six-year-old collecting exclusive cards from inside boxes of fruit rolls and other snacks. The two children traded and gifted cards to complete each child's desired collection. They then carried rubber-banded packs to play dates where each child carefully unbound and displayed, in planned arrangements, those cards that related to the theme for the afternoon's playtime. It was as if the trading cards were tools that helped the children make sense of their thoughts, their play, and their imagined world. In the early and mid–twentieth century, two authors noted a street game called grotto, or grottoes, that was played by children in London. One author noted that grottoes was a May sport in which children created square, round, or heart-shaped decorative displays of "picture cards and oyster-shells and old scent bottles or anything else that looks pretty"[1]; the other author describes the flowers and "old curios and pieces of bric-a-brac" as "miniature exhibitions."[2] While one author attributes the children's efforts to "just a dodge for mumping halfpennies" from an adult passersby,[3] the other recognizes what matters in the game of grotto is in fact "the activity of showing" or of exhibition.[4] In this activity of showing, whether for "mumping

halfpennies" or as a seasonal pastime, the children turned their attention, as did the five-
and six-year-olds we observed, to collection, planning, and audience approval.

Sometimes we collect and display objects for the "wonder" of the collection, sometimes for the knowledge the collection contains. In the sixteenth century, exhibitions
"gathered by princes, popes, merchants, scholars and even tavern-keepers" were displayed
in Cabinets of Curiosity.[5] These exhibits varied in content with the interests and resources
of their collectors and might occupy the space of a small cabinet or of one or more large
rooms. The collection within a Cabinet of Curiosity might contain a wide-ranging set
of objects, such as plants, animals, rocks, minerals, fossils, cultural objects, artificial
works or products of technology, artworks, medals and plaques, and copies and casts.
Some collectors traded, gifted, sold, and shared their collections and objects within their
collections to increase the value or usefulness of each collection. The beginning of popular exhibitions is associated with fairs held for and by persons traveling for religious
observances. As a temporary means to purvey provisions to visitors, the fair became a
means of exchange not only of goods but also of social practices, ideas and information.

Against this background of the exhibition as a popular means to share in the pleas-
ures of display and viewing it is an easy step to consider exhibitions as a mechanism by
which libraries enhance their visitors' experience. Exhibitions can inspire curiosity, wonder, and delight, and initiate learning about the library's collection. Exhibitions, too,
can display rarities that draw in visitors who might not otherwise come into the library.
Much like subject headings for books, an exhibition can pull together different views on
a topic and display how knowledge on that topic is organized and disseminated.

For over a century, librarians have been mounting exhibitions, and these exhibitions are credited with increasing public access to the libraries' collections, serving as
hooks to stimulate reading, and contributing in the broadest sense to public education.[6]
As one librarian said, "We like to do exhibits; it is fun, allows creativity, shows off materials, slips in some education along the way."[7] Another librarian observed "students especially are more media conscious and more readily seduced by a good exhibition (or even
a bad one) than many books.... Exhibitions can function to lead library patrons to books.
Moreover, librarians might look upon exhibitions, whether major installations or several cases, as additional means of discourse which allow creativity in the profession."[8]
Exhibits draw visitors, and librarians see exhibits as adding value to the library experience, both for the visitor and for the librarian. One curator and educator observes, "Public interest in library exhibitions is growing" and nothing short of a revival of exhibitions
in libraries is taking place across the nation.[9] One striking testimonial of the public's
interest in library exhibits was documented in a 1989 user survey when over 22 percent
of the visitors to the Central Research Library of the New York Public Library stated
that they came for the purpose of visiting one of the exhibitions.[10]

Are libraries, however, prepared to avail themselves of this increased interest in
exhibitions and this opportunity to use exhibits to increase access to materials and information and to promote learning and literacy? Can they meet the expectations of patrons
for whom exhibits are a major factor in library visits? Do they have the knowhow to
expand the interest, attractiveness, and educational value of exhibits for all patrons?
Where do library staffs gain basic skills in mounting an effective exhibition?

Most libraries do not have an exhibitions staff and rely instead on staff with shifting responsibilities, or a committee,[11] or on the staff member with "the greatest 'knack' for it"[12] to develop and install exhibitions. In late 1993, a discussion thread arose on EXLIBRIS listserv (<exlibris@library.berkeley.edu>) under the subject line "Library Exhibits." The general message in the thread was that exhibits commonly are in cases and have low to no priority and are handled by paraprofessionals, non-professionals and recreational groups or are assigned to a staff member, sometimes with a specific number of exhibits to be created. In addition, some exhibits that seek to explore current issues have been undertaken as collaborations with groups beyond the library.

Seven years after the 1993 "Library Exhibits" message, another EXLIBRIS listserv posting, on Wed, 7 Dec 2000 and titled "the history of library exhibits," asked, in a series of survey questions on "the museology of libraries and the future of library exhibitions," if library professionals were sufficiently equipped by their master of library science degrees to mount effective exhibitions. Responses seemed to focus on courses in rare book and special collections with mention of an exhibition planning exercise in one rare books course.[13] One respondent observed "Probably the only way you can learn to curate an exhibition is by curating one."[14] Another respondent suggested that a course "devoted to the skills and philosophies behind exhibitions"[15] is needed in library schools.

A review of websites of American Library Association accredited programs found few opportunities for library science students to study the theory and practice of museum work or exhibitions. A search of Books in Print (in print, out of print, forthcoming) for titles relating to exhibits in libraries turned up 29 relevant titles (published 1958 to 2003). Only one title (1997) in the past ten years appears to provide exhibition theory and techniques for librarians. This extends Donald Tanasoca's observation over 50 years ago that "There is a shortage of trained exhibit librarians, so acute that most libraries are unaware of it."[16]

Skills Librarians Need

With rare opportunities to learn exhibition skills in master of library science programs, and little literature addressing these skills, it is time to develop continuing education opportunities and supporting materials to teach librarians about planning, implementing, and promoting effective exhibits and exhibitions. To address these gaps in education and the literature, we decided to ask museum staff what knowledge and skills librarians needed to mount effective exhibitions. We also asked museum staff and librarians about the kinds of exhibits best suited to libraries.

To elicit the opinions, we developed a Survey Concerning Making Exhibits. From hands-on experience and the literature on exhibitions, 14 categories of skills were derived, with subskills listed under each to provide a definition or a clarification of the broader category. Participants were asked to score each skill category as critical, helpful, or unnecessary. From a list of options (education, entertainment, collection access, other), participants were asked to select the main purpose of a museum and the main purpose of a library. Participants were also asked whether libraries should have exhibits and what kinds and whether museums and libraries should partner to create and display exhibits.

The survey was distributed in a posting to two museum and two library listservs: MUSEUM-L, a general museum listserv (3,330 subscribers); ISEN-ASTC-L, a science and technology museum listserv (944 subscribers); PUBLIB, a public library listserv (5,000 subscribers); and PUBYAC, a public library youth services listserv (3,482 subscribers worldwide). Museum staff returned 52 usable surveys and librarians returned 18 usable surveys. The disparate number of returns from the two sets of subscribers could be attributed to the librarians' lack of sufficient expertise and experience in exhibitions and thus a perceived lack of relevance of their knowledge to the survey.

Museum staff members participating in the study hold positions as curator (five), director (four), educator (seven), and evaluator (two); and in exhibits (nineteen), collections (two), and other (thirteen). Eighty-seven percent of the museum staff participants mount exhibits as a major component of their jobs (60 percent) or have mounted a few exhibits (27 percent).

Librarians participating in the study hold positions as director (five) and archivist (one); and in adult services (two), reference (two), youth services (three), and other (five). Seventy-two percent of the librarians have mounted a few exhibits (56 percent) or mount exhibits as a major component of their jobs (17 percent).

Differing Views

Museum staff and librarians agree that money management skills (67 percent and 56 percent, respectively) and an established purpose and theme for the exhibition (94 percent and 89 percent, respectively) are critical for nonmuseum personnel planning an exhibit. Museum staff feel time management (81 percent), exhibit theory (65 percent), exhibit and label design (56 percent), and conservation (58 percent) are also critical areas; librarians feel that spatial considerations (61 percent) and planning the programming and accompanying material for the exhibit (67 percent) are, in addition to money management skills and an established purpose and theme, critical areas. Librarians indicated that fabrication (construction) and installation techniques are either unnecessary or are better to outsource (56 percent).

What can we determine from this data as to the vision of exhibits in libraries? Museum staff seem to view exhibits in libraries as 1) utilizing and applying museum theory, 2) requiring management, and 3) worthy of preservation. Librarians seem to view exhibits in libraries as requiring 1) space management, and 2) orchestration for visitors. Further, librarians seem to view exhibits as being simple, such as bulletin boards and table displays (56 percent do not view fabrication and installation techniques as critical or helpful skills); while museum staff conceive of more complex exhibits for libraries so that fabrication and installation techniques are critical (40 percent) or helpful (27 percent).

What is striking in the data is that accessibility, educational theory and evaluation are not viewed as critical considerations. This suggests that visitor access, educational value of exhibits, and tested quality of exhibits are not viewed as constraints or are viewed as inherent in completed exhibits. From learning theory, we know the population is about equally divided among visual learners, auditory learners, and kinesthetic learners. Books, journals, and online databases support those who learn by reading and writing. Exhibitions, informed by educational or learning theory, can extend learning in the library to those who learn through demonstrations, listening, and doing. Likewise, evaluating exhibitions for usability and educational value with a range of potential visitors will help ensure that the exhibits librarians mount are effective in fulfilling their purposes across a range of ages and learning styles.

From the survey questions considered thus far, we might be tempted to suggest that libraries and museums have different primary purposes and therefore the utilization, function, and types of exhibits would be necessarily different in libraries compared to museums. The question of fundamental purposes in an interesting one and one that we did ask both librarians and museum staff. Specifically, we asked whether the main purpose of museums and libraries is education, entertainment, or access to the collection.

Museum staff and librarians agree that education is the primary purpose of both libraries (62 percent and 61 percent, respectively) and museums (81 percent and 72 percent, respectively). Both feel museums are more focused on education of the visitor (81 percent and 72 percent, respectively) than are libraries (62 percent and 61 percent, respectively) and that libraries are more focused on access to their collections (52 percent and 50 percent, respectively) than are museums (35 percent and 28 percent, respectively). Museum staff feel, however, that museums offer a greater focus on entertainment (19 percent) than do libraries (10 percent), while librarians feel that libraries offer a greater focus on entertainment (28 percent) than do museums (22 percent).

The perception of which institution is more focused on entertainment is interesting, and we will look quickly at how others perceive museums and libraries in relationship to entertainment. Listings for both museums and libraries are commonly classified under "Arts and Entertainment," in newspapers, but how does entertainment figure into their agendas? Judith Dobrzynski, in a *New York Times* feature article on the increased interest in art museums and record-setting attendance at many exhibits, claims "Much museumgoing is ... [s]imply social.... It's entertainment, not enlightenment or inspiration."[17] A library system in the St. Clair County (Michigan) Library System sponsored a program called "Reading for Entertainment" to appeal to students in grades K–8; however, the "entertainment," it seems, were the free movie passes the children received for every five books they read. Reading itself, nevertheless, has long been recognized as a pastime or entertainment. Cathleen Towey of the Port Washington (N.Y.) Public Library underscores the importance of the library's role as reader's advisor in aiding and enriching the lives of its patrons: "People of all ages actively seek out stories.... Stories, both true and invented, help us make sense of our lives, or temporarily exchange our daily narrative for a more interesting one."[18] And Sandy Whiteley, editor of ALA's *Reference Books Bulletin*, reminds us "The role of readers' advisor is one of the oldest played by librarians."[19] The role of readers' advisor can be carried out through a number of vehicles, including exhibits. Library programs, from readings and story hours to magicians and storytellers, provide entertainment as well as opportunities for education. Entertainment attracts visitors, thus giving the visitor the opportunity and the attitude to experience more: inspiration, enlightenment, learning, and the motivation to return. It is understandable that both museum staff and librarians recognize and appreciate that entertainment, while tertiary to education and access, is still a part of the appeal of museums and libraries if not a function of their institution.

But are exhibits beyond the bulletin board and glass display case really that appropriate for libraries? Some feel "exhibits" in library terms should conjure up visions of simple displays while "exhibits" in museum terms should conjure up elaborate if not expensive and sophisticated visions of installations such as of Matisse cutouts or a Viking village. Certainly if we use the titles of books about library exhibits published between 1958 and 2003 we could surmise that library exhibits were best kept to book displays, thematic bulletin board displays, and a few tabletop 3-D displays. There does seem to be a fundamental difference between libraries and museums in the terms used to discuss exhibits. Titles of books under Bowker subject "library exhibits" seem to prefer the term "displays." Some titles mention bulletin boards or clipart or wall space in addressing library exhibits. Title of books under Bowker subject "museum techniques" contain words such as "curating" and "exhibiting." Other titles tell us museum exhibits are about "designing meaningful experiences" or "developing museum audiences" or address "learning in museums" or "shaping knowledge." We might expect, then, that museum staff, when asked if libraries should have exhibits, couch their response by envisioning "exhibits" in museum terms. And so we asked them.

Museum staff (88 percent) and librarians (100 percent) overwhelmingly agree that libraries should have exhibits. Librarians view library exhibits primarily as bulletin boards (100 percent) and secondarily as exhibits of artwork (94 percent) or exhibits in glass display cases (94 percent). Museum staff view library exhibits primarily as exhibits of artwork (85 percent) or exhibits in glass display cases (85 percent) and secondarily as bulletin boards (79 percent). Hands-on exhibits and exhibits with movable parts are viewed by both librarians (50 percent and 39 percent, respectively) and museum staff (58 percent and 52 percent, respectively) as least appropriate for libraries, although museum staff see them as more appropriate for libraries than do librarians. Both librarians (89 percent) and museum staff (77 percent) rated traveling exhibits as appropriate for libraries.

Responses on the survey suggest that librarians and museum staff, like the book titles summoned with Bowker subject "library exhibits," tend to view exhibits in libraries as displays on bulletin boards and in glass display cases or on the wall and select less often as appropriate for libraries exhibits that include installations, eyes-on moveable parts, or hands-on interaction with the exhibit. But it is clear that exhibits are appropriate in libraries.

Training Is Needed

To sum up the survey of museum staff and librarians, findings suggest that a range of exhibits is appropriate for libraries: 2- and 3-D; hanging and encased; interactive and mechanical; and traveling. Both museum and library staff support partnerships to create and display exhibits and agree that the primary focus for both museums and libraries is education, that access to their collections is a secondary focus, and that entertainment plays a part in the function of both institutions.

Librarians, based on findings from the study, do not have the same view as exhibition specialists on what knowledge is needed for nonmuseum personnel to mount an exhibit. This suggest that while "the only way [librarians and library staff] can learn to curate an exhibition is by curating one,"[20] that is not necessarily the most effective or efficient path. Beyond two agreed upon core needs (know your topic and know your budget), librarians' ideas of what constitutes essential skills and knowledge to mount exhibits do not match well with what museum staff feel librarians need to know.

A Need for Exhibitions and Exhibit Librarians

There are more public library buildings in the United States than McDonald's restaurants; visits to public, school, and academic libraries number more than twice the attendance at movie theaters and more than three times the visits to state and national parks.[21] In 2002, libraries were visited 3.5 billion times.[22] If we speculate that, overall, only 1 percent of the visitors came to the library to visit its exhibits each year, we could project there would be approximately 35 million visits annually to library exhibitions. This would mean: more than one American in ten is visiting the library for its exhibits. Clearly, libraries have a substantial opportunity to open and enhance their collections through exhibits that may extend access to materials to a wider audience through interpretation, translation, illustration, and other techniques, as well as providing better support for those who retain information best through demonstrations, listening, and doing.

Tony Bennett, in *The Birth of the Museum*, gives us an interesting perspective on libraries and exhibitions. For the individual with insufficient literacy skills, he observes, the library becomes a museum and books the artifacts in it.[23] This suggests that library exhibitions could be used as a tool to help increase literacy by using learning theory to integrate pictures, sound, and words into exhibits. Bennett further observes that museums, and therefore exhibitions, have characteristics in common with both parks and fairs that make them enticing. Like parks, exhibitions can introduce a more relaxed atmosphere. Like fairs, exhibitions can provide distraction from the customary daily lives of visitors and an opportunity for new experiences. Like both parks and fairs, exhibitions can be designed to provide a kinesthetic experience as the visitor moves from object to object, display to display. In exhibitions, learning need not be limited by literacy level.

While we can envision creative and energetic librarians — like Erma Loveland at Abilene Christian University — who "like to do exhibits,"[24] staff with exhibit quotas, and paraprofessionals and nonprofessionals and recreational groups constructing exhibits for the library, we still come around to the fact that enthusiasm or obligation are not sufficient. Exhibitions need to be curated — researched for knowledge conveyed, justified in terms of other activities in the library, written and designed using time-honored principles, their items displayed for their value as exemplars of the goals of the exhibit.

Exhibits also must be guided by library policy; for, like acquisitions and collection development, exhibits can become a site of political contestation. In May 2002, Mayor George P. Wuerch of Anchorage, Alaska, objecting to a portion of a gay pride display a year earlier at the Anchorage Public Library, issued a directive limiting library exhibits in content and location, "asserting that the [directive] had the immediate effect of law." The 2001 exhibit included "decorating the library elevators to make them look like closets." After ordering the exhibit removed, banning all displays from groups outside the library, the city justified its actions on the grounds of public safety: "Library patrons going into or out of the elevators would have symbolically 'come out' of the closet or taken their beliefs about homosexuality 'into' the closet."[25] The Anchorage Assembly (City Council) later rejected Mayor Wuerch's directive and recommended that exhibits be allowed with a range of views and allowed throughout the library.[26] The library received a court order to reinstate the exhibit. As with banned books, we may find that political influences attempt to set library policy on exhibitions. Libraries need to define and set defendable exhibitions policies. As with challenged books, some patrons or community members may find displayed material offensive. Libraries need to define and set procedures for challenges to exhibitions or exhibit materials.

Challenges may also come concerning the suitability of an exhibit to the institution's mission or to the intellectual integrity of the exhibit itself. The American Museum of Natural History in New York City came under criticism for its exhibition "Spirits in the Steel: The Art of Kalabari Masquerade." Critics questioned whether an exhibit perceived as an art exhibit belonged in a natural history museum. Andrea Barnwell, director, of the Spelman College Museum of Fine Arts, took the stand that "in taking this exhibition the museum asserted its commitment to 'challenge the boundary between anthropology and art.'"[27] Enid Schidkrout, however, observes that when boundaries between disciplines are blurred and the exhibit curators seem to be imposing their "own particular insights and approaches" on the displayed objects, "the intellectual baggage, the incredible stereotypes, the fears and prejudices that people have in approaching any subject in an explicitly comparative way are truly monumental."[28]

Opportunities to Increase Access to Collections

With some basic knowledge and skills in hand, librarians can successfully seize upon opportunities, through exhibits and exhibitions, to increase public access to their collections, stimulate reading, increase literacy, and contribute in the broadest sense to public education, thereby demonstrating both the role and the importance of the library in the life of the community. Library exhibits can take on a variety of forms from complex installations that are designed and built by museum staff as traveling exhibits to homegrown projects utilizing local talent and addressing a local interest or need. Library exhibits can occupy a glass case, a wall, a table, a room, or electronic space. Library exhibits can be designed for visitors to view or to interact with.

These illustrative examples demonstrate some of the possible variety of exhibits mounted in libraries:

Boulder Public Library: The Boulder 'Colorado' Public Library was the first stop, in February 2002, for the national traveling exhibit organized by the Minnesota Children's Museum and the American Library Association, "Go Figure!" "The exhibit introduces early math concepts such as sorting and measuring through kid-sized environments inspired by familiar children's books. *Go Figure!* is designed to bring the exciting world of math and its everyday uses to children two to seven years old and their parents and caregivers."[29] Another national traveling exhibit, "Make It Move," also began its national tour at Boulder Public Library. "Make It Move" was designed and circulated by the Oregon Museum of Science and Industry in Portland. "Make It Move" explores the mechanics of motion by inviting visitors to experience how simple machines help make things move. A child-size crane and excavator, spinning tops, levers, pulleys, gears and a variety of interactive puzzles are all included. Visitors [could also make] a ball move through a 'gravity track' they build themselves, consisting of paddle wheels, loop-to-loops, mazes and other challenges."[30]

University of Kansas library: Locally produced displays have also caught the attention and curiosity of visitors. "Lost in the library? Stop floundering — follow the fish" utilized six display cases in the University of Kansas' Watson Library to raise awareness of the library's expanding bibliographic instruction program and "Reference Assistant," an expert system that directs students and faculty, without the help of a reference librarian, to frequently needed reference books. The displays used a fish motif combined with drawings and sense of humor of a student assistant. In the display, to illustrate "Take a Self-Guided Audio Tour. Pick up the Audiotape at the Reserve Desk" an illustrated fish wore headphones over its gills and had a cassette player tucked under one fin.[31] This display series was low cost and effective.

Arizona State University Libraries: Maxine Reneker, then associate dean for public service at the Arizona State University Libraries, used Sherlock Holmes as the archetype for an exhibit that led students through the process of gathering information in the library on the popular fictional detective and his creator.[32] While the questions posed focused on Holmes, Watson, and Sir Arthur Conan Doyle, students could apply the sources and the process used to locate answers to other questions. That is, the student could transfer the learning from this question set to sets of questions on another topic.

Westminster High School library: Westminster (Colorado) High School library held the exhibition "Help Yourself— Looking at Teenage Problems" which included a week of activities, films, displays, audiovisual materials, posters, bookmarks, and free materials for students. Teenage social problems were addressed from a self-help approach to promote the library as a resource that meets students information needs, personal as well as academic.[33]

University of California, Santa Barbara library: Exhibitions can also be designed and curated as an intellectual activity of scholars. For example "Microcosms: Objects of Knowledge (A University Collects)" began as a two-part exhibition, symposium, and graduate seminar in 1995 and 1996 organized by professors Mark Meadow and Bruce Robertson of the Department of History of Art and Architecture at the University of California, Santa Barbara. Meadow and Robertson questioned why the University of California's physical collections, among the largest university collections in the world and estimated at over $30 billion replacement value, had been the subject of little scholarship about the history, purpose, and future of university collections, let alone any consistent policy within the university about the development, conservation, and research purposes for a collection of these physical objects. "Microcosms" includes: an exhibition that is both an "example of collecting objects as a means towards universal knowledge" and an exploration of "the current use of the same objects in the university;" a collection of related essays; and a web-based memory of the exhibition.[34] This is a rich example of an exhibition that explores the institution's collection practices, doing so by using cabinets of curiosity as the display technique.

These examples of library exhibitions have, we hope, roused your eagerness to gain or increase your exhibit knowledge and skills. But before we examine the exhibition process, we want to look at some of the theories that support exhibit work.

2

Exhibit Theory

The desire to collect things as well as the desire to show the collected items to others have been called "natural ... 'instincts' of people [that] seem to be universal and timeless."[1] There is evidence that humans have been collecting and exhibiting things for about five thousand years. Sometime after 3000 B.C., written records began to be collected and arranged into what are now recognized as the early beginnings of archives. "[W]hat began as a collection of records-government, temple, business, or private-gradually grew into a library as other materials of historical, literary, or informative nature were added."[2] Early library collections were treated in a variety of ways: as spoils taken back as treasure to some conquers' homelands, as resources for scholarly study in temples and schools, as leisure reading material housed in rooms at public baths, and even as ornaments of fashion or status in private homes.[3] According to Kevin Flude, one of the earliest museums we have found is in the ruins of a school in Ur, the ancient city of the Sumerian civilization that was settled almost 3,000 years ago; a room in the school was set aside as a museum and housed objects that were 1,600 years old.[4] In the first half of the third century B.C., the great Museum of Alexandria was established as a configuration of buildings, connected by a columned walkway, that included an observatory and botanical and zoological gardens as well as a library estimated to contain 500,000 to 600,000 volumes.[5]

Both libraries and museums are grounded in our instinct to collect. Traditionally, libraries are concerned with information while "museums are concerned with objects."[6] Today we distinguish between libraries, as collections of information resources in print or in other forms that are organized and made accessible for reading or study[7] and museums, as "public institutions dedicated to preserving and interpreting the primary tangible evidence of humans and their environment."[8] That is, libraries are organized for access to their materials while museums are organized to interpret their materials in the context of that specific organization.

Museums, archives, libraries and digital libraries are collectively called memory institutions as each collects a portion of the memory of society. Exhibits, displays, and exhibitions are communication tools or vehicles of memory institutions that allow the public to access the memories these institutions hold. An exhibit is an array of cues (images, text, sound, resources, artifacts) that are purposely brought together and structured to illustrate a chosen theme and to achieve a desired effect[9]; this is in contrast to lists, such catalogues and indexes, that identify the existence of the individual items. Generally an exhibit is a collection of items that are considered as a unit while an exhibition generally occupies more physical space than an exhibit and might consist of a collection of exhibits. A display, in contrast, is a collection of objects that offers the visitor little more than a title and perhaps identification labels. While displays can inform by means of labeling, exhibits and exhibitions can educate a visitor by means of more complex presentations. This is a subtle but important difference. A glass case displaying an array of Toni Morrison novels under a banner "Novels by Toni Morrison" informs the viewer visually in much the same way a list of authors and book titles would inform lexically. We would call this a display; the objects have a lexical or indexical relation. In the same glass case, however, the same books might be arranged with documents, drafts, manuscripts, excerpts from correspondence, photographs from the author's life or of relevant subject matter, headlines from the period of the novels' settings or compositions to illustrate events that might have influenced and shaped the novels. We would consider this an exhibit because it is telling a meta-story, a story of how a story emerges. The materials presented provide a context for the novels and the novels provide a focus for the exhibit.

Displays, exhibits, and exhibitions all have the same rationale: to instruct through presentation. It is critical to determine the motivation for the presentation and then to follow good exhibit practices in fulfilling that purpose so that the presentation will provide the intended experience for the visitor.

Good Exhibit Practice

Why would we want to have an exhibit in the library? Seven reasons for exhibits in museums[10] can be applied to libraries. First, the exhibit allows us to use artifacts, signage, and activities to tell a story to visitors; for example, a story of influences that shaped a town through a series of photographs spanning its frontier beginnings to today. Second, the exhibit allows us to tell a story that cannot be told where it occurs; for example, the story of family life in a different time through artifacts found in a typical home. The exhibit can bring artifacts and stories to the visitors; for example, eating utensils and customs from other cultures. Fourth, the exhibit can incorporate and protect real artifacts; for example, delicate or rare text. The exhibit can bring extremes into human scale; for example, scale models of the universe or of a cell rejuvenating. The exhibit allows visitors freedom to pace themselves, to move quickly or slowly through the exhibit, to focus closely on a portion and scan the rest. And lastly, the exhibit, once mounted, frees staff to engage in other activities; that is, the exhibit becomes the teacher, the educator, always on duty as visitor after visitor views, questions, considers, and understands. It is this last rationale that we think the most intriguing; for example, consider a room dedicated to permanent exhibits focusing on teaching visitors about use of the library and library materials and resources: a kind of bibliographic instruction arcade with exhibits for various age and interest groups. This could become a form of one-on-one information literacy instruction that the library staff, given the constraints of their other duties, might be hard pressed to provide to every visitor.

In moving from idea to exhibition, there are four principles of good exhibit practice that apply to any exhibit, whether in a museum or in a library: the exhibit must 1) attract the visitors' interest; 2) inspire the visitor's confidence; 3) reward the visitor for their time; and 4) do these in a pleasing way and in good taste.[11] Both attracting visitor interest and rewarding the visitor for their time spent with the exhibit will be discussed in the next chapter under learning theory and human needs. Measuring visitor satisfaction will be covered in chapters 5 and 6.

The means of exhibits are the objects displayed; to have an exhibition, objects must be collected. The objects could come from the library's collection of books and artifacts, or the objects might be gathered from other sources, including other libraries. There are two basic ways to go about collecting objects: 1) decide on a theme for an exhibit and then collect objects to fulfill the proposed goals of the exhibit (this is similar to gathering materials from one's own collections, databases, and inter library loan to write a paper); and 2) decide on a general theme around which the library would like to collect objects and then plan exhibits around the objects in the library's collection (this is similar to collection development in a specific discipline or subject area). Whether the collecting or the exhibit planning comes first, the library, or more specifically the curator or collector for the library must have a collecting plan. A collecting plan requires that criteria be developed for the objects to be collected and decisions made on whether they are to be held temporarily for a specific exhibit or permanently in the library's collection. These criteria should be based on the theme around which the objects will be collected and should also consider the educational value of an object as well as its investment value, size, and handling and storage needs. Careful thought must be given before any object is accepted on loan: loans, or donations, should not have unusual conditions (beyond matters of handling, storage, conservation, insurance) and should not be accepted for unspecified periods.[12] The collecting plan should include criteria regarding objects and criteria regarding information. No doubt both objects and information about objects will be collected. Some of the information will be about the ability of the library to borrow an object at a future time. What information should be collected about the object and borrowing stipulations and procedures to arrange the loan? At what level of authority will the information be gathered? At what point and to whom will the library send a letter of understanding confirming the information gathered and expressing interest in borrowing the object? Some of the information will be about the object itself. What information about the object will be gathered? At what level of authority will it be gathered? Will collaborating evidence or sources of collaborating evidence for gathered information be requested?

One author commented that a good exhibit was a collection of well-written labels with the best available specimens to illustrate each label.[13] While other authors might argue with this label-centric perspective of exhibit development, what does strike a chord of commonsense in this perspective is that without defined boundaries of a theme and a concrete idea of what the exhibit is to do for the visitor, a collection of objects may become a set of odds and ends vaguely held together by an uncertain topic.

A Plan for Collecting for Exhibits

A collecting or exhibit plan begins with a statement or abstract of what we want the exhibit or collection to accomplish. For example, we might state "A collection of handcrafted clothing produced locally will be used to illustrate the influence of recent economic growth on the spirit of the community." Let's stop a moment and consider the wording of this goal. Three concepts are assumed: locally crafted clothing expresses an attitude that changes over time; local industrial or financial growth can be divided into periods with unique characteristics; and the local community has a collective spirit that can be illustrated and that changes over time. We now have a very good idea of the kinds of objects we would like to collect: locally crafted clothing (items, reconstructions, photographs) with a sampling at specific year intervals and over a given period; representations (headlines, photographs) of industrial growth with a sampling at specific year intervals and over a given period; and representations (photographs, circulars, lapel pins and badges, headlines) of community spirit (community celebrations, community response to events) with a sampling at specific year intervals and over a given period. With the plan in hand (limited by other constraints such as size, value, etc.), collecting can begin. After items have been gathered from the sampling periods, each of the categories (clothing, industrial growth, community spirit) can be organized by year, and then we can observe any patterns that emerge. For example, one to two years following each expansion in local industry, the town's July Fourth celebration grew by adding events, and the themes from the expanded celebration were carried out in novelty aprons made by the quilt club and auctioned annually at the celebration to benefit the local hospital. Determined criteria, such as the aspects of community spirit to be illustrated, or the most significant changes in local industry, guide the selection of objects as well as the sampling period and intervals.

In our cycle of collecting we are also researching; and every good researcher knows the value of keeping a research notebook or diary. A collecting or research notebook or diary serves as a storehouse for sketches or photographs of or notes on collected items and facts about the items such as where it was found, dimensions, special handling or storage needs; unstructured observations about the items collected with perhaps notes on similar items that were found but not selected for collection or about links among the found items; and descriptions of the context and conditions under which the items were found and collected. The collecting diary is used to keep short memos or ideas about the theme or the planned exhibit. The collecting diary records the process of developing the exhibit by documenting perceptions and insights as they unfold. In addition to serving as a storehouse for explanatory comments and photographs and drawings as well as written reflections, ideas, and insights leading to an exhibit, the collecting diary also serves as an inspiration for reflection on the exhibit's boundaries and what the objects and the exhibit can convey to the visitor.

As the collection begins to take form toward accomplishing the goals set for collecting and before all objects are collected, plans for the size and scope of the exhibit should be finalized as these plans may impact the final collecting.

A Plan for Preparing Exhibits

The first step in preparing the exhibit is to understand your audience. Perhaps borrowing from the literatures would help to explain what is involved in understanding your audience. Each visitor comes to the exhibit with a repertoire or background of knowledge and experiences of life, and perhaps with the assumed experience of having visited exhibits before. Exhibits are designed with gaps in information that the visitor is expected to fill from their background of knowledge and experiences. By filling in the gaps, the visitor is able to see the exhibit as meaningful. If the visitor does not have the needed pre-existing experience, the story that the exhibit tries to tell may lack consistency or meaning for that visitor. Testing the exhibit (see Chapter 6) can serve nicely to match the background needed for understanding the exhibit to the background of the expected visitor and helping to make the exhibit successful by identifying any gaps that are not filled by the visitor's previous experience.

Two additional early steps in preparing the exhibit have been started with the collecting plan: to plan ahead and to develop one theme for the exhibit. "A powerful exhibition idea will clarify, limit, and focus the nature and scope of an exhibition and provide a well-defined goal against which to rate its success."[14] The idea should tell just one story and be covered in a one-sentence statement of what the exhibition is about. The statement should have a subject, an action, and a consequence and should not be vague or compound.[15]

Once designed, an exhibit can be assessed for the knowledge it contains and resulting desirable changes in attitude and in behavior. For example, to assess the effectiveness of a behavior change exhibit on environmentally responsible behavior, the environmental psychology lab (EPLab) research group at the University of Michigan tested an exhibit at the Brookfield Zoo near Chicago using three methods: theoretical analysis, attitude assessment, and behavior experiment. The conclusions from this comprehensive analysis suggest visitors are receptive to receiving messages while visiting exhibits, an exhibit can influence visitors' interest in responsible behaviors, and follow-up intervention is needed if long-term behavior change is expected. In assessing learning afforded by the exhibit, the EPLab research group used a framework based on exhibit theory and principles from education and psychology. Six evaluative criteria were used: information, presentation, engagement, motivation, participation, and physical space. In assessing Information, researchers wanted to know if the visitors gained an understanding of the issues and behaviors intended. Presentation asks if the exhibit exposes visitors to concepts in a manner that is sensitive to their learning needs. Engagement assesses whether the exhibit helps visitors feel excited about and interested in the concepts in the exhibit. Motivation measures whether the exhibit develops the visitor's sense of responsibility or caring in the areas that the exhibit designers planned. Participation indicates whether the exhibit offers visitors opportunities to physically and cognitively explore the issues or themes presented by the exhibit. Physical space determines whether the exhibit provides visitors with an environment conductive to interactions and learning.[16] (Evaluation will be covered in detail in Chapter 6.)

Some authors seem to suggest that a good exhibit goes beyond presenting information to visitors; a good exhibit translates or interprets knowledge from the language of the scientist or researcher or resource expert into the language and experiences familiar to the visitor.[17] This may involve choosing appropriate metaphors for presenting complex concepts. In other words, a good exhibition is a good storyteller.

Interpretation or translating knowledge is also viewed as a communication process that reveals meanings and relationships to the visitor through first-hand experiences with objects, artifacts, or natural landscapes or sites.[18] Hands-on experience is needed to actively involve the visitor; however, hands-on exhibits must also be minds-on exhibits. That is, the visitors must understand why they are interacting with the object; the visitors must be directed to focus on a task with the object.[19]

In planning, the two hardest questions to answer are Why would a visitor want to know this (i.e., the information that the exhibit is presenting)? How do you want the visitors to use the information the exhibit is presenting? The purpose of the questions is to focus the exhibit planner on the visitor and to help ensure that the exhibit is not being planned for the interest of only one person: the exhibit planner.[20]

The Psychology of Exhibits and Exhibitgoers

A visitor only has so much energy to put into his exhibit experience: This amount of energy, in the form of time and physical and psychological effort, is called exhibit load.[21] As the visitor expends energy in an exhibit, his interest level begins to drop off. That is, in expending energy on an exhibit through looking, listening, or interacting, the visitor becomes "psychologically tired and overloaded with information and stimuli." This causes the visitor's interest to wane. A visitor, it is estimated, will reach exhibit overload in about 45 minutes and then head for other entertainments such as a gift shop or food area.[22]

Different kinds of exhibits require different energy levels and, therefore, have different interest-holding abilities. Interactive or hands-on exhibits generally have the highest load on visitors while viewing paintings and collections behind glass generally have the lowest load on visitors.[23] However, research has shown that people are more interested in dynamic, animated, changing stimuli (such as found in hands-on and eyes-on exhibits) than in inert stimuli (such as found in text and photographs). This means that although interactive or hands-on exhibits require more energy, they also carry more interest to a greater number of people. When a number of exhibits will be displayed, it is better to have a diversity of load types that can be arranged to move the visitor from a more restful or lower load beginning exhibit to a move active and high load exhibit and then finally to a rest period of lowest load exhibits.[24] That is, an exhibition should be choreographed to alternate periods of higher activity of exhibit load with periods of lower activity or exhibit load.

Universal Design Principles Foster Interaction

Each visitor will have his or her own style of approaching and interacting with an exhibit. A visitor's interaction style is the observable pattern of behaviors carried out when nearing a given type of display. The pattern of behaviors may be based on characteristics of the display or characteristics of the individual or a combination of both. We could say that where there is conflict between the characteristics of the display and the characteristics of the individual, access to the display is limited for that individual.

Originally compiled in 1997 by a working group of architects, product designers, engineers, and environmental design researchers, the Principles of Universal Design[25] provides guidelines that can be applied to exhibit design to make exhibits more cognitively and physically accessible to visitors. Not all principles are applicable to every exhibit. And, as one title exclaimed, "designing for accessibility doesn't have to be expensive or complex. It can be easily."[26] The goal is to design exhibits with the principles of universal design in mind and to try to make each exhibit as accessible as possible to the expected visitor. The seven principles of universal design are equitable use, flexibility in use, simple and intuitive, perceptive information, tolerance for error and low physical effort.[27]

Equitable use involves designing both the intellectual content and the physical presentation of materials so that they are useful to and approachable by visitors of diverse abilities. This may involve taking into consideration that visitors have different learning styles and learning strengths, that visitors come in different heights and therefore require different viewing levels, or that visitors have varying abilities to decipher colors (such as distinctions between red and green). Other considerations might be placement of signage so both taller standing adults, adults in wheelchairs, and shorter standing adults may easily read the text; and placement of visuals so both adults and school-aged children may easily view them.

Flexibility in use involves designing to accommodate a range of preferences and abilities by providing choices for the visitor. This might involve presenting information as written text such as through a label or narrative poster as well as on an audio recording or as an interactive model or drawings as well as a written description. This might also involve designing to allow the visitor to control his pace through an exhibit. The organization of information in an exhibit can aid the visitor in controlling his pace through it. For example, an exhibit might convey six major points. Each point could be represented by a variety of methods: a group of objects or photographs or other graphic representations; a short phrase in large titlelike print; a paragraph or two that can be read a few feet away; and an assortment of detailed passages that require closer reading. A visitor may then chose to move quickly through the exhibit reading only the large print titles or more slowly reading the summary narratives or very slowly reading all detailed comments. A visual display can be organized in a similar fashion using a few large or prominent representative images with groups of more detailed or varied images that the visitor can choose to spend time studying or examining closely.

Simple and intuitive design should be easy to understand regardless of the visitor's experience, knowledge, language skills, or current concentration level. This may involve arranging information consistent with its importance or stating the who, what, why, when, and how of an issue in a few larger print sentences and then expanding details in a more lengthy narrative. Simple and intuitive means that an exhibit is consistent with visitor expectations and intuitions; for example, lines on the floor directing the visitor through an exhibit are a shade of green and circles to mark information stations are a shade of red (rather than vice versa). Simple and intuitive exhibits accommodate a range of literacy and language skills by using commonly understood terms rather than technical terms, subject-verb-object sentence structure, and shorter sentences; and eliminate any unnecessary complexity.

Perceptive information involves designing to communicate necessary information effectively to the visitor regardless of the visitor's sensory abilities. Designing for perceptive information might include using larger print; using various modes-pictorial, verbal, tactile-for redundant presentation of essential information; and providing adequate contrast between essential information and its surroundings, for example through use of color, texture, or pattern;

Tolerance for error involves minimizing hazards and the adverse consequences of accidental or unintended actions. Low physical effort involves designing for efficient and comfortable use with a minimum of fatigue while using a reasonable operating force and maintaining a neutral body position. For example, an exhibit that requires lengthy viewing would likely be uncomfortable and have increased physical effort for visitors standing through its duration. A rail for leaning or benches for sitting would require lower physical effort and would therefore increase visitor comfort. Exhibits installed on tabletops may require taller visitors to lean forward to view or interact with the exhibit, increasing physical effort and discomfort. Exhibits should also minimize repetitive actions and sustained physical effort.

Size and space for approach and use involves providing for approach, reach, manipulation, and use regardless of visitor's body size, posture, or mobility. This includes making components comfortable to reach for seated or standing visitors, and providing a clear line of sight to important elements for the seated or standing visitor. Exhibits that anticipate families need to allow space for maneuvering strollers. The National Center for Chronic Disease Prevention and Health Promotion reports that during the past 20 years Americans have been getting bigger[28]; to allow equitable use, therefore, display space must be designed to accommodate larger sized visitors.

"There is no way to make every part of an exhibit accessible to every visitor. Exhibit developers have to consider competing needs ... creating exhibits that are meaningful and fun for as many people as possible."[29] It may be helpful, however, to make a list of the prevalent diverse needs of the library's service community and try to incorporate these needs in planning each exhibit.

The Museum of Science, in Boston constructed a web resource explaining its method of exhibit development. That process includes consideration of universal design (accessibility) for exhibits.[30] The Museum of Science presents the general considerations of accessibility in the form of questions that may be more understandable to beginning exhibit designers: Can you get to it? (considers safety, barriers, path of travel, and placement of components); Can you find it? (considers visual, audio, and tactile directions to and within the exhibit); Can you see it? (considers lighting, colors, labels); Can you reach and use it? (considers exhibit height and dimensions and manipulation and reachability of controls); Can it reach you? (considers readability and consistency of narratives and multi-sensory presentations of the same ideas); and Is the space comfortable? (considers seating, lighting, noise, and layout).[31]

Types of Exhibits

Exhibits can be classified into three basic types: art exhibits, history exhibits, and science exhibits. Art exhibits display objects that are valued for their own sake as unique and highly unusual productions of gifted individuals. History and science exhibits are concerned with typical, common, quantity-produced, and natural objects that are primarily valued not for themselves but rather as examples of the natural world and of human cultures.[32]

Certain topics or objects seem more suited to certain forms of exhibit activities. Art exhibits tend to be displays that the visitor views, although the Philadelphia Museum of Art hosted an exhibit of art for the blind that intended the visitor to interact with the art object. Though the visitor may be inactively looking at the exhibit, the exhibit may be active; for example through use of film or light displays or moving display behind glass. Science exhibits tend to suggest more opportunities for interactive exhibits in which the visitor has an action to perform. However, "exhibits can take on a variety of forms.... All it takes is interest, imagination, enthusiasm, and energy."[33]

Robert Gardner describes exhibits in terms of how the visitor interacts with the exhibit. These five classifications of exhibits are useful for considering the variety of exhibits that could be displayed in a library: exhibits to see, eyes-on exhibits, hands-on exhibits, interactive exhibits, and puzzles.[34]

Exhibits to see are useful for explaining. Exhibits to see utilize examples in the form of photographs, illustrations, models, and other visuals that permit careful observation but do not involve manipulating the materials. Both printed text and audio recordings can be used to direct the visitor's observations and describe the events the exhibit depicts. An example of an exhibit to see is Gunther von Hagens' "Body Worlds: The Anatomical Exhibition of Real Human Bodies" (Museum of Science and Industry, Chicago, February 4 to September 5, 2005). In this exhibit, the visitor was able to examine more than 200 plastination specimens of entire bodies and individual organs.[35]

Eyes-on exhibits are useful for displays that contain materials that undergo change. Eyes-on exhibits encourage visitors to come again and again to observe changes over repeat visits, for example, over an hour or a day or a week. Eyes-on exhibits offer intriguing possibilities for family or children oriented exhibits in public or school libraries. An exhibition on the coming of spring might contain exhibits of germinating seeds or a butterfly emerging from a cocoon. An exhibit on time might show the workings of clock gears.[36]

Hands-on exhibits are useful if you want the visitor "to do something with materials rather than just observing and reading about them."[37] The Discovery Room for children and families at the Idaho Museum of Natural History on the campus of Idaho State University, Pocatello, is one example of a hands-on exhibit. The Discovery Room permits families to see and touch fossils, shells and other specimens from nature. The Discovery Room also contains games, puzzles, and table games about science. Other activities include grinding grains and playing with masks from around the world.[38]

Interactive exhibits are useful for displays in which you want the visitor to perform actions that will lead them to an "answer to a question, or to the discovery of a pattern or law of nature."[39] "For Babies and Me" at St. Louis Children's Museum is a unique exhibit area for children under the age of 2. The exhibit includes a peek-a-boo house, baby-sized gym, and a toddler-size school bus. The exhibit incorporates child development information for the caregiver.[40] An interactive exhibit that would appeal to children from toddler to adult is an exhibit on the art of pop-up books complete with displays of pop-up mechanics constructed of heavy materials and operated manually with a lever.

Puzzles are useful for displays that "encourage people to use their analytical abilities, sometimes to test their senses, and to challenge their ideas."[41] The "Crime Lab Detectives" exhibit at the Montshire Museum of Science in Norwich, Vermont (January 22 to May 8, 2005) gave visitors an opportunity to take on the roles of crime investigator and forensic scientist. Through this exhibit, visitors look for clues, scrutinize the evidence, and record their findings as they try to determine the identity of a neighborhood burglar. Visitors are then encouraged to share their observations and determine which suspect committed the crime.[42]

In addition to being classified by types of interaction, exhibits can also be classified by their permanence and residency, that is, as permanent, temporary, or portable or traveling.

The permanent exhibit is planned and constructed to be a mainstay attraction in the library. Through the years, new knowledge of visitor needs and ongoing upkeep may bring about modifications or modernizing of the permanent exhibit, its lighting or labels or colors, the traffic patterns around it, or elements of its contents.[43] One example of a permanent exhibit is The Kids' Café at the Northeast Louisiana Children's Museum in Monroe. The Kids' Café, sponsored by the Louisiana Restaurant Association, "recreates a true-to-life restaurant environment where each child can explore the different types of jobs found in a restaurant. Kids can see what its like to be a Server, Dishwasher or even a Chef!"[44]

Temporary exhibits, lasting perhaps one to six months, have become increasingly important in encouraging regular and repeated visits by visitors. Temporary exhibits permit new material, perhaps borrowed from other groups or organizations to be introduced and has the benefit of also stimulating revisits to the permanent exhibits.[45] Otter

Tail County Historical Society in Fergus Falls, Minnesota, maintains permanent exhibits that introduce key aspects of Otter Tail County's past and use temporary exhibits to give "an in-depth look at specific themes, events, time periods and individuals from the county past."[46] One such temporary was "To Your Health: Otter Tail County's Public Hospitals" (February to October 2004) which included memorabilia from each of the five county hospitals.

Portable or traveling exhibits can be temporary or permanent in nature, can emerge from collaborations among institutions, and provide a mechanism for sharing nationally with more remote communities and internationally with countries undergoing rapid social and cultural change.[47] Two examples of portable or traveling exhibits are "Playing with Time" and "Amazing Feats of Aging."

"Playing with Time" is a collaboration between Red Hill Studio and the Science Museum of Minnesota (with major funding provided by the National Science Foundation). It opened in March 2002 in St. Paul at the Science Museum of Minnesota and is traveling throughout the country until 2009. Playing with Time "takes visitors on a journey to the unseen world of natural change and shows events that happen too fast or too slow for humans to perceive."[48]

"Amazing Feats of Aging," supported by a grant from the National Center for Research Resources, National Institutes of Health, is a traveling exhibit from the Oregon Museum of Science and Industry in Portland. The exhibit explores the mysteries of why and how animals and humans age and permits visitors to "look into the future as [they] watch [their] face age up to 25 years." Visitors may discover the biological secrets of aging, how animals age, how scientists can double the life span of certain animal species, and observe cells aging at different rates.[49]

Certainly within the various kinds of exhibits and examples of exhibits, there lie possibilities for libraries to collaborate, seek funding, and develop traveling exhibits that focus on information and library skills as well as kinds and use of resources.

Notwithstanding these classifications, some libraries, in their exhibits policies, define types of exhibits in a manner to support their exhibits policies. The J. Paul Leonard Library at San Francisco State University defines two types of exhibits: major and mini. "Major exhibitions are generally done by guest curators.... Mini exhibits are those that are displayed in the permanent exhibit cases in the Library entry or lobby and run for shorter periods of time than major exhibitions. Mini exhibits may be curated by Exhibits personnel, library staff, student groups, faculty, or guest curators."[50]

The Value of Exhibits

It is in our nature to collect things. We also like to engage in the activity of showing collected items to others and gaining their approval of our efforts. A pleasing exhibit, however, is not a chance outcome of planning. There are principles governing good exhibit practice and there is a psychology surrounding both exhibits and exhibit-goers.

Exhibits have been a vehicle for us to share our accomplishments (4-H and county fairs) and to explore cultures and industries outside our everyday experience (World's

Fairs, museums, zoos, and trade fairs). Exhibits have entertained us (circuses and sideshows) and allowed us to entertain others (backyard shows and grottoes). Exhibits appeal to children and adults, engaging us with sights, sounds, smells and tastes, and things to do. Exhibits have a wide-ranging and plentiful history. Yet, it is the future of exhibits that may prove to leave a greater mark on this history.

The relaxed, accommodating, and self-directed structure of an exhibit has been found to be a supportive environment for learning. Some believe exhibits are a more successful teaching strategy than traditional methodologies. Exhibits, as effective educational tools for teaching, are gaining increased attention and likely will become one beacon on the educational landscape.

3

Learning Theory

Over the past 25 years, there has been increased attention to the educational role of exhibits. This has resulted in a reevaluation of the relationship between visitors and exhibits.[1] We might liken this to the changes in the orientation of televised advertisements from entertaining propaganda aimed at potential buyers to providing a service to viewers by also being informative about a product and its uses, giving rise to the informercial. As some commentators have noted that a large body of educational research shows that traditional teaching methodology is ineffective in today's environments[2]; that is, the more traditional lecture, being predominantly verbal seems to need supplemental techniques to grab and hold the attention of the listener; multi-modal presentations (sound, visuals, activities) appeal to today's students' learning preferences, giving rise to what some have called "edutainment."

Some writers have linked informal and self-directed learning in museums with recent progressive ideas in education.[3] Two essential components of progressive education are respect for diversity (including abilities, interests, and needs) and critical, socially engaged intellect.[4] The self-paced, multimodal (seeing, hearing, doing) format of exhibits facilitates visitors in adjusting their contact or experience based on their interests and current knowledge. The visitor may move about exhibits, revisit portions of an exhibit, move at different speeds within the exhibits, and choose to focus on information presented as text, visuals, sound recordings, or interactive tasks. From research we do know that "exhibitions ... appear to lead to learning, do result in some change in the visitor that is often remembered with pleasure and can influence future behavior"[5]; play is a significant learning activity[6]; and "students would learn more if they were able to be involved in meaningful physical activity," that is, there is a "need for 'minds-on' as well as 'hands-on' ... activities."[7]

Because exhibits are, in today's world, effective educational tools in learning, we should look at theories of learning and decide how they might apply to the design of exhibits in the library. Theories of learning fall into or overlap four general areas of human growth or nature: physical growth, mental growth, spiritual growth, or social emotional growth. Certainly there are more theories, theorists, and practitioners of theory of learning than are covered here; we have chosen theories that we feel are more widely known, still enjoying tested popularity, and are therefore possibly familiar to you. We will begin with some overarching theories that can apply to all exhibit visitors. As with the previous chapter on exhibit theory, the goal is not to apply each theory to every exhibit project. Rather, the idea is to select a couple of ideas that can be applied to an exhibit project. We hope you will return to this chapter as you develop the practice of presenting exhibits.

Learning as a Reward That Encourages Visits

The first theory we will consider links future behavior ("Shall I visit the exhibit?) to return on past behavior ("What did I get out of my last visits to exhibits?"). Behavioral theorists such as Thorndike and Skinner found that rewards received in connection with a behavior will strengthen that behavior. That is, if a visitor received benefit from visits to exhibits, that visitor will be more inclined to visit exhibits again. We can view the benefit or reward a visitor receives from an exhibit as gaining new knowledge, greater understanding, aesthetic pleasure, leisure entertainment, or mental engagements. A well-designed exhibit that rewards the visitor with learning or enjoyment can serve to strengthen their interest in visiting other exhibits. Part of the decision to visit an exhibit, then, is based on experience with or benefit from past exhibit visits. Visitor benefit, therefore, needs to be planned into the exhibit.

Another behaviorist, Robert Glaser, tells us that people are motivated by what makes possible or supports satisfaction of needs (and what satisfies need can be viewed as benefit). Each individual, according to Glaser, has four fundamental needs: to belong (to be involved with their environment), to have power (to feel important, have recognition, be skilled and competent), to have freedom (to be independent and have choices), and to have fun (to feel enjoyment, to learn, to have laughter). These needs, particularly the unsatisfied needs, control a person's behavior. By creating exhibits that satisfy, at least for the duration of the exhibit, one or more of these fundamental needs, we are creating motivation to interact with the exhibit, and, in so doing, exerting control over the visitor's attention. Certainly some satisfactions for these four fundamental needs can be planned into exhibits, and, good exhibit design should include engagement (the visitor feels involved with the exhibit), intellectual power (the visitor feels skilled and competent as a result of interacting with the exhibit), freedom (the visitor has a choice of different ways to gain knowledge through the exhibit), and fun (the visitor finds the exhibit enjoyable to interact with).

While need satisfaction may motivate the visitor to engage with or to revisit an exhibit, satisfying a current need may not be sufficient for the exhibit to also be a learning experience. George Hein tells us "routine experiences that do not challenge and stimulate us may not be educative.... It is not sufficient for experiences to be 'lively, vivid, and 'interesting'; they must also be organized to be educative."[8] To help ensure that our exhibit is organized, and therefore able to be educative, we will turn to a behavioral theory practitioner, Madeline Hunter, who is known in education for her systematic approach to lesson design.

Designing Exhibit Content

Hunter found that to enhance and maximize learning, the learning experience needs to be planned or designed utilizing a methodology that has been effective across the different developmental stages (grade levels) and socioeconomic backgrounds of the learners, involving suitable subject matter, and teaching or presentation style. In designing or planning the lesson, there are eight elements that need to be considered. We will apply these eight elements to planning the intellectual content of the exhibit. Intellectual content design should be undertaken as a planning phase separate from the design and planning of the physical exhibit itself. In designing the exhibit's intellectual content, each of the following elements should be considered:

(1) What short activity or prompt might be devised to focus the visitor's attention on the exhibit, marking the beginning of the exhibit's message?

(2) What is the purpose of the exhibit? What will the visitor be able to do with that knowledge? How will the visitor be able to show he has gained the desired learning?

(3) What vocabulary, skills, and concepts will be utilized in the exhibit? Will these be imparted to the visitor through discovery, reading, listening, observing, interacting?

(4) Can you devise a graphic form or model depicting the knowledge to be learned from the exhibit?

(5) Can you develop techniques that will permit the visitor to check their understanding of the concepts or skills presented in the exhibit?

(6) Can you design a segment that leads the visitor through a guided practice of the new learning? Can this utilize a trimodal approach (hearing/seeing/doing)?

(7) Can you design activities that permit the visitor to practice the new learning, skills or understandings on their own?

(8) How can you review or wrap up the exhibit's goals, marking the conclusion of the exhibit's message?

The point Hunter is making is the point made by system-designers: the bulk of the work is in the planning-the construction and installation are just a fulfillment of the plan.

As an example of this methodology, let's design an exhibit for kindergartners who will be introduced to the nonfiction collection in their school library and asked to gather information from books for an oral report on an animal. The goal for the exhibit is to excite students about finding information and to do so utilizing subject material and techniques that can be reused in years to come. The librarian and teacher decide killer whales would make a good prompt for the student's attention and decide to focus on the intelligence and other human-like characteristics of these mammals. The exhibit will

be titled "Two Mammal Families" and will depict how killer whales and people are alike, that is, explaining some shared characteristics of mammals. The librarian and teacher decide to use four vocabulary terms for the four concepts to be shown in the exhibit: intelligence, socialization, language, and family. These topics will be conveyed through photographs and cartoonlike drawings and through a short audio reading of statements on mammals, specifically killer whales and dolphins. The art teacher provides cartoon-like renderings of the four topics using the gathered photos of killer whales and people engaged in problem-solving activities, social activities, communicating activities, and family activities ; the art teacher also suggests, for a picture to accompany the exhibit title, a whimsical drawing of killer whale calves (babies) and children sitting in desks at school. For testing understanding, the exhibit includes a board matching game with feedback (using wire, batteries, and small bulbs): a picture of killer whales and of peo-ple will each be placed on the board connected to a probe. Cartoons of characteristics that mammals do and do not possess will also be mounted on the board. When a probe touches a depiction of a characteristic of a mammal, the bulb will light. The art teacher also creates a two-page independent activity for students: one page contains a two-col-umn table with the picture of a person heading one column and the picture of a killer whale heading the other. On the second sheet are squares depicting characteristics mam-mals do and do not possess. The children may cut out the pictures that represent char-acteristics of mammals, paste them in the appropriate column on the first sheet, then color the pictures. The exhibit concludes with a collection of books on killer whales and paper animal tracks from the display to shelves containing books on animals.

In designing the content for "Two Mammal Families" the librarian and teachers have determined the goals of the exhibit (introduction to nonfiction), have planned a prompt (whimsical caricature of two mammals — killer whales and humans — in school) to focus the child's attention on the exhibit, and have established the vocabulary and concepts (intelligent, social, language, and family) to be used and the graphic forms (photographs and drawings) to depict these concepts. Three modes (seeing, hearing, and doing) are utilized to engage the senses and accommodate individual children's innate learning preferences. A match game is used both to give the child guided practice (bulb lights up for correct match) and to practice on their own (handout). To concretely link the exhibit and its goal, animal tracks lead the child from the exhibit to the nonfiction collection on animals.

A well-planned exhibit can satisfy fundamental intellectual needs as identified by behaviorist models: to be involved with their environment, to be skilled and competent, to have choices, and to have fun; and that by doing so the visit is rewarding. This in turn strengthens the inclination to visit exhibits. (Likewise, poorly planned exhibits that do not reward the visitor can reinforce a behavior of exhibit-avoidance.) In addition, a time-tested planning structure like Hunter's lesson design will enhance and maximize the learning a visitor can receive from an exhibit.

We now know that the intellectual content of exhibits needs to be systematically planned to maximize learning and to reward visitors for their visit. We will now look at how basic needs and cognitive development influences a visitor's ability to focus on or to grasp the concepts presented through the exhibit.

Basic Needs Can Influence Learning

We will consider basic human needs through Maslow's Hierarchy of Needs. Maslow identifies five levels of need: physiological needs including food and sleep; need for psychological and physical safety; need to belong; need for self-esteem; and need for self-actualization. Each need level must be satisfied before the next level can be attained. If we consider the exhibit as an environment or ecosystem, we can follow a visitor through it using Maslow's Hierarchy. The most basic needs are physiological needs, including hunger and thirst. We might want to dismiss this as not being relevant to exhibits; but lets imagine that our visitors arrive at the exhibit having not recently eaten or very thirsty; their attention may be directed toward their hunger and thirst and they may be unable to give the needed attention or focus to the exhibit. (The U.S. Department of Agriculture established that in 1997 over 12 million households in the United States were "food insecure." Research has linked hunger to lower test scores and behavioral problems. In short, "Hungry students can't learn."⁹) If the exhibit's environment has the means to satisfy some of these lower level needs, then good signage such as to water fountains and food areas would be helpful in assisting visitors with satisfying these needs before they begin to interact with the exhibit. Likewise, a quick trip to an exhibit before a child's usual snack or mealtime may not be the best time for engaging the child's attention or focus. Given that the physiological needs are reasonably met, Maslow tells us the visitor must now need to feel safe, both physically and psychologically. In terms of the exhibit, this means the exhibit needs to be located in a well-lighted and highly visible area with defined boundaries and rules of conduct regulated through signage or design, must have sturdy construction, and should have sufficient cues or signage to give the visitor psychological comfort in how to access, move through, and exit the exhibit.

Once the needs at these lower levels are reasonably well satisfied, the visitors will be able to turn their attention to needs at the higher level. The higher levels on Maslow's scale coincide with needs identified by Glaser and include acceptance or affiliation, self-esteem and self-actualization. By considering the repertoire of the visitor, that is knowledge and experiences the visitor is likely to bring to the exhibit, the designer helps to make the visitor feel affiliated with the context and content of the exhibit. By designing the exhibit to provide, for example, verification or feedback on a new skill or understanding gained from the exhibit, the exhibit can help build self-esteem. The highest level of need is that for self-actualization (aesthetic and/or cognitive), that is, the need to be all that you can be in terms of use of imagination and thinking. It is interesting to note that people enjoy being exposed to activities that satisfy needs that are otherwise unmet. Therefore, a well-constructed exhibit can, at least for the time in the exhibit, help visitors to bridge over deficiencies in their lives and to experience higher levels of need satisfaction. This may seem like a lot to keep in mind and strive for when designing the learning environment of the exhibit. Your goal should be to attend to one or a few of these in each exhibit, rather than to every consideration mentioned in this chapter. Repeated work on designs of other exhibits will make it increasingly easier to apply aspects of theories of learning and will allow you to increase your ability to apply learning theory to the exhibits you create.

Visitor Age Can Affect Design

Now lets turn our attention to the effect of visitor age on learning and exhibit design. The age or level of cognitive development of the expected visitor does need to be considered in exhibits. As a general rule, visitors fall into two broad cognitive skill levels: emerging (under approximately age 14) and developed (over approximately age 13). According to Piaget,[10] during late childhood (approximately ages 6 to 13), cognitive processes become adultlike except in speed of operation. This means that exhibits designed for the average adult should be appropriate for visitors as young as approximately age 14. Exhibits designed for children under age 14, however, need to take into consideration the specific age and approximate cognitive skills of the children expected to interact with the exhibit.

To show how cognitive development comes into play in planning exhibits, let's begin by drawing on Piaget and others and apply their work to exhibits. We will begin with newborns and look at how they might interaction with exhibits and where we might want to construct exhibits for infants.

Exhibits for Infants

Public libraries, from Atherton Library in San Mateo County, California, to Delphi Public Library in Delphi, Indiana, to Bixby Memorial Free Library in Vergennes, Vermont, have begun offering lap time story hours for caregivers and infants. Libraries may want to design an exhibit that would interest infants participating in lap time story hours (this might be a good opportunity to create a permanent exhibit to attract to the library each new group of newborns, and their caregivers, in the community). Infancy spans birth to the appearance of language, about 2 years of age. During this time babies are concerned with coordinating movement and action and in discovery of their bodies. Let's also remind ourselves, for the purpose of input into an idea for a permanent exhibit, that a child is born with the ability to make the range of human sounds; however, this ability is developed through actually hearing the sounds. This suggests that one possible permanent exhibit for infants might be one based on sounds of a variety of languages. An interactive exhibit could be constructed so that pressing an image would activate a short narrative in a given language. The interactive aspect would support gaining coordination as well as retaining the ability to make native sounds in many languages by hearing those sounds. Since infants are also discovering their own physical self (feet, hands, toes, etc.), we might design a touch exhibit with shapes of feet, hands, and other objects that when touched would play a sequence of simple sentences about that object, cycling through two or three languages, such as "Clap your hands. Aplauda las manos. Clap your hands. Applaudir vos mains. Clap your hands. Klatschen Sie Ihre Hände. Clap your hands. Applaudire le sue mani. Clap your hands." Such a multilingual permanent exhibit could serve as a welcoming link between the public library and various cultural or ethnic groups in the community, giving a sense of affiliation, and encourage early introduction to the library.

Infants (birth to the appearance of language) need to be exposed to a variety of experiences that help them make sense of the world; and they need to hear language. The Pickle board books by Lynn Breeze: *Pickle and the Ball, Pickle and the Blanket, Pickle and the Blocks*, and *Pickle and the Box*, help introduce the infant to common household objects and interactions with these objects. A simple exhibit for infants might provide copies of these board books and objects from these books, encouraging the caregiver to read the books to the infant and assist the infant in interacting with objects that are named in the books. The infant's basic needs (warmth, companionship) can be established with cuddling during lap time story hours and caregivers reading books aloud. Discovery of the physical self can be facilitated with books such as Helen Oxenbury's *All Fall Down* and *Clap Hands*. As the infant gains control of their hands and legs, they can mimic the actions as these books are read aloud. Books can be used to help develop large motor skills by letting the child handle and open the book. Keeping in mind these needs and the skills infants are learning to master, we might plan a reading environment with rocking chairs and other comfortable chairs for two, with cases of books and books on tape (including in multiple languages), and interactive exhibits that combine developmental skills with exploration. Using the installations in the Cotsen Children's Library housed within the Firestone Library at Princeton University as inspiration for ideas for creating literature-based interactive exhibits for infants, we might think of a reading environment as an exhibit itself. For example, a permanent installation based on *Good Night Moon* could include a rocking chair (for infant-caregiver read alouds) next to the bookcase filled with books for reading. The bed might be modified into an oversized reading chair for two and developmental activities could be incorporated into the other objects in the room such as the dollhouse and telephone and radio. An installation based on, for example, *Good Night Moon* could be accomplished along a wall, nestled in a corner, or installed in an open area. It could become the backdrop for programming for infants with caregivers as well as programming for parents, babysitters, and teachers.

For Preschoolers and Kindergarteners

During early childhood (approximately ages 2–4), children are busy discovering the environment. This child's play centers on exploration and questions of how and why. These questions can lead to exhibits that help the preschooler discover answers. Children of this age take activities quite literally and often explain things that happen by giving life to inanimate objects. An exhibit might be designed around "The day little bear's fire truck tripped him." The fire truck could demonstrate the hows and whys of the mechanics of a few moving objects from a rolling truck to a falling bear that lost its balance. The fire truck could also introduce both books on trucks such as Byron Barton's *Trucks* and *Machines at Work* and stories such as *The Little Engine That Could* and *Mike Mulligan and His Steam Shovel*.

The child in early childhood likes concept books dealing with time (before-after), distance (near-far), size (tall-short), mass (big-small), color, shape, differences between "between" and "through." These preferences may be used as themes for exhibits that will appeal to children this age; for example, oversized books of permutations that change a portion of a figure to create depictions (with words) of large, small, tall, short, near, far, big, little. Exhibits could present puzzles that include matching games between objects and sounds or objects and words (star, square, circle). Nursery rhymes and folk tales that humanize animals are also popular with this age group; colorful depictions of humanized animals might be designed into moveable and pop-up displays that introduce children, for example, to handling and care of books.

Between the ages of roughly 4 and 7 (middle childhood), children become able to react realistically to the environment and are able to project themselves into other roles and think in terms of other people. Exhibits that explore the lives of others such as "If I were a farmer" would be appropriate for these children. During middle childhood the child begins to recognize the differences between how things look and how they really are. Exhibits designed around classic problems or puzzles that this aged child is just becoming able to grasp might include "Which is more?" This classic puzzle might be shown with the same volume of liquid being poured into differently shaped containers or rows of the same number of objects, each on an expanding band that would result in the objects being spaced differently. Simple tangram puzzles might be used as an activity that linked successful construction of stylized shapes with completion of a clue that marks in the collection books about that object. An interactive exhibit based on Pat Hutchins' *The Doorbell Rang* would appeal to this age child who seems to count everything; it also introduces division.

The child in middle childhood is gaining reading skills, perhaps entering this stage with only rudimentary knowledge of letters and their sounds and leaving it with the ability to read a book. These children need praise to verify adult approval as they move toward greater independence. Exhibits with interactive tasks can be designed to automate praise when a task is successfully accomplished.

The child in middle childhood likes stories in which the characters experience conflict; that is, it is important for this child to hear stories about characters whose actions throw them into opposition with others. This child can learn through characters what it is to take on more responsibility for their actions. Children of this age like a good balance of realistic fiction (particularly with characters to which the child can relate) and fantasy (particularly fantasy and stories that apply human characteristics to animals). In middle childhood children see characters (and issues) in absolutes: all brave, all cunning, etc.; but is able to understand more fully developed characters that talk about feelings and motives. These characteristics might suggest an exhibit that begins to introduce decision-making and consequences, perhaps in choose-your-own-decision style. For this age child, collaborative exhibits can be used to bridge classroom activities with resources in the school library media center and between the school and the public library.

For School-aged Children

During late childhood (roughly ages 7–11), the concepts of time are more fully developed and the child is now able to understand ideas about the past, even the historical past. The child in late childhood begins to move beyond one-dimensional thinking and is able to relate one event to a system of interrelated parts, for example, from a beginning to an end, suggesting the beginning of the ability to handle flashbacks and to think in terms of the future.

During the end of late childhood (about ages 9–11), children are very interested in examining the rules that govern their lives, including questioning traditional ways of operating, and asking what happens when conventional wisdom is questioned. Exhibits can be designed to address the child's new ability to work through a problem. Children in late childhood are determined to master tasks that are set for them; they need to show that they are competent and constantly measure themselves against their peers.

Exhibits that teach mastery of new tasks are very important for the student in late childhood. Children at this level favor mysteries and puzzles, and they can benefit from historical fiction and biographies of real people, stories with flashbacks and future time, and chapter books. These characteristics should guide exhibit themes and design.

During adolescence (roughly ages 11–15), the young person is able to formulate theories about physical and social aspects of life, to understand and empathize with others and to be more aware of their relationships within the family and within the community. The adolescent is focused on a search for identity (both personal and cultural). These characteristics can be utilized in exhibits to enable the young person to think beyond immediate experiences and to theorize about a variety of things including universal concerns and beliefs that expand the young person's view of the world.

Exhibiting for a Range of Ages

We do need to keep in mind the relationship between these levels of development and the ages associated with each level. The developing child does not jump from one developmental level to another at the appointed age. The ages suggested for each developmental level, rather, suggest where the majority of children at the given age are likely to be in terms of skill and ability levels. A portion of that age group, however, will still be at earlier stages and a portion will have advanced to later stages. To appeal to the broader range of children in a given age group, exhibits should include activities aimed at a range of developmental levels.

Vygotsky's Zone of Proximal Development (ZPD) suggests how an exhibit can appeal to a range of developmental levels. The Zone of Proximal Development is marked at the low end by performing a skill with assistance and at the high end by performing the skill alone. Within the Zone of Proximal Development, a child learns to manipulate ideas and skills independently by being assisted in varying degrees, as needed by the child at that time. That is, a child is able to perform tasks when assisted that they could not perform on their own. For example, consider a child who is unable to tie shoelaces. However, by mimicking the steps performed by another, or by following each step as reminded verbally, the child is able to complete the task. Another form of assistance is to use reminders in the form of questions, for example, "Where do we lay the right lace?" "How do we make the right lace go under and over the left lace?" Assisted performance permits the child to successfully accomplish tasks they are not yet able to accomplish independently. An exhibit, therefore, can be extended to additional age or developmental levels by including both activities that can be accomplished alone and with assistance. Hunter's methodology for designing learning experience, recall, includes planning both practice activities that the visitor can accomplish with prompts or assistance and practice activities that the visitor can accomplish alone.

For Young Adults and Adults

Now we will turn our attention to adults, or, more specifically, to those over approximately 13 or 14 years of age. An aspect of adult personality or behavior is cognitive style; that is, each adult has a preferred way of thinking or processing information. One adult may scan material while another focuses closely on each detail. One adult may reflect on what is learned while another is impulsive and moves quickly to another concept. Exhibits can be designed to facilitate individual's different intensities of attention to material. For example, an exhibit that uses a complete take-away message for the title or heading of a longer, more detailed description, allows for the scanners to easily grasp the key points while giving the detail seekers additional material to explore. Some adults tend to merge memories of similar events while others recall the distinctiveness of each event. Design techniques such as using different background colors for different event presentations may aid those who merge similar ideas with keeping needed distinctions between ideas. Adults will also differ in their speed and adequacy of forming hypotheses and responses from presented material; therefore, to facilitate the range of visitors, designs should facilitate the visitor in moving through the exhibit at their own pace.

Other theories of learning suggest that displays, to appeal to more adults, should include elements of concrete experiences, reflective observation, abstract conceptualization, and active experimentation.[11] Adult visitors to museums and libraries are generally motivated learners and the informal learning opportunities offered by exhibits best meet these learners' needs. That is, the success of exhibits for adults is not found in what they learned but how they were able to learn or explore within the exhibit.[12] Informal, self-directed learning is facilitated by exhibits that support: essential skills of literacy and numeracy; information location and retrieval; goal setting; time management; question-asking behavior; critical thinking; and comprehensive monitoring and self-evaluation.[13]

We know that adult learning is different from children's learning in three ways: adults are more experienced in taking responsibility for their own lives; adults have accumulated a broader and deeper repertoire of experience, giving them more models for making sense out of new experiences; and adults are generally motivated to learn in the hopes that it will enable them to more effectively cope with or more fully enjoy their lives.[14]

Family Learning and Exhibits

Through stories, reminisces, discussions, and mentoring, members of a family exchange their experiences, knowledge and values, creating a shared family culture. As members of the family gain new knowledge and relationships, they may bring them immediately into the family culture or share them at a future time or repeatedly over time.[15] The family's shared culture creates potential for learning within the family; that is, each member is a gateway through which learning can reach all family members. Research has further found that families evolve learning agendas and that those agendas include specific interactions within and external to the family unit.[16]

Exhibits, then, are an opportunity for families to enrich their family culture by engaging in mentoring, discussion, reminisces, and stories prompted by the artifacts and content of exhibits, perhaps with sentimental or affectionate feelings for this informal style of learning. Exhibits can become a tool for lifelong family learning, providing stimuli for family conversations that may begin before the visit and extend well beyond the visit, in fact, becoming part of the shared experiences that can serve as experience-based examples for other discussions or problem-solving or to fuel further exploration of topics.[17] Further, learning seems to be based in experience or knowledge; that is, "learning proceeds primarily from prior knowledge and only secondarily from the presented materials."[18] Exhibit visits, then, give families the opportunity for some members to share their knowledge and experience that other members lack, helping to extend learning to all family members.

Family visits to exhibits provide the child with the opportunity to share with the adults in the family competency and confidence gained during a visit to the exhibit.[19] The adults will also have opportunities to guide and praise the child's learning as well as take on the "role of mediator, asking questions, supporting children's ideas and prompting their learning process and understanding."[20]

Family-oriented exhibits, however, need not be complex or difficult to hold the interest of the adult members. It has been found that complex or difficult exhibits "get visitors' awe and respect but not comprehension."[21] The better exhibit will have very few goals, perhaps even one, and will address those goals in a number of ways so that more members of the family (a wider range of ages) will experience what it is that the exhibit planners set out to accomplish.

An exhibit cannot hope to be all things to all people. However, decisions on how information will be presented in an exhibit will impact which visitors will be attracted to and stay focused on the exhibit, as well as what impression the visitor will take away with them from the exhibit. Keeping in mind how people learn will help the exhibit designer plan increased access to the intended experience or knowledge.

4

Status of Exhibits in Libraries

Members of the public seem to know that display and exhibit areas in libraries are valuable communication, educational, and business tools. From articles on and notices of displays and exhibits, we begin to feel the range of exhibits citizens request in libraries. Historians and archeologists have looked for library exhibit space in which to display their research. Hobbyists have looked for showcases in which to display educational and artistic displays of gourds and of quilts. Special interest groups, clubs, and organizations have looked for bulletin boards and exhibit walls on which to raise awareness of issues, events, and people. Artists have used library exhibit space for their exhibitions. Alexandra Nechita (*Outside the Lines*, Longstreet Press) recalls that her first art exhibit was in a library: Now she sells her paintings in galleries for $50,000.

The American Library Association seems to know that exhibits are valuable promotional and outreach tools for libraries. In the promotional description for one of its publications it states: "It's no secret that well-executed exhibits in libraries and museums can make attendance numbers skyrocket.... A great exhibit can be the hook that brings people to the door for the first time."[1]

But do libraries promote exhibits as one of their valuable tools? One way to measure the status of exhibits in libraries is to look for the prominence of exhibits on libraries' websites. To do this, we decided to look at one public library in each state. For each of the states (and the District of Columbia), one city was chosen randomly (from an online map of the United States that labeled only a few cities in each state). Using www.publiclibraries.com and Yahoo, the URLs were obtained for the public libraries in the 51 selected cities or towns.

Prominence of Exhibits

The homepage of each public library website was examined for mention of exhibits or exhibitions. Where events links were found (but no mention of exhibits), the link was followed to see if mention of exhibits could be found on the linking webpage. When no mention was found through other logical links from the homepage, a site map or site index or site search function, if available, was used to locate any mention of exhibits.

Of the 51 public library homepages, just under 10 percent (5 out of 51) of the library websites gave homepage prominence to exhibits using the terms "exhibit," "gallery," or "display." Three of the 51 (6 percent) listed "exhibits" (only two with links to another page, the third simply stated "Interesting exhibits are just one reason to visit the [library]"). A fourth homepage gave the name of the gallery space. A fifth mentions "displays" on the homepage but gives no link to additional information.

In looking at linking webpages, just under 22 percent (11 out of 51) of the library websites had some mention of exhibits or displays on webpages that linked from the homepage by following "events," or "programs." Five (10 percent) contained mention of exhibits by following Events (4) or Program (1) from the homepage. A sixth mentioned lobby displays; a seventh mentioned Now on Display (however, there were no entries under the heading); and an eighth mentioned "This month's events/Art in the library." Two contained lists of events that included mention of exhibits. And an eleventh site mentioned that programs were held in the Exhibition Gallery, however, no exhibits were mentioned.

Of the 16 public library websites (31 percent) with some mention of exhibits or a phrase suggesting exhibits on the homepage or a page linked from the homepage, two were links to policies governing displays and exhibits in the library, and one linked to a philosophy stating that the curated exhibitions promote the library's special collections and services. Of the ten libraries (20 percent) that listed an actual exhibit, nine libraries seemed to have exhibits other than a bulletin board or display case and one had a display case that collected objects around a theme. Of the ten exhibits and displays, five were of fine art (including local, nonprofessional artists), two of performing arts, one of a historical theme, one of natural history, and one about a sports team.

Using a site search function and/or a site map or index, four additional instances of exhibits were found: one listing both fine arts and theme-based exhibits; one to a research library and an exhibit gallery; one to an historical exhibit; and one as a note about an associated exhibit on a webpage focusing on a workshop event. Eighteen (35 percent) of the library websites did not have site searching or site maps.

In summary, based on the 51 public library websites, one selected from each state plus the District of Columbia, 27 percent (14) appear to have advertised exhibits (or displays) with half of the exhibits displaying fine arts works and half displaying theme-based materials including the performing arts, crafts, history, nature, and sports.

Eighteen (35 percent) of the 51 library websites had some mention of exhibits or displays (recall, some were links to policies and some listed no exhibits). In looking at the distribution of public libraries with known exhibits, based on geographical location, in the Northwest (including Alaska) one out of 6 libraries (17 percent) has exhibits; in the Southwest (including Hawaii) 4 out of 5 libraries (80 percent) have exhibits; in the North Central 3 out of 11 libraries (27 percent) have exhibits; in the South Central 3 out of 8 libraries (38 percent) have exhibits; in the Northeast 4 out of 15 libraries (27 percent) have exhibits; and in the Southeast 3 out of 6 libraries (50 percent) have exhibits.

Policies on Library Exhibits

In additional searches of these 51 websites, few policies on exhibits were found. Of those found, libraries tended to employ exhibits as a means to educate visitors about library resources and community events. One library uses exhibits to provide "places for persons or organizations to share interests and ideas" while another uses exhibit space to "enhance the visual environment" of the library, providing for "the enjoyment of the visual arts" and "spaces for artists and community residents to share creative talents and information." One library utilizes exhibits as a way "to create understanding of the role of libraries in education and economic development."

The Policy Manual of the American Library Association calls for libraries that maintain exhibit spaces and bulletin boards for outside groups and individuals to "develop and publish statements governing use" of those spaces; these policies are "to assure that space is provided on an equitable basis to all groups which request it."[2] Further, policies governing exhibit space should be written in "inclusive rather than exclusive terms;" that is, what is permitted rather than what is not allowed.[3] In "Exhibit Spaces and Bulletin Boards: An Interpretation of the Library Bill of Rights,"[4] the American Library Association reminds us that exhibit spaces and bulletin boards should conform to the Library Bill of Rights. Exhibits in libraries should "endeavor to present a broad spectrum of opinion and a variety of viewpoints" and "should not censor or remove an exhibit because some members of the community may disagree with its content."

In looking at exhibit policies of libraries beyond the 51 surveyed, we find that, where extensive policies have been developed; they include an application for use of exhibit space. More comprehensive exhibit policies include:

- exhibit guidelines and purpose
- general guidelines for content in displays
- criteria for use of the exhibit space
- description and size of exhibit spaces
- procedure for requesting display space
- policies on the library's right to refuse an exhibit or exhibitor that does not meet these policy guidelines
- policy on the sale of exhibit items during the exhibit; using library materials in displays
- conservation considerations
- installation and dismantling of exhibits; security
- general supplies needed or allowed to set up an exhibit
- signage

- publicity
- follow-up and clean-up
- fees if the library must dismantle the exhibit
- exhibit application form and timing of request procedures
- procedures for filing concerns about a current exhibit.

Some policies carry a statement that the library's policy is in agreement with the American Library Association's Library Bill of Rights; some state the library board has adopted them or the applicable article(s); and some make no mention of the Library Bill of Rights. Applications for use of exhibit space include:

- name of exhibitor and contact information
- title of exhibit
- space requirements
- number of pieces to be exhibited
- dates requested
- specific space requested
- information for publicity
- agreement to pay a given fee if the library must dismantle the exhibit
- need for other library facilities in addition to exhibit space (and location of procedures to request use)
- waiver of insurance
- dated signatures of the exhibitor and of the librarian.

Every library with display or exhibit space needs to develop a policy to guide the use of that space. Those policies should be in agreement with the *Library Bill of Rights*.

Professional Competencies and Exhibit Work

While many if not most libraries have display if not also exhibit space, knowledge of and skills in exhibit work are not generally included in job descriptions for librarians. It is, therefore, of interest to ask, What competencies in exhibit work, if any, are desirable?

In looking at professional competencies for librarians, as established by the professional divisions of the American Library Association, we find recommended competencies that directly or indirectly suggest that knowledge and skills in arranging or creating exhibits are appropriate staff development opportunities if not required basic skills. Specifically, we reviewed competencies for four groups of librarians: librarians serving children in public libraries,[5] librarians serving young adults,[6] reference and user services librarians,[7] and school library media specialists.[8] In looking at the competencies for each group, we looked for skills or goals that mentioned displays or that could be fulfilled by exhibit work. Under Organization and Design of Services, we find desired skills for reference and user service librarians include creating "displays, tutorials ... and other special tools to increase access to information resources and to motivate users to use them," organizing and effectively displaying information, and designing "services to meet the special access needs."[9] It is desirable for children's services librarians to have competencies that include understanding "theories of infant, child, and adolescent learning and development and their implications for library service," creating "displays ... and other special tools to increase access to library resources and motivate their use," and designing, promoting, executing, and evaluating "programs for children of all ages, based on their developmental needs and interests and the goals of the library."[10] YA librarians should be able to "create an environment that attracts and invites young adults to use the collection" and to "employ promotional methods and techniques that will increase access and generate collection usage."[11] Further, the American Association of School Librarians, in its ALA/AASL Standards for Initial Programs, includes as evidence under Program Administration, "showing expertise in displays, organization, bulletin boards, charts that encourage student learning and reading."[12] Certainly creating engaging exhibits as learning tools is within the scope and competencies of librarians who provide user services and services to children and young adults.

While some knowledge of and skills in exhibit work are within the recommended competencies for librarians, certainly expertise of the level expected for museum staff is not expected. It is of interest, however, to know where there are shared competencies among museum staff and librarians. The International Councils of Museums (ICOM) has developed Curricula Guidelines for Museum Professional Development.[13] In looking at the ICOM Guidelines and the ALA competencies we found seven common areas: assessing and understanding community needs; exhibition techniques as tools for mobilizing community members for the use of their common resources; intellectual access; physical access; educational theory, psychology, and sociology; learning theory; nonvisitors characteristics and visitor characteristics. These areas of potential common knowledge provide a productive space for librarians and museum staff, with each bringing their own unique expertise into collaborations that may benefit libraries, museums, schools, and their communities.

Future of Exhibits in Libraries

While exhibits in libraries will undoubtedly continue to serve their patrons as centers for information and display for special topics and community interests, the educational role of exhibits will take on more prominence. Exhibits in libraries could come to play a major role in increasing information literacy if not also functional literacy.

As a tool for teaching and learning, exhibits seem more effective in today's environments than are traditional teaching methodologies.[14] Some institutions have supplemented their librarian-led information literacy instruction programs with web-based tutorials, in some cases by linking to TILT (Texas Information Literacy Tutorial), which delivers units on kinds and locations of sources; selecting and searching best sources; and locating, evaluating, and citing sources.[15] Exhibits can go beyond this, offering the advantage of informal and self-directed learning and providing constant interaction between the visitor and the library's environment.

Exhibits as venues for teaching information literacy skills afford the potential for collaborations among libraries, schools, and museums, and their communities. Public libraries and public schools might collaborate, for example, on creating portable exhibits on the Big6 Skills[16] or Super3 (the early childhood version of the Big6 Skills)[17] information literacy models or the Research Cycle[18] strategy for seeking and using information. Exhibits might first be used in the schools in conjunction with formal introduction or teaching of these methods, then displayed at the public library to assist students using the public library to research topics for school assignments.

A library might design permanent exhibits to foster information literacy by exploring, on a rotating basis, topics such as information sources, information use, information seeking, and evaluation of information sources. A consortia of libraries and museums might apply for funding, such as to the Institute for Museums and Library Services (IMLS), the U.S. Department of Education (DOE), or various foundations, to design and build a series of traveling exhibits to facilitate teaching information issues and skills or to design a series for reproduction and use by other libraries. Public or academic or special or school libraries might partner with museums to create exhibits on resources and on searching in specific subject areas. Community groups might partner with local public, school, or academic libraries to create exhibits that feature sources and guides to portions of the collection of special interest to these groups.

Library exhibits can reach out to the community and provide informal information education that is flexible to different learning styles and to a range of learners from challenged to talented, children to adult learners, and nonliterate to literate to nonnative speakers. Libraries can reach out to groups that might not otherwise have access to the knowledge and skills afforded through exhibits.

5

The Basic Exhibit Process

There are a number of different kinds of exhibits you can have at your library. No matter which kind you plan to have, you can use the basic exhibit process outlined in this section to make things go smoothly. These ten steps are designed for beginners. The Comprehensive Exhibit Process is described in Chapter 6 and recommends a specific order and adds some optional aspects of exhibits, such as programming, not addressed here.

The ten steps will prevent you from becoming overwhelmed. For your first exhibit you should start small. With each exhibit, you will gain knowledge, experience, and confidence that will inspire you to go a step further on your next exhibit. In addition, throughout the Comprehensive Exhibit Process section, a hypothetical exhibit is used to illustrate many of the steps. The following symbol is used to mark these examples, making them easy to find:

All exhibits can be created using the following steps:

1. Determine why and how you will be making an exhibit.
2. Decide on an exhibit theme.
3. Review administrative concerns.
4. Develop and design the exhibit.
5. Prototype the exhibit.
6. Write and design the exhibit labels.
7. Prototype the exhibit again.
8. Fabricate and install the exhibit.

9. Publicize the exhibit.
10. Evaluate and document the exhibit before deinstallation.

Step 1: Determine Why and How You Are Making an Exhibit

Before making an exhibit, you must know what your goals are and what resources you have to put toward it. When these are established, a plan must be created to help the project run smoothly.

• Identify your goals. (See also Chapter 6, step 1.1.1.)

The first step to any exhibit is to define why you are making it; all other decisions hinge on these goals. The theme, style, design, and kind of exhibit you make will change to meet different goals. For example, if your goal is to showcase the library's rare special collections, you won't worry about designing the exhibit with space to display circulation materials; but if one of your goals is to promote reading or circulation, you will want to have circulating materials on display with the exhibit. If your library hopes to promote itself as an institution central to its community, it should concentrate its exhibits on themes that are relevant and important to that community; if, however, the goal is simply to educate or entertain patrons, it can make or hire exhibits on any number of themes, even (or maybe especially) those about far-off places and ideas. Your goals can change for different exhibits, but it is important to identify what they are for each individual exhibit to focus the exhibit development and provide a basis for an evaluation of the exhibit's success.

• Know your resources. (See also Chapter 6, step 1.1.2.)

The size, extent, and kind of exhibit you can make depends on the availability of funds, staff, space, and time. You must determine how much of each of these you can devote to the exhibit before you begin to develop it. Answer the following questions:
1. Budget: How much money can the library spend ? Will it be able to raise further funds through grants, sponsorships, donations, or other means?
2. Staff: Which staff members will be working on the exhibit and how much time can they spend on it? Are there any volunteers who could commit to this project?
3. Space: Where in the library will the exhibit be located? Is there more than one possible space?
4. Time: Is there a specific date on which the exhibit needs to be up? How much time is there to prepare?

• Develop a plan of action. (See also Chapter 6, step 1.1.4.)

After answering the questions and identifying your goals, develop a plan. This plan should include a budget (see a sample budget in step 1.5.1 in Chapter 6), an assignment of staff and volunteer responsibilities, and a schedule or timeline. Pay particular attention to those tasks that rely on the completion of another task; make sure these are appropriately accounted for in the timeline. A planning checklist and sample timeline like the ones in Chapter 6, step 1.1.4, can help you develop your plan.

Step 2: Decide on an Exhibit Theme

What kind of exhibit you will have and what it will be about are obviously important decisions. Researching your audience as well as the theme will help you narrow the theme to one "take-home message" that will guide the development of a successful exhibit.

• Choose a general exhibit theme and kind of exhibit. (See also Chapter 6, step 1.1.3.)

With your goals in mind, decide what your exhibit will be about and what kind of exhibit it will be. In some cases, your theme will dictate what kind of exhibit you'll have, but some themes could be addressed using more than one kind of exhibit. These might be an art show, a display of books or other objects, a historical exhibit, a hands-on exhibit, a traveling exhibit, a combination of any of these, or more. If you choose to rent a traveling exhibit, read more about that process in Chapter 7.

• Research the theme. (See also Chapter 6, step 1.2.1.)

Once your general theme is set, do some research to find out what things you could say about that topic. You won't be able to say everything, so you want to narrow your focus to the most effective, important, or interesting aspect.

• Know your audience and tailor the exhibit. (See also Chapter 6, step 1.2.2.)

One way to narrow your theme is to tailor it to your audience. A good exhibit provokes thought or an emotional response in the visitors; it prompts them to make connections with their own lives and what they know, and can generate new ideas, awareness, or attitude. To do this, an exhibit must resonate with the visitors and there is no better way to do make this happen than to relate the exhibit to the visitors' lives. You must always keep the visitors in mind when developing an exhibit. Ask yourself, "What is the best way to reach this audience?" If you do not know your audience, you won't be able to answer.

You can find out about your audience through front-end evaluation, the process of interviewing or surveying your visitors to focus your exhibit on their needs. You can find out such things as what topics they are interested in, what they would like to know about a specific topic, what they know about that topic, how they feel a topic relates to their life, or how they feel emotionally about a topic. This kind of evaluation can also tell you what they like and don't like to see, what they expect to see, and what they wish they could see in exhibits in general as well as in this one in particular. Through such questioning you can determine what level of information to include in your exhibit; there is no sense repeating what most people know, but you need to provide adequate background if your topic is complex or not well known so your visitors won't be lost. Also, knowing whether there are any areas of your theme that are particularly locally relevant or important can be invaluable in developing a successful exhibit.

• Write a theme sentence. (See also Chapter 6, step 1.2.3.)

After narrowing your theme and before you begin developing the exhibit in earnest, write the message you want visitors to take home from the exhibit in one sentence. Articulating the take-home message will force you to fully understand exactly what you want the exhibit to be about and help you focus all aspects of the exhibit on this message. The labels, the design, the title, the objects, and all the other elements of the exhibit should work toward expressing this message.

Step 3: Review Administrative Concerns

There are four main administrative concerns in exhibit work: funding, contracts, insurance, and security. Not all exhibits will require all of these things, but they are of extreme importance and mustn't be disregarded.

• Funding (See also Chapter 6, sections 1.5, 2.5, 3.4, and 4.5.)

As for any other library service and program, funds can be raised to pay for an exhibit entirely or to supplement the budget. In addition to grants and donations, sponsorships can be considered. Needless to say, it's important to make sure funding for exhibits is secure before the project gets under way. As with all projects, funds must be allocated appropriately and spending should be reviewed throughout. Use the sample budget in Chapter 6 step 1.5.1 to guide you.

• Contracts (See also Chapter 6, sections 1.6, 2.6, 3.5, and 4.6.)

If you are renting a traveling exhibit or exhibiting objects on loan, contracts must be signed. The owner of a traveling exhibit will provide a contract; the lender of objects may. Either way, the library must be sure to keep a record of the receipt, condition, and return of such objects. A loan agreement form is a simple way of doing so. It includes the names and contact information of the lender and borrower, a list of the objects on loan, their condition and value, and any requirements of the lending institution for conservation, security, or insurance. (See a sample form in Chapter 6, step 1.6.3.)

• Insurance (See also Chapter 6, sections 1.7, 2.7, 3.6, and 4.7.)

Additional insurance must be considered for traveling exhibits, and any exhibit of collections whether owned by the library or borrowed from another institution. The insurance required for a traveling exhibit will be specified in the contract. Individuals lending items to the library may require additional insurance to cover their value. Even if the lender requires no such insurance, it may be in the library's best interest to get it anyway. Such a determination can be made with the help of the insurance company. Whether additional insurance is needed to cover exhibits of the library's own collection is another question for the insurance company. Presumably these objects are covered by the library's insurance policy, however, they may be covered for storage only, not display. Display increases the risk of damage and therefore may necessitate additional coverage.

• Security (See also Chapter 6, sections 1.8, 2.8, 3.7, and 4.8.)

Security issues vary among libraries, creating different needs when it comes to exhibit safety. Levels of security needed depend on an individual library's community and atmosphere, the kind of exhibit, the location of the exhibit, and the value of the items on display. Security measures can be as simple as placing the exhibit in view of the front desk, posting "do not touch" signs, and placing objects under glass, behind barriers, or in locked cases. More serious measures include alarmed cases, regular monitoring by a security guard, video monitoring (or signs indicating such), and a permanently stationed guard.

Step 4: Develop and Design the Exhibit

There is much to think about in the development and design of an exhibit. Most important is the question of how best to convey the take-home message. One aspect crucial to success is accessibility: The exhibit message must reach as many visitors as possible. The items you choose to display and create also affect how well the message is conveyed. Whatever you display, you will need to consider whether conservation measures are necessary and work this into the exhibit's design. Throughout development, ask yourself how the exhibit will say what it needs to say, what visitors will see and do at the exhibit, and what elements will best get across your message. Remember, everything you plan should support the take-home message.

• Understand successful exhibit strategies. (See also Chapter 6, step 1.2.4.)

An exhibit differs from a book; it is more than words. To successfully convey its message, an exhibit must rely on a number of elements including labels, images, objects, and hands-on elements and use varied methods of communication. The best exhibits work by provoking thought in the visitor and are most effective when this thought relates in some way to the visitor's life and experience. A visitor should be able to understand the message of an exhibit without help from an "expert." Exhibits that encourage interaction and discussion between visitors often have a lasting impact. Finally, active and real experiences in an exhibit are most engaging and hold the visitor's attention, allowing more time for your message to sink in. For a successful exhibit, show your visitors how the theme relates to their lives, get them to talk about it with each other, show them real things, and give them something to experience.

• Consider accessibility. (See also Chapter 6, step 1.2.5.)

Accessibility is one of the most important considerations in exhibit development: You want your exhibit to reach everyone. Planning an accessible exhibit pays great dividends; you not only end up with an exhibit that can be used by those with disabilities, but an exhibit that is more effective for everyone. There are three major kinds of disability you should consider when developing your exhibit: sensory, motor, and cognitive.

1. To make an exhibit accessible to someone with sensory disabilities (blindness, low vision, hearing impairment) think in terms of providing experiences for the ears and the hands as well as the eyes. Exhibits are often visually based. This not only excludes those who can't see, it gets boring for those who can. Adding aural and tactile as well

as visual experiences opens the message of the exhibit to more people and enriches the overall experience for everyone.

2. Motor disabilities include but are not limited to wheelchair use and varying degrees of arm and hand paralysis. Plenty of room should be left around the exhibit for wheelchair navigation, labels should be placed at a height that can be read by seated visitors, and all interactive devices should be operable by those without full use of their hands.

3. Visitors with cognitive disabilities may have a hard time understanding labels. Think about the language you use in your labels and about what message is conveyed by your exhibit without them. Since much of the public also reads few or no labels, you will increase your chance of reaching everyone by making them short and telling plenty of story without them.

• Consider conservation. (See also Chapter 6, step 1.2.6.)

Conservation must not be ignored if you are displaying objects in your exhibit. Materials including paper, wood, textiles, and others can be damaged by light, temperature and humidity levels and changes, the chemical off-gassing of exhibit fabrication materials such as paints, and pests. If the objects are from the library's collection you may know how they should be treated, and this treatment should not change or change only minimally while they are on display. If the objects are being borrowed, the lending institution may require certain conservation measures. If you are unsure of the needs of the objects, seek the advice of an expert.

• Determine whether related library materials will be displayed. (See also Chapter 6, step 1.2.7.)

One way to tie your exhibit to the library and potentially increase circulation and interest in the exhibit theme is to display related materials from the circulating collection with the exhibit. These can continue to circulate during the life of the exhibit or be part of the exhibit themselves, out of circulation until the end.

• Create an initial design. (See also Chapter 6, step 1.3.1.)

Having developed ideas of what will be in the exhibit, you can put together a design. The design can play an important part in reinforcing the exhibit's message. Would it help to set a mood or evoke an emotion? Are there colors, shapes, or textures that relate to your theme? What aspects of the exhibit do you want to place emphasis on? Design also makes an exhibit attractive (or not!). Try to design with variety so as not to bore the visitor, but be consistent and avoid a cluttered, jumbled feeling. Don't forget to include lighting in your design; if people can't see the exhibit, they won't get the message.

Step 5: Prototype the Exhibit (see also Chapter 6, step 1.3.3)

You've arrived at one of the most important steps of the exhibit process: the prototype. Building a prototype of your exhibit (or just part of it) lets you test your ideas to find out if they work. It's absolutely essential to do this because until you try it, you never know whether that "perfect" idea is really so perfect. Prototyping should be an ongoing process during the development of the exhibit. You will test an idea, tweak it, test it, tweak it, and so on until you get it right. If you keep an open mind throughout this process and are willing to make changes when it seems like your original idea doesn't work, your exhibit will turn out much better.

In this initial round of prototyping, you want to find out if there are any problems with your plans for the accessibility, location, size and layout, lighting, attractiveness, and usability of the exhibit. To test these aspects build a prototype of the exhibit with the actual tables and cases that will be used, with cardboard boxes and tape, by taping dimensions on the floors and walls, or through a combination of these methods. Include mock ups of display items, titles, labels, hands-on devices, and design elements. Evaluate this prototype with the following kinds of questions. Is their enough space around the exhibit? Will it be navigable (for multiple people, or those in wheelchairs)? Does everything to be included fit in the exhibit space? Is the arrangement attractive and meaningful or crowded and confusing? Is there room for labels near the things they are interpreting? Is anything too high to read, see, or reach (for seated visitors as well)? Is there enough light on the exhibit? Do the colors and other design elements work as you envisioned? Are there visual, tactile, and aural experiences? Do hands-on parts of the exhibit work as planned? Ask other staff members to help you if you like, but at this stage you can answer many of these questions yourself.

Step 6: Write and Design the Exhibit Labels (see also Chapter 6, section 2.2.)

Making labels can be a lengthy part of the exhibit process. Because labels are one of the primary vehicles for the take-home message it is worth spending the time to get them right. A brief discussion of the label making process including planning, writing, editing, and designing is provided here. More suggestions and detail are given in Chapter 6.

• Plan the labels (See also Chapter 6, section 2.2.1.)

There are a number of kinds of labels with different purposes. Interpretive labels that can help convey the message of the exhibit include titles; introduction labels which introduce one idea, an area of an exhibit, or related objects; identification labels used to describe basic information about individual items, captions which interpret those items; instruction labels which tell the visitor to do something with a hands-on component and explanation labels which explain what happens when they do it. You do not need to use all these kinds of labels, only the ones that help the visitor understand your message.

It's important to keep in mind that visitors don't always begin at the beginning. They often float around the exhibit reading labels at random. Therefore each label must stand alone, not relying on the previous ones to make sense. In addition, repeating your message on labels throughout the exhibit will increase the chance it will be seen by a visitor and will act as reinforcement.

• Write the labels (see also Chapter 6, step 2.2.2)

Labels make an exhibit meaningful to visitors, but only if they're read. It's important to remember that people won't read labels if they appear overwhelming and most visitors skip labels that are too long. Labels must be short and focused and not provide too much information. The most important role of a label is to support the exhibit's take-home message. There may be all sorts of fascinating peripheral information you would like your visitor to know, but if it does not help them understand the main message, it will detract from the success of your exhibit. As you are writing, ask yourself if the words increase or divert attention from the main message; it will help you stay focused.

To increase meaning and interest, write labels that relate exhibit content to the visitor's experience both in the exhibit and in life. Labels should point out and interpret things that the visitor can see, touch, hear, or smell in the exhibit. They should also explain the content of the exhibit in relation to things that the visitor knows and has experienced in life. In addition, it's extremely important to write labels in a style that everyone can understand. This means using simple language; short, simple sentences; the active voice; and everyday vocabulary.

• Edit the labels (see also Chapter 6, step 2.2.4)

Write your first draft of the exhibit labels and then begin to slash away at them. You will be surprised at how much you can take out without losing meaning. Often cutting words and extraneous information actually clarifies meaning. It doesn't matter how well a point is made if the label doesn't get read, so always keep in mind that a visitor is more likely to read a short label. Once you have a draft you feel is as short as it can be, show it to your coworkers and see if it makes sense to them. Do they get the point? Are there sentences they don't understand? Words they find confusing? Sections they don't see the point of? If so, revise some more.

• Design the labels (see also Chapter 6, step 2.2.5)

The design of the labels also contributes to whether they will be read. A crowded label with small type on a dark background is not very inviting or readable. An uncluttered look with margins and plenty of white space, on the other hand, draws the eye to the label. For labels to be accessible, they must have large type (20 point, even larger if read at a distance) in a clear font and have good contrast; never print type over an image, even a grayed out one. Labels throughout an exhibit should have a consistent design; all labels of one kind should have a standard look (e.g. all captions should have the same size, shape, color, font, etc.) and the different kinds of labels should be linked by common design elements. A label's purpose also affects its design. Titles are typically short, but very large so they are the first thing read. Introduction labels usually have larger font than other labels to attract the visitor's initial attention. Captions and identification labels are small enough so they don't dwarf the item they describe, and are placed close to the item so the relationship is clear. Instructions can be written in numbered lists to make them easy to follow.

Step 7: Prototype the exhibit, again
(see also Chapter 6, section 2.3)

We know you're thinking, "Didn't I already do this step?" Hopefully you did, but since it is an important, ongoing process, now you have to do some more. There are two major differences this time: You are going to be testing everything about the exhibit including the content of the labels and you are going to be testing the exhibit on other people, including visitors. As you continue to develop each part of the exhibit, whenever you find yourself wondering what the best thing to do is or speculating about whether an idea will work, test it. Testing can take the form of asking formal or informal questions or simply observing people use the exhibit. When you are struggling in the rough initial stages, get help from your coworkers; go to the public in the final stages, once you think things might be just right. The goal of testing is to find out whether the design, text, hands-on elements, images, objects and all other aspects of the exhibit that make sense to you also make sense to other people. You will be amazed at how often something you think is perfectly clear will be lost on someone else. Accept that if a number of people have problems with the same thing, no matter how much you like or understand it, it needs to change for the success of the exhibit. Prototyping is a time to set aside your ego.

Eventually you will have developed a complete (albeit not polished) exhibit that makes sense to you; you should feel it works well, is clear, and delivers its message. With this relatively accurate prototype, you can test the exhibit as a whole rather than in its individual components. Seeing the exhibit all together for the first time can give you a good sense of whether the design is consistent throughout; if the labels are readable and the objects visible; and if the exhibit is well-lit and things aren't in shadow. Review the exhibit's accessibility again, and look for safety hazards such as loose electrical cords, hot lights, choking hazards, cane or bump hazards, moving parts, and sharp angles and edges (see Chapter 6, steps 2.3.4 and 2.3.5). Observe and question visitors to find out the following things. Are they able to navigate and use the exhibit without confusion? Is the flow of information clear? Are they coming away with the right message? Are there any problem areas? When you talk to them, make sure they understand you are testing the exhibit, not them.

Step 8: Fabricate and Install the Exhibit
(see also Chapter 6, section 3.2.)

Once you've prototyped the exhibit within an inch of its life and are satisfied with the final design, you can go ahead and build or put it together. You'll need to buy all necessary materials including label supplies, decorative elements, mounts and supports, exhibit cases, lighting, electronic components, tools and equipment, fasteners, and finishing products. Any fabrication being outsourced (such as large-format label printing or exhibit cabinetry) will take a certain amount of time and must be factored into the schedule. There are a number of styles of label. Labels behind glass do not have to be mounted or laminated, but they should be printed on stiff, thick paper such as card stock. Those that visitors can touch need to be protected; details about how to do so are provided in Chapter 6, step 3.2.4.

Installation can often take longer than you anticipate. Depending on the size of your exhibit, you may want to arrange for help from coworkers or volunteers. Things will go faster and more smoothly if you collect all potential installation tools including hangers, Velcro, screws, levels, etc. in one place at the beginning of the day.

Step 9: Publicize the Exhibit (see also Chapter 6, sections 1.10, 2.10, 3.9, 3.10, 4.9, and 4.10)

If people don't know about an exhibit, they won't come to see it, so advertise, advertise, advertise! How you advertise depends on the size, length, target audience, and theme of your exhibit. Start by always mentioning your exhibit on the library website and in the library newsletter. In addition, you might consider creating posters or brochures for distribution to the community. Always include the exhibit on community events calendars online, in print, or on local public access cable stations. Don't just send press releases to local newspapers and community or neighborhood newsletters, invite them to write news stories or offer to write stories for them. In addition, you can create public service announcements for local radio or television stations; take out paid advertisements; and send postcards to individuals or letters to local organizations and groups who might have a specific interest in the exhibit theme. For large exhibits, you might want to consider holding a opening to which you invite the press.

Step 10: Evaluate and Document the Exhibit Before Deinstallation

Evaluating the exhibit will help you improve both it and future exhibits, while documentation will prove handy for use in public relations and fund-raising.

• Evaluate the exhibit. (See also Chapter 6, steps 4.3.2 and 4.3.3.)

As soon as you put the exhibit up, spend some time observing visitors using it. Look out for problems you didn't catch during prototyping and fix those you can right away. You may find problems with labels or lighting that are easy to fix.

Throughout the life of the exhibit, you can evaluate its success using methods such as interviews, surveys, or observation of visitors. You want to find out not only whether your exhibit effectively conveys its message, but which parts of the exhibit were most successful at doing so, which parts were visitor favorites, whether the exhibit got people talking, and whether visitors actually enjoyed the exhibit. Make sure you are measuring the right things by relating the evaluative questions to your original objectives. In addition, gather circulation data on circulating library materials displayed with the exhibit and if possible keep track of the number of visitors to the exhibit.

• Document the exhibit. (See also Chapter 6, step 4.3.4.)

Always keep a record of the exhibits you have created or hosted. At the very least, take pictures which can be used in library public relations materials such as the annual report, can act as inspiration for future exhibits, and can prevent you from repeating ideas and designs too soon. Keep a file for each exhibit in which you collect these pictures, the exhibit evaluation, publicity materials such as posters and news stories, the final budget, sponsor information, an analysis of the effectiveness of security and publicity, and receipts from outside vendors for work done on the exhibit (fabrication, printing, etc.) plus an indication of the quality of this work.

6

The Comprehensive Exhibit Process

In this section, we cover, step-by-step, everything you might need to consider when making an exhibit. Depending on the size and extent of your exhibit, however, some of the steps may be unnecessary. We indicate which ones are essential for every exhibit and which ones are important only in certain situations. (If you are bringing in a pre-made exhibit or traveling exhibition, you will be able to skip many of the steps in this process. Chapter 7 details a modified process.) As you read you will notice some spaces in which you can record information about your library. Using these spaces will make this book a specific reference source about your library, handy for any employee involved in exhibit work, and invaluable for your overall exhibit program. In addition, there are sample forms and examples to help you take care of some of the tasks during the exhibit process.

 We have created a hypothetical exhibit to illustrate some of the steps in the process. Whenever you see the symbol to the left, we'll be talking about this example exhibit. Sometimes it describes things we did right, other times, things we did wrong.

Many different tasks from design, to administration, to writing, to promotion, to fabrication are required to make an effective exhibit. It is the rare person who has all the needed skills. Because of the range of work involved, a team approach is often the most successful. We have split the tasks in the exhibit process into four main areas: administrative work, programming, publicity, and the exhibit work itself. If you are working in a team these may be the logical divisions of labor; one of your coworkers may take care of one of these areas for the library. Almost everyone who works on exhibits recommends working in a team, especially when brainstorming for theme and design ideas, and evaluating the exhibit. Even if you are solely responsible for the exhibit, ask some of your coworkers for assistance at different stages of the process.

The exhibit process is split into four parts corresponding with each stage of the project: the beginning idea and preliminaries, development and design, fabrication, and installation to deinstallation. Each of these parts is split into the four work areas. This should allow each member of the team to quickly and easily identify her responsibilities. If you are making the exhibit alone — don't worry, you can do it! — these divisions will help you organize your work.

If you are working in a team, it's a good idea to meet regularly to take stock of how things are going and to make important decisions. These meetings can be weekly or called as needed, whichever works best for your organization. We begin each part of the exhibit process with a section called Taking Stock that will help guide these meetings. If you are working alone, it is a good idea to use these sections to review what has been done, make changes as necessary, and reconfirm the next steps. Remember that when working in a team, there should be one person who is responsible for overseeing the entire project. This person should make up the exhibit process timeline, call meetings, coordinate the different members of the team, and be the go-to person for questions and decisions.

It's impossible to say how long it takes to develop an exhibit; it differs for each one. How long each of the stages will take depends on the kind of exhibit you are making, how involved it is, the number of people working on it, your level of inspiration, and the other responsibilities you have in your job. The important thing is to identify your time frame up front and plan accordingly. Only practice will give you a sense of how long things take, but until then, keep in mind that everything takes longer than you think it will (in exhibit work as in everything else!).

Part I — The Beginning Idea and Preliminaries

1.1 Taking Stock

1.1.1 Identify Your Goals

Before you can start thinking about your exhibit (let alone making it), you must identify your goals. Why do you want to have an exhibit or display at the library? Many things about your exhibit process (the kind of exhibit, its design, its promotion, your programs, and the time frame) will differ depending on what your goals are.

Here are some possible goals:[1]

- To educate or inform visitors about a specific topic.
- To entertain visitors.
- To display part of the library's collection (book or otherwise).
- To promote reading.
- To market the library's resources.
- To promote circulation.

- To play a central role in your community.
- To encourage people to come to the library.
- To celebrate or commemorate an event.
- To teach people how to use the library.
- To give community organizations/members a public space in which to showcase their work or communicate a message.

Write down your goals for the exhibit and refer back to them throughout the process of creating the exhibit, always asking yourself "How will this part of the process, section of the exhibit, or program help us meet our goals?"

 Our hypothetical exhibit was created at the hypothetical Granitetown Public Library (based on the real Aldrich Public Library in Barre, Vermont). The library has a history collection of photographs, manuscripts, and artifacts relating to the quarrying and carving of the vast supplies of granite that are the basis of Granitetown's economy. Our initial goal in creating an exhibit was easy: We wanted an opportunity to show off our local history collection. It seemed a shame that all those wonderful photos and interesting items sat in boxes where most people didn't even know they existed. There were two additional goals for the exhibit though: to show the library as a center of the community by telling the story of the town's major industry and to complement an upcoming exhibit of contemporary stone carving. The library is one of the main preservers of the town's history. An exhibit would not only bring the story of that history to life for the residents, it would show them how central the library is to the life of the town. Combining a history exhibit with the planned art exhibit had the potential to reach a new audience: teaching those in the art world about industrial history.

1.1.2 Know Your Current Resources

What kind of exhibit you make depends greatly on the resources you have at your disposal. Budget, staff availability, time, and space all influence what you will be able to do.

Budget: Find out approximately how much money you have to work with and whether there will be the possibility of raising more.

Staff: Identify the staff member with the primary responsibility for seeing the exhibit project to completion. Find out who else (staff members and volunteers) will be available to work on the exhibit team, what kinds of jobs they can do, and how many hours they can put in. Keep track of volunteers interested in helping out with exhibits below.

Space: Take a walk around the library to determine where an exhibit might go. Your

Exhibit Volunteers

(List artists and woodworkers, students, designers, and other community members, their telephone numbers, and what they like to help out with.)

_____

_____

_____

_____

_____

_____

_____

_____

_____

_____

_____

_____

_____

_____

_____

_____

_____

_____

_____

_____

_____

_____

_____

_____

_____

_____

_____

library might have only one small spot in which to put a table, or maybe it has an entire room waiting to be devoted to an exhibit. Identify where you are able to put an exhibit at the current time. There is no point in dreaming of a traveling exhibition if you work in a one-room library, but don't sell yourself short; use your imagination as you look around. Maybe that odd corner by the door would be perfect for a display, or, failing floor space, what about hanging things? Pay attention also to what sort of pre-existing setups you have: unused tables, glass cases, etc. Possible spaces for exhibits in a library include:

- Wall display cases (free-standing or built-in)
- Horizontal, flat display cases
- Tables (free-standing, against walls, or on the ends of stacks)
- Walls (in hallways, community rooms, bathrooms, etc.)
- Portable walls
- Bulletin boards
- Community rooms
- Easels
- Tops of low stacks
- Open floor space in large rooms
- Ceiling (for hanging exhibits)
- Outdoors (for sculpture or very temporary exhibits)

The potential locations for the Granitetown Public Library's exhibit were limited. The library is small and in an old building that barely allows room for the stacks needed for the collection. There is no central foyer or built in exhibit cases that would suit an exhibit, however, three potential exhibit spaces are available in the newer part of the building: a small art gallery, a multipurpose room, and a large hallway linking the new and old buildings. The multipurpose room is frequently used for programs and meetings, so although part of it could be devoted to an exhibit, the exhibit wouldn't be available to visitors when the room was being used; not an ideal situation. The art gallery was reserved for the art exhibit. The hallway linking the old and new parts of the building, while large enough to accommodate an exhibit with cases and wall displays, is on the basement level, an area without much foot traffic and far from the companion art exhibit. Since we wanted to put the art and history exhibits near each other, we looked in the area around the art gallery room. An open space leads to the entrance to the art gallery. The space was smaller than we were planning on, but it had one long blank wall along which an exhibit could be built. Most importantly, this wall led directly into the art gallery; visitors could learn about stone carving's past, just before they stepped into its present.

List possible exhibit areas in your library below.

Time: Ask yourself when the exhibit must go up? This deadline gives you an idea of how complex your exhibit can be. If you only have a day, you can't build Rome. If you have no deadline, you can plan something more involved. Additionally, ask yourself for how long the exhibit will be on display? If it is long term, you will have to think about using appropriately lasting materials which may take more time and money.

1.1.3. Decide What Kind of Exhibit to Have and What Its Theme Will Be

Now that you know your goals, general budget, time frame, and space availability, you can make an initial decision about what kind of exhibit you want to make and what it will be about. Your theme might dictate the kind of exhibit you have, or vice versa. Just get a general sense of what you want to do here; later on you'll have a chance to research and further develop the idea. Some of the kinds of exhibits you might choose include:

- Book exhibits
- Art exhibits
- Historical exhibits
- Displays of items other than books
- Hands-on exhibits
- Bulletin boards
- Traveling exhibits
- Displays in local business windows

If you are planning a book display to highlight the library's collection, you might think about exhibiting books on a certain topic at a related local business (for instance books on gardening in the hardware store window or books on raising and training pets in the veterinarian's waiting room).[2] The displays can combine items sold by the business with books available at the library. It's a great way to reach people who don't use the library and give them a reason to start. One surprising example is the library display created by the Traverse des Sioux Library System at a Minnesota farm Exposition. Books were displayed right next to "manure spreaders and combines" and the library passed out 3,000 copies of a booklist spreading the word about library resources.[3]

 Our general theme was predetermined by our goals and local history collection: the exhibit would be about the granite industry. The granite industry is alive and well in Granitetown. As one of the world centers for quarrying granite, the town fosters an artisans community of stone carvers. In the early days of the industry, these carvers focused on traditional work, carving buildings, tombstones, and civic sculptures. More recently,

Pre-existing and Potential Exhibit Spaces in Our Library

(Include a description of each space — dimensions; lighting; location; in public areas, in stacks, in separate room; cases, tables, etc.)

_____

_____

_____

_____

_____

_____

_____

_____

_____

_____

_____

_____

_____

_____

_____

_____

_____

_____

_____

_____

_____

_____

_____

_____

a growing number of carvers have turned their focus to fine arts sculpture. Clearly, a number of different kinds of exhibits could focus on the theme of the granite industry: book, art, history, hands-on, etc. The library had already planned an art exhibit showing the work of local stone carvers. We had to decide what the second part of the exhibit would be.

We could display books. In addition to historical books in the archives, the circulating library collection has a number of more recent books about stone quarrying and carving. The combination of old, leather-bound books and glossy, color coffee-table books could potentially make an attractive exhibit to showcase and generate interest in the library collection. But our local history collection has much more than books. It includes many photographs; records, letters, and other manuscripts; and perhaps most excitingly some old stone carving equipment including tools and masks. We could create an exhibit of artifacts and pictures instead of books—a true history exhibit. We definitely wanted to show off some of these tangible items—things people can imaging using, not just reading. And even better than just imagining using something is being able to use and touch it, so we tried to think of ways to make an exhibit that wasn't just under glass to be looked at. Could any of our items be touched? Maybe the stuff from our archives was too delicate, but perhaps we could borrow some modern-day tools from the stone-cutters displaying their work in the gallery.

After considering all our options, we decided that a combination of approaches would suit our exhibit best. We knew it wouldn't be solely an exhibit of books because one of our goals was to show our local history collection. So we would display photos and artifacts behind glass to protect them. But we didn't want it to be a static exhibit experienced only through looking and reading. We wanted people to get involved, to get more interested. So we set our minds to creating some basic hands-on elements to pull people in and make it more accessible. In addition, we definitely wanted to display related materials from our collection to take advantage of people's interest and encourage them to take out books as soon as they felt inspired.

1.1.4. Develop a Plan

You've answered all the preliminary questions, and can now make a plan. Using the deadline for when the exhibit needs to be up and the following planning checklist, sketch out a timeline or schedule of the tasks required and the deadlines for each. Highlight those tasks and deadlines that are dependent on previous tasks being completed. You may not know all your deadlines yet — that's okay, just put them in the timeline tentatively and make it a priority to figure them out as soon as possible. This timeline should be created (and adjusted) by the leader of the exhibit team for use by all its members, and should be reviewed at each "Taking Stock" meeting.

The plan of action can take a number of different forms. It can be as simple as a calendar on which you mark important dates, deadlines, and blocks of time in which to complete various tasks. More complex exhibits that rely on ordering or gathering materials from many outside sources, or on the work of many different staff members might require a more formal schedule. One such scheduling tool is a Gantt chart which provides a visual schematic of the time frame for a project (an example follows). In addition to recording general and specific tasks and deadlines, you can use these charts to note who has responsibility for each task and which tasks depend on the completion of other tasks. The charts can be hand drawn or made using specialized project management software such as Microsoft Office Project or any of a number of products available for free download on the Internet. Whatever method you use to keep track of the exhibit schedule, the planning checklist below will help you remember to add everything before its too late.

1.2 Beginning the Exhibit Development

1.2.1 Research the Topic

You've decided what your exhibit is going to be about and now comes the fun part; you get to find out all about that topic. You're all librarians, so we're not going to detail the myriad ways to find information on a topic! Suffice it to say that the more you know about something, the more ideas you will have for an exhibit about it and the more accurate your exhibit will be. But, of course, you have to rein yourself in sometime, so keep a close eye on that timeline.

We looked through our archives to determine what materials we had and read some history books to find interesting topics about stone cutters and the granite industry. We had no trouble creating a list of potential topics for our exhibit; it included silicosis, working conditions, unions and strikes, Labor Day, the Italian immigrant community, methods of stone cutting and granite quarrying, tombstones and other community monuments, and our granite around the world. With so many possibilities it was time to take the next step to decide which was the best option for this exhibit. We liked a lot of the exhibit topics and it was hard to throw some out. We placated ourselves by keeping the list of the topics on file for use in future exhibits. Those topics we loved could be done later on.

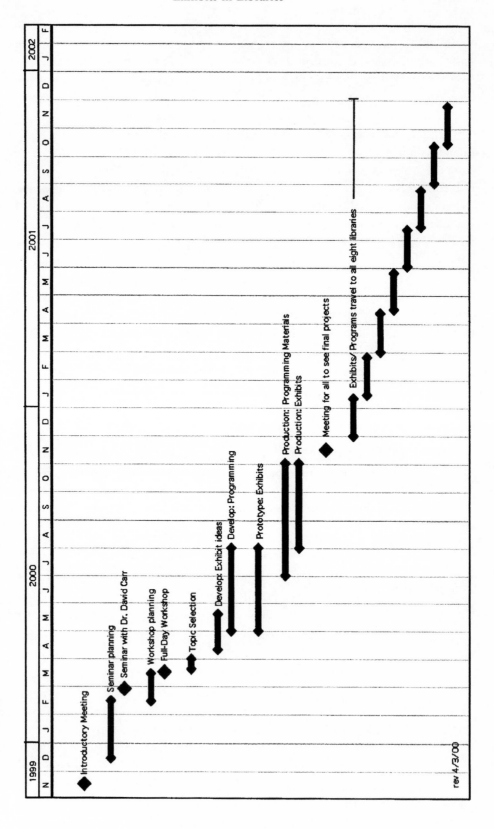

Science in the Stacks • Project Timeline

Planning Checklist

To do immediately:

☐ Set exhibit opening and closing date and reserve exhibit space.
☐ Identify exhibit goals.

To do in the planning stage:

☐ Research exhibit topic and audience and narrow theme.
☐ Determine conservation needs.
☐ Consider accessibility.
☐ Develop initial exhibit/design ideas and prototype.
☐ Review costs of materials and get quotes on outsourced items.
☐ Create budget and begin fundraising, determine needs for contracts, insurance.
☐ Create publicity plan and determine media deadlines.
☐ Generate program ideas

To do in the design and fabrication stage:

☐ Plan, write, edit, and design labels.
☐ Prototype and evaluate exhibit.
☐ Finalize exhibit design.
☐ Order outsourced items and materials and fabricate exhibit and labels.
☐ Write and send publicity materials.
☐ Finalize program ideas, set dates, and reserve space, staff, and equipment.

To do the week of the exhibit opening:

☐ Clean and prepare exhibit space and prepare for installation.
☐ Receive traveling exhibit or loaned items and check condition.
☐ Install exhibit.
☐ Collect program materials.

To do during and after the exhibit:

☐ Maintain and clean the exhibit and monitor the environment for conservation.
☐ Evaluate and document the exhibit.
☐ Host opening event and hold programs.
☐ Deinstall the exhibit.
☐ Return loaned items.

Other important dates to include on your schedule:

☐ Last dates to order materials and outsourced items (to get them on time).
☐ Important meetings.
☐ Program dates.
☐ Arrival and return dates for traveling exhibits or loaned items.
☐ Media deadlines for publicity materials.
☐ Staff vacations/days off that might impact the schedule.

1.2.2 Know Your Audience

Identifying your audience will help you develop the exhibit concept and allow you to tailor the design. If you are making exhibits for the children's section, you will want to write and design for children. If the exhibit is aimed at young adults, you won't want to design for children! In a public library, you will usually be designing exhibits for the general public, so know who your general public is. By knowing who lives in your community and what is important to them, you can create exhibits to meet their unique needs and desires.[4] Choose exhibit topics that are relevant to community interests or make your exhibit topic resonate with members of the community by tailoring the information offered in the labels to their shared knowledge. Keep track of exhibit topics related to the community.

One way to find out about your audience is through front-end evaluation, a method of interviewing visitors to determine what they already know about an exhibit topic and what they would like to know about it. When you create an exhibit, you assume visitors know a certain amount about the topic to begin with. The information you provide in the exhibit is based on this assumption. If you assume incorrectly, your exhibit will fail; if you think visitors know more than they do, the exhibit won't provide enough information for them to understand it. If, on the other hand, you don't give them enough credit, your exhibit risks being boring or, worse, patronizing.[6]

To perform front-end evaluation, approach a visitor, tell her you are planning an exhibit about your topic and are trying to find out what people already know and what interests them about it. If she is willing to talk, ask her questions like these:

- What do you think of when you think of this topic?
- How do you define the topic?
- At an exhibit on this topic, what would you want to see, do, find out about? What would you expect to see, do and find out about? Are they the same?
- How would you feel at an exhibit on this topic?
- Do you have any questions about the topic?
- What experience have you had with this topic?
- Do you have any special interest, knowledge, or training in the topic?[7]
- Would you want to go to/look at an exhibit about this topic?
- Identify specific technical terms related to this topic and ask about those: Do you know what the terms mean? Do you ever use these words? When?
- Read short samples of text or show pictures relating to your topic and ask: What does this make you think of?[8]

Brief interviews with a variety of your visitors using questions like these will provide information about what they already know, what they would like to know, and what their attitudes are about a subject. This information will help you begin to narrow what you will attempt to say in your exhibit. You may find out if you have to make things more basic than you thought as well as the following types of things; what concepts are shared knowledge and could be used as a focal point and what ones will need to be defined or eliminated; what experiences (hobbies, family histories, school and job-related)

Special Interests of Our Community

(Include local holidays, celebrations, or commemorations; names, birth dates, and details of local heroes and celebrated citizens of the past; famous local happenings [5]; names and contact information for local historical societies and other local organizations and special interest groups.)

exist that you could use as a "hook" in your labels;[9] whether the topic brings up certain emotions in people that you could explore in the exhibit; and interesting ideas about how the topic relates to the lives of people in your community.

Since one of our goals was to show our citizens what an integral part of the community the library is, we chose a topic that was related not only to the community's history, but to its present: the continually evolving industry of stone carving. The contemporary art show was the perfect cornerstone of this exhibit. To know what story should be told by our exhibit, we needed to find out what people already knew and thought about granite and stone carving, so we did some front end evaluation. We asked library patrons, "What's the first thing you think of when you think of Granitetown granite?" A variety of answers were given, but a large proportion of them centered on one of the town's famous cemeteries, Hope Cemetery, filled with marvelous tombstones displaying the art and craft of stone carving. No wonder it was mentioned so often, since it is one of Granitetown's biggest attractions.

We also wanted to find out what kinds of things we could include in our exhibit that would resonate with visitors, so we did some more research. It turned out that some of the tombstones in Hope Cemetery are not just beautiful examples of stone carving, but tell important historical stories. One tombstone tells, without words, the heartbreaking story of silicosis, the lung disease that historically killed many stone cutters. We showed patrons pictures of this tombstone; many recognized it, but few knew the story behind it. We asked them what they knew about silicosis; only about half knew what it was. This sounded like a promising topic to us, so we conducted further research about silicosis. What we found amazed us. While reading about silicosis at the World Health Organization website, we saw that it still exists in the stone industry in China. During our interviews, patrons, like us, had spoken of the disease in the historical sense, as something that no longer existed. We had found a current-day hook to help our visitors relate to the exhibit.

Our front-end questioning turned up some other interesting information about our audience. A large number of patrons either had family or ancestors or knew someone who had family or ancestors in the granite industry. Since so many people knew someone in the granite industry, we thought hearing the memories of granite workers would be a powerful link to our audiences lives. We decided to enlist the help of the local historical society which has many members who work in or are retired from the granite industry. Maybe we could interview them; including their memories in the exhibit might resonate with our audience.

1.2.3. Narrow Your Theme

Through researching your topic you will have found all sorts of fascinating information, but your exhibit needs a focus if it's going to be successful. This focus has been called the "big idea"[10] or the "take-home message." Everything in your exhibit from objects, to images, to hands-on elements, to labels, to the title should help the visitor walk away with that idea or message. This means you might not get to include everything that's interesting (gasp!). We'll talk more about this later when you work on the exhibit labels; for now, though, make sure that you have articulated the big idea of your exhibit, what you want people to walk away understanding. You should be able to state it in one sentence.[11] Write it down and keep it in mind as you continue developing the exhibit. Everyone working on the exhibit should be aware of it.

In addition to your take-home message, creating objectives for your exhibit will help you focus its development and evaluate it when the time comes. There are many different kinds of exhibit objectives. You might want visitors to come away from your exhibit having learned a specific piece of information. Maybe you want them to have experienced an emotion. Perhaps you are hoping your exhibit will prompt them to take some sort of action. Objectives can be as basic as wanting the exhibit to make visitors think about a new idea or make them want to come back to the library. In writing objectives, it's important to keep in mind how exhibits work. The purpose of an exhibit is not necessarily to teach specific information. Rather, they tend to be most successful at arousing interest, awareness, or emotions; changing attitudes; imparting general knowledge; and helping people make connections between ideas to encourage informal learning. Objectives such as these are likely to be most successful. Whatever your objectives, make sure they are specific. Having specific objectives will help you develop exhibit ideas and labels that can meet these objectives.

After our front-end evaluation we decided that the story of silicosis would be a good way to narrow our general exhibit theme of granite carving. Our research showed that in the first half of the 20th century, silicosis was epidemic in the Graniteville region because the granite industry used no dust-catching safety equipment. The average life expectancy for a granite worker was 42 years. Not until the 1950s were workers able through strikes to get laws passed requiring the provision of safety equipment that prevents silicosis. Our big idea was: stone cutters in the granite industry died early of silicosis until their fight for better working conditions was successful.

1.2.4 Know What Works

As you research, you'll think of many exhibit ideas. Some will be realistic possibilities, others won't. It's a good idea to learn what kinds of things work well as an exhibit so you can narrow down your list of ideas and not waste time on flights of fancy or sure losers. These are a few key points to keep in mind:

- The exhibit stands alone.
  An exhibit must be able to be used by an individual or group without outside assistance. If an educator or an explainer is needed to facilitate the user's experience, it is not an exhibit, but a program. Certain ideas work better as programs (or handouts or posters) than as exhibits.

- The exhibit is not just a collection of words.
  I'm sure you've all been to an exhibit that looked like a wall full of never-ending text with a few pictures thrown in here or there. How does that make you feel? Like turning around and walking right back out again, right? An exhibit is not a book, and it shouldn't try to take the place of a book. Visitors at exhibits don't want to read pages upon pages; if they did, they would relax with a book at home. An exhibit should offer a different experience. Certain topics can only be explained using a lot of words or are not able to be explained using any method besides words. These topics are not good choices for exhibits.

- The exhibit provokes thought
  "Ideally a visitor walks away [from the exhibit] with something to think about. If we can relate the content of the exhibit to something in a visitor's own life, so much the better. Often a good exhibit doesn't actually impart any hard information, but instead let's the visitor make connections with other exhibits, other phenomena, books, and past experiences. This can happen while the visitor is interacting with the exhibit, or it can happen two months later."[12]

- The exhibit focuses on the visitor's experience.
  Exhibits are most successful when they focus on the visitor, not just on transmitting specific content. They can do this by providing something for the visitor to do or experience, displaying real objects for the visitor to look at (or touch) and discuss, and including labels written to help the visitor notice things and relate the information in the exhibit to their previous experience. In this way, an exhibit will keep visitors' attention longer and be more likely to provoke thought.

- An exhibit should focus on the real.[13]
  Seeing real things or engaging with real phenomena is a more powerful experience than "secondhand" ones like viewing pictures of objects or reading descriptions. When possible, you should strive to have real objects or present real experiences in your exhibit. It will strengthen the visitor's experience.

- The exhibit is accessible to a wide variety of people.[14]
An exhibit that everyone can be interested in, use, and enjoy is the ideal. An exhibit shouldn't exclude any group or individual based on age, disability, education-level, previous experience, culture or ethnicity, or background from its audience. Your aim should be an exhibit that can be appreciated or enjoyed at many different levels and by many different people.

- The exhibit promotes interaction.[15]
An exhibit that causes visitor's to interact with each other (whether they are discussing it, showing each other things they have found, manipulating something together, or working something out together) is likely to provoke thought, help them make connections and relate the exhibit to their lives, and give them something to take away from the exhibit.

- It's feasible to make the exhibit.
While you want to be creative, you must also be realistic and accept when an idea is beyond your capability (because of money or time or the physical laws of the universe).

We used these criteria as a checklist to brainstorm exhibit ideas and determine their appropriateness. These are the things we decided would (and wouldn't) work given each of the criteria.

Stand alone: Since the exhibit was about stone carving, we liked the idea of letting people try it out. We reasoned that if they could feel what it was like, they could appreciate the art all the more, and understand where the stone dust that caused silicosis came from. It didn't take us long to decide that this wasn't feasible within the confines of an exhibit. It would require a complex design of enclosed plexiglass boxes with special arm holes to allow people to use the sharp tools safely. In addition, the kinds of power tools that cause noticeable dust would be too loud and dangerous to use in an exhibit. This kind of activity would be better as a program, perhaps a stone cutting demonstration with an opportunity to try your own hand at it. The exhibit needed hands-on activities that did not require supervision or major safety measures.

More than words: Already having decided that the exhibit would be based on photographs and artifacts interspersed with things to touch, we weren't worried that it would turn out to be an exhibit of words, words, words. In addition, the art exhibit would have only one short introductory label and one identifying label for each work, hardly any words at all. We did, however, think about how to get our message across without the written word and came up with the possibility of recording our granite workers' memories rather than writing them and brainstormed ways to put special emphasis on those photos with more emotional weight.

Provokes thought: We planned to try to provoke thought through three methods of relating the exhibits message to the visitors' life. We felt a discussion of working conditions and worker's rights would be inherently understandable to visitors since almost everyone has or has had a job. It would be our goal in the exhibit labels to get people thinking about their own working conditions. We hoped including the memories of town residents would be another link to the visitor's life, especially if we could contrast older workers' memories of how things were with talk of how things are now. Finally, by bringing in the present day situation in China's granite industry, we could show that the problem isn't just one of history and get visitors thinking about how far we have come locally, but how far we still have to come globally.

Visitor experience: It was important for us that the visitor experience consist of more than just reading labels. The art show would be inherently experiential: the nature of art is such that a visitor experiences emotions, appreciates skills, and makes connections with their own life. We had to think about how to provide experiences in the history side of the exhibit. We decided that touching granite samples might help visitors imagine what it was like for stone cutters to work in this medium. In addition, since safety equipment is necessary when working with granite (to prevent silicosis), we thought having a dust-filtering mask for visitors to try on would give them a sense of what it feels like to work as a stone cutter.

Real phenomena: Besides the artwork in the show, we wanted to bring as much real life into the exhibit as possible. Being able to try on a dust-filtering mask is a more real experience than simply looking at one. When touching granite dust, visitors could much more easily imagine what it was like to breath it in. Memories from local people next to their pictures are very real; some would be familiar to our visitors, people they see around town. Recording them speaking instead of printing their stories on labels, would contribute to a real feeling—their voices, some with Italian accents, and their laughter would come out in a way not possible in a printed quote.

Accessible: It was thinking about accessibility that finally settled our minds to include our granite workers' stories as recordings rather than labels. We wanted multisensory experiences in the exhibit. Objects and labels are typically visually oriented, but we wanted our exhibit to be meaningful through sound and touch as well, another reason it seemed important to offer experiences besides that of reading and looking.

Promote interaction: We hoped that our exhibit topic, so tightly linked to our community, would naturally encourage discussion. In particular, we thought that the emphasis on the local workers and the well-known cemetery would cause recognition and get people talking.

In a study by Alt and Shaw[16] of museum visitors' attitudes towards exhibits, visitors listed what they felt distinguished an ideal exhibition. As you are planning your exhibit, think about how it can meet those characteristics:

- The exhibit appeals to all ages.
- It's clear what you're supposed to do with the exhibit and how to begin.
- The exhibit's message comes across quickly and is easy to understand.
- The exhibit grabs and holds your attention, gets you involved, and makes the subject come to life.
- The exhibit gives just enough information, presents it clearly, and makes a difficult subject easier to understand.
- The exhibit allows you to test yourself to see if you understand the points it's making.

1.2.5 Accessibility

You want your exhibit to be accessible to as many people as possible, so you need to consider the differences between people in your audience. There are lots of different disabilities, both physical and cognitive, as well as different backgrounds that affect how a person experiences an exhibit. It's necessary to keep these in mind when developing and designing your exhibit. As you are generating the initial ideas for an exhibit it's especially important to consider sensory and cognitive accessibility and background as these challenges are often partially solved in the development of the exhibit (and the writing of labels) rather than in its design. Here is an introduction to accessibility issues. They will be discussed in further detail later in the exhibit process.

Sensory disabilities: The sensory disabilities of blindness or low vision and deafness or hearing impairment are quite common. People who are blind or have low vision are at a particular disadvantage at exhibits which tend to be highly visual, made of things to look at and labels to read. The challenge in making an exhibit accessible to people with these disabilities is to include experiences that are tactile, aural, and visual. Think of ways to communicate your big idea in all three ways: visually (through objects on display, labels, graphics, etc.), aurally (through recorded sounds, speeches, stories, and labels; video with sound, etc.), and tactually (through things to touch or manipulate). If your exhibit is primarily visual (as many displays of objects or art are), maybe you could have a model representing the objects on display that can be touched, or an audio description of the items.

We looked at our exhibit ideas overall to see how well they provided different sensory experiences. The visual sense, usually the easiest, would be served by photos, text labels, and the sculpture in the art show. Spoken histories would provide an experience for the ears. Unfortunately, these recorded memories would not be accessible to visitors who were deaf or hearing impaired. We realized that since we were interviewing older residents, their stories might be of special interest to other older residents, the very people who are most likely to be hearing impaired. Since this was such an important part of our exhibit, and one that would take some work to create, we decided we wanted it to reach as many people as possible, so we would offer a printed version of the stories in a laminated sheet that could be carried around for those who couldn't or did not want to listen to them. We planned to let people touch samples of granite and try on a dust-filtering mask. Touchable samples of granite were one way to make the sculpture part of the exhibit more meaningful to people who are blind. Since the sculptures themselves could not be touched, we planned to get different kinds of granite samples: rough, unfinished granite, polished granite, granite carved with letters and flowers, and granite dust.

Cognitive disabilities: People with cognitive disabilities may not have the full ability to read and understand the information in a label. As you develop the exhibit, ask yourself what someone will be able to get out of it if they cannot (or do not) read the labels. Will the big idea be accessible without them? How could your design facilitate understanding without the labels? Later we will discuss how to write labels to maximize accessibility. Since many people who *can* read labels don't, addressing this challenge will make your exhibit more effective for everyone.

Motor disabilities: Motor disabilities vary widely from the use of a wheelchair or walker to limited mobility or complete paralysis of hand(s), arm(s), or the upper body. The important things to keep in mind early on are that there should be enough room for easy movement around the exhibit, that objects to be touched and viewed should be at the correct height, and that interactive devices should be able to be reached and manipulated with a closed fist and with minimum pressure or stretching.

Background: Your visitors vary in gender, ethnicity or race, age, and life experience. Think of how your exhibit topic might be meaningful to different groups. (If need be, do some interviewing to find out.) Use these ways as "hooks" to help people relate to the exhibit. Recognize exhibit topics that might have an inherent bias and try to develop the exhibit to avoid it. For instance, an exhibit about sports might end up feeling like a "boys" exhibit, but there's no reason it has to. In addition, watch your own bias when writing labels and choosing exhibit topics.

The best way to make your exhibit accessible and meaningful to many people is to consider these differences early on in the planning stages. You will find that making an exhibit accessible to a person with a particular disability often ends up making the exhibit better for everyone. For instance, leaving enough space around an exhibit for comfortable use by a wheelchair user also means there's enough space for a parent with a child in a stroller. Providing a tactile experience in an exhibit as well as a visual one not only makes it more accessible to someone who is blind, but provides an additional, enriching experience for everyone. These are just two ways that greater accessibility can improve your exhibits overall — there are many more. Get in the habit of thinking about accessibility right up front: it will improve your exhibits and can save you from some embarrassing and avoidable moments later on.

1.2.6 Consider Conservation

Find out right at the beginning of the process if the items you want to display will require any conservation measures as this will affect the materials you can use in the exhibit and its design. If the items will be on loan, work with your colleague responsible for the administrative details of the exhibit to determine the display requirements of the lending institution. If the items belong to the library, you may already know their conservation requirements. If not, seek advice from a conservation expert at a local museum, historical society, or state library or archive. Alternatively, consult the published information on conservation; one excellent series of technical leaflets is available on-line from the Northeast Document Conservation Center at www.nedcc.org/leaflets/leaf.htm. Their 1999 leaflet "Protecting Paper and Book Collections During Exhibition" addresses many areas of conservation and offers a bibliography of further reading and sources of supplies. In addition the American Association of State and Local History publishes a leaflet titled *Exhibit Conservation: Strategies for producing a preservation-responsible exhibition* available for purchase at www.aaslh.org/leaflets.htm. Both leaflets address the following issues:

Temperature and humidity: Maintaining a constant, appropriate temperature and humidity protects against mold, chemical deterioration, and physical damage of items on display.[17] Fluctuating levels can be particularly damaging. A range of 45 to 55 percent relative humidity and 65 to 75 degrees Fahrenheit is best.[18] Most climate-controlled libraries (with central heating and air conditioning) will be within this range. Make sure that any outdoor air entering the library does not affect the exhibit area[19] and that the exhibit lighting is not generating heat. You can monitor the temperature and humidity of your exhibit case with a thermohygrometer.[20] These can be purchased from companies that sell scientific instruments or preservation materials, including major library suppliers such as Gaylord. They can cost from $30 to hundreds of dollars. Humidity control measures such as silicone packets can also be purchased at these places.

Light: Different kinds of objects can withstand different levels of light. There are three classes of object: specially sensitive (paper, textiles, etc.), sensitive (paintings and painted objects, organic materials), and relatively insensitive (stone, glass, ceramics, metal, inorganic materials). Appropriate light levels for these classes are 50 lux, 200 lux, and 300 lux, respectively.[21] These are minimum levels erring on the side of caution; it may be unnecessary to keep the lighting this low in your exhibit. If you are displaying objects that have specific lighting needs, you may have to use a light meter. Ultraviolet light is the most damaging, so avoid direct sunlight and use ultraviolet filters on your fluorescent and track lights, and do not train light directly on very sensitive objects.[22] The damaging effects of light are cumulative and irreversible.[23]

Off-gassing of materials: All materials have the possibility of releasing chemicals into the air. This is called off-gassing. Some materials are very stable and don't off-gas anything. Others off-gas harmful chemicals that can damage display items. Because of this it is important to know what materials are safe to use when building display cases, painting exhibit rooms and mounts, and making cloth linings or paper decorations or labels. Anything included in a display case must be safe. Many woods, paints, papers, textiles, and other materials are not. The technical leaflet mentioned above discusses specifically what materials are safe and which ones to avoid.

Pests: Insects can do serious damage to organic materials. They are not always easily visible. It may be necessary to keep food out of the exhibit area or include pesticides in the exhibit case, however pesticides themselves can be damaging.

Items important or fragile enough to need conservation, obviously should not be available for the public to touch. Items on display specifically for hands-on use, however, must still be protected. The public can be amazingly hard on exhibits and anything they touch must be tough and mounted for protection. Work under the assumption that if an item can be easily removed from an exhibit, it will be. There are varying ways to protect an item. An item displayed for its texture can be mounted below plexiglass with a hole through which visitors can reach to touch it. An item available for manipulation by the visitor (for instance, a magnifying glass) should be tethered to the exhibit with plastic coated wire. No matter how well protected they are, over time almost all hands-on items will degrade. For instance, magnifying glasses will become scratched and the texture of wood, textiles, and other materials will be rubbed away. For long-term exhibits, plans must be made and funds dedicated to maintaining or replacing these items.

In our exhibit we displayed labels and photos, granite sculptures, some metal tools, and some dust-filtering equipment. We did not use any original photos in the exhibit, only scans, so we didn't have to worry about their conservation. The tools and equipment were displayed behind glass. Light and temperature was not an issue for the granite samples and sculptures, but food was—grape juice stains granite, too—so we did not allow food in the art gallery. The items to be touched had to be anchored properly to prevent any damage to them or the visitor. The mask available for visitors to try on was not one from our collection of early granite industry equipment, but rather a present day version on loan to us from a local granite company.

1.2.7 List Collection Connection Materials

Displaying a collection of library materials that relate to your exhibit theme is a great way to encourage people to learn more about the topic and use the library resources. Throughout the book we refer to them as "collection connection" materials. If you are planning to display collection connection materials with the exhibit, begin choosing them now. Try to choose a wide variety of materials including books, videos, audio books, magazines, etc. Include items that will appeal to all ages, backgrounds, and interest levels; if your library has a children's section, don't forget related materials from there. If your library does not have enough variety in its collection, think about interlibrary loan or purchasing new material to supplement the exhibit.

Decide whether the materials will be for circulation or display only. If the materials are integral to the design or content of the exhibit you will want them to stay in place. Otherwise, allowing them to circulate takes advantage of interest generated by the exhibit. If you do this, it's a good idea to have a sign indicating the materials are for circulation so people will know they can take them off display.[24] If visitors will not be able to check out the items choose materials you will feel okay taking out of circulation for the duration of the exhibit. If the exhibit will be up for longer than you want materials out of circulation, make groups of different materials and put each on display for a portion of the exhibit time. This will highlight more of the collection while allowing most of the materials to continue to circulate.

1.2.8 List Your Ideas

It's time to sum up all of your ideas. There are a number of things to include. If you haven't thought about the first five things on this list yet, do it now before you move on. The final two, exhibit and label design, will come up again later.

- What kind of experience do you want the visitor to have? Is the exhibit supposed to be scary, funny, sad, or have any other emotional pull?

- What do you want the visitor to do at the exhibit? Are you hoping they will look at things and admire them, touch things, play, make choices and try different things out, talk to each other, do things together, etc?

- What do you want the visitor to leave the exhibit thinking about? Or what is the most important thing that they get out of the exhibit?

- What items do you want to display (if any)? Do they require conservation?

- What are your overall ideas for the exhibit?

- What ideas do you have so far for the exhibit design?

- What ideas do you have for label copy and design?

Once you've made your lists, decide which of your overall ideas seems like the most worthwhile to take forward. You don't have to choose just one; sometimes it's a good idea to take a couple of ideas to the next step to see which one works best, and some exhibits are made up of more than one component.

 Our ideas for the different parts of our exhibit story included:

- A description of silicosis including statistics on deaths.
- The story of Louis Brusa, a stone cutter who died of silicosis. Before he died, he carved his own tombstone for Hope Cemetery, a life-size sculpture of his wife standing by him as he lies dying.
- Discussion of the workers' twentieth century fight for improved working conditions.
- The current silicosis epidemic in China.

Our ideas for different things to include in our exhibit to tell the story included:

- Recorded interviews of the memories of stone cutters.
- Displayed stone cutting tools and equipment.
- A dust-filtering mask available for trying on.
- Granite samples for touching including rough, polished, carved, and dust.
- Photographs of the Brusa monument, stone cutters at work, the working conditions and safety equipment inside the granite sheds during different decades, and the strikes that helped lead to industry changes.

1.2.9 Request Items to Borrow

If you hope to borrow items from another institution or individual, you need to set that process in motion soon. Send a letter to that institution including a list and description of the items you want to borrow, the purpose of the loan, and how, where, and when they will be exhibited. The more you include about your qualifications and ability to safeguard the items, the more likely you are to be able to borrow them.

1.3 Beginning the Exhibit Design

1.3.1 Sketch Initial Ideas

Now that you have settled on some exhibit ideas, it's time to start the design. Make a brief sketch of your design ideas. If you are working on a display of items, sketch their relative locations and where their labels will go. If you are working on an interactive exhibit, think about what the components will be and how they will be used (for more on interactive or hands-on exhibits, see chapter 8). Your sketches don't have to be complicated or even to scale at this point; just get your ideas down on paper. As you brainstorm design ideas, consider these things:

Theme: Is there a way to relate the design to your exhibit's theme? How can you use color, props, lighting, and label design and fonts to help reinforce your exhibit's big idea? Can you think of a visual "hook" to attract visitors that says something about the exhibit content?[25]

Emotion: Are you interested in setting a specific mood or drawing out an emotion in the visitor? Will certain colors, lighting styles, label fonts, or props help evoke such a mood or emotion? Is there a reason to try to evoke an emotional response with this exhibit? Is this reason worth additional effort or expense?[26]

The topic of our exhibit was a sad one: a decades-long history of early death for most of the men in our community. In particular, the story behind the Brusa monument and the monument itself are sad. To acknowledge the inherent sadness in the design of the stone and help visitors notice it since they are not looking at the actual tombstone but rather at a picture of it, we enlarged the picture of the monument and spot lit it directly, allowing the areas surrounding it to go dark.

Labels: What kinds of things will you want to say on they labels? How much room will they take? How many will you need? How will they be integrated into the exhibit?

Design is a combination of five elements: color, line, shape, space, and texture. The decisions you make about each and the way they work together when you combine them determine how attractive, inviting, and successful your exhibit is. There are certain principles of good design that you should be familiar with: balance, emphasis, simplicity, variety, and unity. Your goal is to combine the five design elements to follow the five design principles and support your big idea. We discuss each element of design briefly below, followed by a description of each principle of design. If you don't know a lot about design, get help from a volunteer or staff member who does. If you are on your own, read the following hints, look at some books about design, start simply, and always ask others if they think the design is attractive or inviting. As with everything, you get better at this the more you do. If you want to get help, look around for local art or architecture students (from high school to college), department store window and interior display designers, theater designers or technicians, or commercial artists who might be willing to volunteer.[27]

Consider the following elements of design as you think about your exhibit. Ask yourself how your choices about each can support (or detract from) your big idea.

Color: Color can evoke a particular feeling or idea. Certain colors or combinations of colors have meanings or associations. What does red make you think of? Black? Yellow? Combinations of colors work in different ways: some clash, some complement. You should choose colors that relate to the purpose and theme of the exhibit. In some exhibits, you will want to use colors that "match." In others, clashing colors will add to the meaning of your exhibit. Some exhibits will call for traditional color choices, others for more creativity. If you are displaying objects, choose a background color that will show the objects to their best advantage, not detract from them.

Line[28]: There are two kinds of line: visible lines, that are drawn, and invisible lines, created by the relationships between items. Use them in your exhibit to provide order, make relationships between items clear, and tell the visitor's eye where to look. Borders and boundaries focus attention on what's inside them. Lines or arrows used as links show that items are related. Dividing lines separate and organize information. Decorative lines can add meaning or mood to your exhibit: think about the different feelings evoked by a squiggly line, a diagonal line, a jagged line, a curved line, etc. Borders can be made out of patterns or pictures that relate to your exhibit theme.

Shape: Shape is one of the most instantly noticeable parts of a design. The overall shape is created by the exhibit itself (often rectangular). The other shapes you use in the exhibit, both two and three dimensional, should relate to each other, the overall shape, and when appropriate, the exhibit theme. Shapes in an exhibit can appear intentionally (you cut out a circle as a background) and unintentionally (the text of your label looks like a triangle). As you design, step back periodically and look at the big picture — are there any unintentional shapes that you can fix?[29]

Space: The items in an exhibit are arranged in three dimensional space. The exhibit has height, width, and depth. (Even a bulletin board, a seemingly two-dimensional space, can have depth, and using depth in a wall exhibit often makes it look more lively and interesting.) How the items in a case, the words on a label, the pictures on a wall, or the exhibit components in a room are arranged will affect the visitor's reaction to them. If not enough space is left, the exhibit will look cluttered or the label unreadable and people will avoid it. Too much space will make the exhibit look unfinished and won't help people make connections between the objects. Just the right amount of space is inviting; people will want to look at the exhibit and read the labels, and if the space is in the right place, it will help them understand the big idea.

Texture: Texture adds interest to your exhibit and can be used to support the big idea. Consider how textured papers (crepe, folded, glossy, etc.), textiles (burlap, velvet, denim, fake fur, etc.), and other objects or props (mesh, sand, wood, etc.) might reinforce the meaning or feeling of your exhibit. Even if these things are not to be touched, visitors will make an association.[30]

Now use the following principles of design[31] as a guideline as you choose and combine your elements of design.

Balance: Balance is achieved by evenly distributing the visual "weight" of items in an exhibit (labels, display objects, decorative materials, etc.). A symmetrical display is the easiest way to attain balance, but it doesn't necessarily allow for items to be arranged in the most meaningful way. An asymmetrical arrangement allows you to place your items anywhere, as long as the overall exhibit is balanced. Bigger, brighter, or bolder items are "heavier." This means if you have one large, brightly colored item on the left, you will need more than one smaller, lighter colored item on the right to balance it. Try different layouts to see which looks best. Through trial and error you will eventually develop a sense of balance. A well-balanced arrangement can prevent a cluttered feeling in the exhibit and the appropriate use of space can help with balance. Don't just spread single items uniformly over a space; place related items closer together and balance these individual clusters to provide meaning through design.

Emphasis: Putting emphasis on an object, a word, or an area of an exhibit will help show the visitor right away which things are most important. Emphasis in labels can be made with borders, arrows, bold type, color, type size, etc. Objects can be emphasized through lighting, their placement in space (higher, further forward, out of line, or isolated from other objects), color (their own or the background they are placed against), the texture on which they are placed, or a line pointing to them.[32]

Simplicity: The design of an exhibit serves a purpose: it supports the big idea of the exhibit and it attracts people. It should do this in the simplest and most direct way possible. Using simplicity as a guideline often means choosing to leave some things out. Any design element not serving the purpose should go. Any element *not necessary* to serve the purpose should go. Getting rid of meaningless clutter allows you to concentrate your energy (and the visitor's energy) on what's important in the exhibit.

Variety: Variety, in design as in life, adds spice. Use it to attract people and to help make your meaning clear. Without it, you'd have a hard time emphasizing things and everything would look a bit dull. But beware of variety: your goal should not be to use as many shapes, colors, lines, textures, typefaces and sizes as possible. Too many differences will make your design look cluttered sacrificing simplicity, accessibility, unity, and appeal, and compromising your meaning. When you are thinking of adding variety, ask yourself if it serves to support your meaning or if it is more likely to detract from it.

Unity: When all your design elements work together for the same purpose, you've achieved unity. All the design elements should relate to one another and to the whole. Repeating certain design elements and being consistent in their use will help you create a unified design.[33] Choosing only design elements that support the exhibit's theme or goals will help.

1.3.2 Think About Display

You must think about how and where to display collection connection materials at the beginning of your exhibit design or you will be stuck with nowhere to put them. They could be on a special shelf next to the exhibit, on the edge of the exhibit table itself, or on a separate display near the circulation desk to act as "impulse items." They could be displayed on book racks, lined up side by side, standing face out, etc. How you display them depends on how many you have, how they are shaped, and what formats they are.

1.3.3 Prototype

At this point you have a basic idea of what you want to do. Now comes one of the most important parts of the exhibit process: prototyping. Also called formative evaluation, prototyping allows you to identify problems before you set them in stone. We cannot stress enough how important prototyping is to creating a successful exhibit. No matter how experienced you are with exhibits, you will overlook and misjudge things as you get caught up in the design process. What seems like a perfect idea in your head can often turn out to be a mess in reality, impossible to make, or worse, confusing to the exhibit user. Prototyping brings you back down to earth and helps you avoid all sorts of calamities and failures.

You will prototype different parts of your exhibit with different goals in mind throughout the exhibit process. This first prototype will help you find out if the location and layout of the exhibit are feasible and meet the initial standards of physical accessibility. These things can be determined using a very basic model. You don't have to get too detailed at this point, although further along in the exhibit process when you are testing your ideas on the public, accurate prototypes become necessary. (Prototyping is not necessary for traveling exhibits; presumably, the lending institution has already taken care of that and are sending you a finished, fabulous product.)

Check location and traffic patterns: First check whether the exhibit's footprint and size will work where you plan to put it. You want to be sure that it will allow plenty of room for visitors to use the exhibit and walk by the exhibit, and that it doesn't impede the use of other library resources. It should also not block doorways and things on the wall or ceiling (light switches, fire alarms, existing signage, etc.) To find this out, you can put the table or case you will be setting the exhibit up on in the planned location and walk around it, pretend to look at and use it, and observe the behavior of your patrons as they pass it. If you don't have the exact base you will use, you can substitute one with the same dimensions or build the shape out of cardboard (cut up boxes and packing tape work great for this). Or, you can simply lay it all out with masking tape: stick the tape on the floor in the correct dimensions of the base. Even a prototype this simple can reveal important information.

Check for accessibility: Once you've laid out the exhibit, check to make sure it is physically accessible. You won't be checking everything to do with physical accessibility at this early stage, but there are some basic areas that are good to think about as soon as possible. The Smithsonian Institution's Accessibility Program publishes the *Smithsonian Guidelines for Accessible Exhibition Design* which provides detailed information (including measurements) about how to make exhibits accessible. It is an invaluable resource. It is available free by writing Smithsonian Accessibility Program, Smithsonian Institution, Arts and Industries Building, Room 1239 MRC 426, Washington, DC 20560; calling (202) 786-2942 or TTY (202) 786-2414; or e-mailing majewskj@si.edu. It can also be downloaded on the Internet at www.si.edu/opa/accessibility/exdesign/. No exhibit maker should be without a copy. It is exhaustive in the areas it covers, but at this stage, you should check the following things. (The measurements given here are discussed in greater detail with illustrations in the above-mentioned book.)

- The route to the exhibit is accessible. (If it isn't, can the exhibit be located elsewhere?)
- The route through the exhibit is wide enough, at least 36 inches.
- There is enough room in front of and around the exhibit to allow a person using a wheelchair to circulate. (There should be about 48 inches in front of the exhibit in order for a person using a wheelchair to face it and 60 inches to turn around.)

- Items on display (and labels) will be visible to a seated person (not too high and no obstructions). (Viewable items and labels in cases should not be higher than 36 inches from the floor. Labels on walls should be between 48 and 61 inches from the floor.)
- If a hands-on exhibit, there is room for a person in a wheelchair to slide their legs under the table and no part of the exhibit to be manipulated is out of reach of a seated person. (There should be at least 27 inches from the floor to the bottom of the table. No controls should be above 48 inches when reached from the front or above 54 inches when reached from the side — with no obstructions).
- Anything kept in front of the exhibit (like a chair or stool) is easily moved.
- The exhibit is adequately lit.
- The exhibit cases, tables, benches, barriers, etc. are not hazards for someone who is blind and uses a cane and nothing hangs too low from the ceiling. (Those who use canes can detect objects with a lower edge of 27 inches or less. Items hanging lower than 80 inches from the floor are possible head-bump hazards.)

Check for general design success: Finally, get a general idea of whether your exhibit idea will work. You will prototype it more accurately later, so for now just make some basic models to show if your idea is possible. If you are planning to display items, use the prototype to make sure that your table or case will be big enough, that the stands will be sturdy enough and display the item at the right height and angle, and that the idea in your head will look good in reality. It's not necessary to use the actual items you will display in this prototype (although if it's practical to do so, there's no reason you shouldn't — working with the actual items will tell you a lot and provide inspiration). Instead you can make cardboard or paper models or use any other objects that are similar in size and shape. Arrange and rearrange these as necessary to answer any questions or concerns you might have. Remember to allow room for labels, titles, etc. If you are making a hands-on exhibit, now is the time to put together a crude version of your first idea for the interactive component to find out what works well and what doesn't. (Find out more about prototyping hands-on exhibits in Chapter 8.)

Remember that prototyping often exposes problems that you hadn't thought about. That's the whole point. So keep an open mind as you are doing it and pay attention to what you find out. When something doesn't work, you must rethink it.

1.3.4 Sketch Revised Design and Layout Ideas

Prototyping your initial design may have given you some ideas for improvement. If so, sketch out your revised design now.

1.3.5 Consider Lighting

Your exhibit will need to be lit. If the objects you are displaying require conservation measures, accuracy in lighting is very important. But even with no conservation concerns, lighting can affect the quality of your exhibit. If you think about and plan for it up front, you won't be stuck at the end with a great exhibit in a dark corner. If you don't know much about lighting, you could seek advice from commercial photographers, theater-light specialists or technicians, electricians, or department store window and interior display persons.[34]

It's most important to have enough light; labels need to be read and objects viewed. If lack of light causes people to squint or feel dull, they will not bother looking at the exhibit. Often the existing ceiling lighting will provide plenty of light. If not, you will have to add other sources of light. As you are looking at the light, make sure you consider not just the ambient light of the room or exhibit area, but the light that will fall on the exhibit directly. For instance, if there is a panel light in the ceiling to the right of the exhibit, there may be enough light for the room, but the exhibit may look dull with no direct light on it. Track lighting that you can direct or individual movable lights that you can attach to the ceiling will come in handy to remedy this situation.

With this kind of additional lighting you can also highlight special items. You might be surprised at how lighting can change the feel of your exhibit from drab to dramatic. Pay attention also to the exhibit labels. If nothing else, these need to be lit well for easy readability. Vertical labels (on a wall or stand-up base) often need additional lighting as the ceiling lights don't hit them at the right angle.

1.4 Review Exhibit Costs

1.4.1 Make a Materials List

List all the materials you think you will need to create the exhibit from your preliminary design including materials for the exhibit itself, for decoration, and for labels. Estimate how much of each material you will need.

1.4.2 Price the Materials

Check your library supplies to see which materials on your list you can get for free. Determine the cost of the other materials by calling around to local stores (or checking on the Internet if they can't be bought locally). When calling around to local businesses, be sure to ask if they will give a discount to the public library. Also, if you have a storage area at the library, find out if buying any supplies in bulk would save you money. But be careful — buy in bulk only those supplies that you will use on every exhibit (for instance, foamcore or laminating sleeves for labels).

1.4.3 Gather Outsourcing Information

If it looks like your design requires that part of the exhibit be made outside the library or calls for supplies that are not readily available locally, call around to find out prices and lead times (how long it will take from the order of an item to its delivery). Remember to ask if the library can get a discount. It's very important to get a sense of price and time frame on this sort of work now, so you can avoid a crisis by ordering on time, or by rethinking your exhibit design to fit within your budget. Although you may have only a vague idea of what you will need (a poster about 4' × 3', a painted box about one cubic foot, etc.), this is enough to get some preliminary estimates (you can get official quotes later on). Builders and other vendors may be reluctant at first to give you an estimate without knowing details (level of finish can make a big difference in pricing), but assure them that for now you need only a ball-park figure. In addition to cost and time frame, ask about what they need from you in order to fill your order (e.g., what kind of computer file can they accept for printing jobs, whether dimensions over the phone are okay or if they need a drawing, etc.). Once you get the estimates, you can check them against your budget and update the timeline with the new ordering deadlines.

Common things to consider having done outside the library include large-format printing, printing of color photographs or pictures (unless the library has a quality color printer), vinyl letters or other specialty signage, custom-made carpentry or woodworking projects (from basic mounts — bases on which to display objects — to fancier exhibit bases, panels, or display cases), or ready-made exhibit systems (walls or cases). Look in the yellow pages to find a list of local vendors. For printing jobs you can look under "printers" and for special signage look under "signs." In their ads, the vendors will indicate if they do large-format printing or vinyl letters, or any other of the processes you might desire. For exhibit components look under "cabinet makers" or, even better, ask a local museum for referrals to the people they use to build exhibits. These builders may be very helpful to you — they'll know about durable materials, might have advice on how to make something less expensively, and may even be familiar with conservation and accessibility standards.

Perhaps you think that there's no way you could afford to outsource these things, but don't rule it out right away; you might be surprised at how little it costs to have labels printed, for instance. Call around; in a few minutes, you will know whether it's within your price range. Remember to ask about discounts or donations and to shop around to see if prices vary. And as with all vendors, you might work with a couple before you find that perfect person who is wonderful to work with. Find them faster by asking others who use these services for recommendations (try calling your local museums and asking for the graphics or exhibit fabrication department).

If these services remain beyond your budget (and for many libraries with no exhibit budget, this will be the case), call around to your local schools. They won't be able to help you with vinyl lettering or large-format printing, but between high school, vocational-technical school, and college woodshops, you might find some students who would be willing to volunteer for the library on some of the carpentry projects (or some teachers who would be willing to offer extra-credit to students for helping you out). Look for community woodworking centers and local craft stores as well: there may be some handy carpenters or hobbyists out there who would love to throw together some basic cabinetry or mounts to help out the library. There are quite a few books with plans for different museum style display units. We list some in step 3.2.2 on fabricating the exhibit. In addition, you might want to check with art schools or classes to find volunteers to help with label and exhibit design.[35]

 Although we had some cases in which to safely display the artifacts from our archive under glass, we needed some new stands on which to display the items for visitors to touch, the mask and granite samples. One of our library volunteers is a

woodworker and he volunteered to make them for us if we sup-
plied the materials. We worked with him on the design and he
helped us decide what materials were most appropriate. We
planned to print our own labels and photos, but purchase the
overall exhibit title in vinyl letters. At this point, we contacted
the local historical society about having a volunteer interview
local stone cutter's about their work, memories, and family.

Record information about outsourcing options on the following pages.

Administration: There are four areas of exhibit administration: funding, contracts,
insurance, and security.

1.5 Funding

1.5.1 Make a Detailed Budget

Use the budget template following to make a budget for the exhibit. Add categories
to it as necessary. Staff time is very difficult to predict accurately, especially when it
comes to creative work. Make your best estimates of staff time, then add some. Be sure
to set aside money (about 15 percent of the total) as a contingency in case your estimates
are off or things go wrong.

1.5.2 Begin Additional Fund-Raising

You will be able to tell by comparing your budget with your exhibit idea if you
have enough money, will need to scale back the exhibit idea, or will need to look for
more money. If the latter, now is the time to begin looking into the possible money
sources.

Sponsorships: Sponsorships are the best way to raise money quickly for a specific
exhibit. The sponsors give the library a certain amount of money in exchange for their
names being used in conjunction with the exhibit: a sign on the exhibit would thank
the sponsors, and their names would be used in all mentions of the exhibit in the library's
public relations materials (such as the website, newsletter, and press releases). The sponsors' names do not have to be included in the title of the exhibit. It is possible to have
multiple sponsors of the same exhibit — even contributing different amounts; just make
sure that each knows they are not the only one, and that the acknowledgement makes
clear the primary sponsor (through name placement or type size).

The benefits of sponsorship are clear: the library gets money (for very little output)
and the sponsor gets publicity and can take a tax deduction of its charitable donation.
This symbiotic relationship can be especially beneficial at a public library where the
sponsor's name can reach a wide array of people and the library might not have much,
if any, money in its budget for exhibits. The dollar amount of sponsorship can vary
depending on the library, community, sponsor, and exhibit. If you are doing something
quite small, a sponsorship of $50 from a small local business might buy all the supplies
you need and be within their budget. If you are a large library putting on a more exten-

Local Vendors for Printing

(Include contact names; phone, fax, e-mail, and addresses; what format they take computer files in and their requirements for the files; if they can accept e-mail files or have an ftp site; general prices on printing; if there is a minimum order; kinds of paper and colors of vinyl, lamination, and mounting offered; other useful products offered; delivery charges and methods; lead time for orders; and any discounts. Once you've used the vendors record how it was to work with them, the quality of their products, and whether the work came in on time. If they were terrible, indicate that the library should never order from them again.)

Local Vendors/Organizations for Carpentry

(Include contact names; phone, fax, e-mail, and addresses; kinds of wood offered; what kind of work they will do; how small a job they will take; delivery charges and methods; lead time for orders; and any discounts. Once you've used the vendors record how it was to work with them, the quality of their products, and whether the work came in on time. If they were terrible, indicate that the library should never order from them again.)

_____

_____

_____

_____

_____

_____

_____

_____

_____

_____

_____

_____

_____

_____

_____

_____

_____

_____

_____

_____

_____

Local Vendors for Specialty Signage

(Include contact names; phone, fax, e-mail, and addresses; what format they take computer files in; if they can accept e-mail files; general prices on vinyl lettering; if there is a minimum order; colors of vinyl offered; other useful products offered; delivery charges and methods; lead time for orders; and any discounts. Once you've used the vendors record how it was to work with them, the quality of their products, and whether the work came in on time. If they were terrible, indicate that the library should never order from them again.)

Budget Template

(Adapted from a budget by Joan Waltermire, Montshire Museum of Science)

STAFF TIME			
Task	Staff Responsible	# Hours	Cost
Exhibit and Collection Connection Development			
Research, determine theme			
Front end evaluation			
Preliminary design			
Find conservation consultants and determine conservation needs			
Obtain cost estimates			
Prototyping			
Make prototype			
Write and design labels			
Test and re-test on staff and public			
Find accessibility consultants, run plans by them			
Revise design and labels based on budget and evaluation			
Exhibit and Collection Connection Fabrication			
Installation			
Exhibit maintenance/cleaning			
Deinstallation			
Programming			
Plan children/YA programs			
Execute children/YA programs			
Plan adult programs			
Execute adult programs			
Administration			
Determine budget available			
Manage budget			
Write and oversee contracts			
Determine and arrange for insurance			
Arrange security			
Fundraising			
Publicity			
Write and design PR materials			
Plan opening event			
Evaluation (summative) and Documentation			

OUT-OF-POCKET EXPENSES	
Item	Cost
Conservation and Borrowed Collections/Exhibits	
Materials and supplies, equipment	
Transportation	
Insurance	
Storage	
Exhibit and Collection Connection Development	
Paid consultants	
Accessibility	
Conservation	
Design	
Materials and supplies for prototypes	
Exhibit and Collection Connection Fabrication	
Materials and supplies, equipment	
Cases, panels, props, stands	
Paid outside builder/fabrication consultant	
Labels (materials, paid outside printing)	
Image reproduction rights	
Book purchases or ILL costs for Collection Connection	
Installation to Deinstallation	
Materials and supplies	
Lighting	
Installation, labor	
Security	
Post-opening modifications	
Deinstallation, labor	
Maintenance supplies (and materials for hands-on exhibits)	
Evaluation consultant	
Programs	
Honoraria, lodging, food for presenters	
Materials and supplies, equipment	
Refreshments	
Publicity	
Advertising	
Opening event (refreshments, invitations, etc.)	
Other	
Postage	
Prints and copies	
Telephone	
Mileage	
CONTINGENCY (15% of total)	

sive exhibit to serve many more people, the sponsorship amount could be much more, hundreds or even thousands of dollars.

When searching for sponsors, don't rule out anyone: consider all of the businesses in your community. But also think in particular of people or businesses who might have a special interest in the exhibit topic. Sponsorship would be a natural fit for them making it easier for you to ask if you are shy about such things. When asking, remember to stress the benefits to them: free publicity at a center of the community — a place where many go, a place that makes them feel good. As you talk to people, keep a record of those who express interest on the next page under "Potential exhibit sponsors."

 Possible sponsors for our exhibit included local granite quarrying companies, stonecutter guilds, unions, or monument sellers.

We mentioned an idea related to sponsorship briefly before: a book exhibit placed at a local business. The business sponsors such an exhibit by providing the space and props (from their own stock) and money (if needed).

Donations of services and materials: One way to meet your budget is not to find additional money, but to get donations of materials and services in kind. Always ask businesses if they are interested in making such donations to the library. They benefit by getting to take charitable tax deductions of the value of the goods or services and as with sponsorship, you can offer them a label on the exhibit indicating that it would not have been possible without their generous donation — nice advertising for their services since their products will be right there on display.

 We needed granite pieces to display and a local quarry and monument company agreed to provide a piece of unfinished granite, a piece of polished granite, a piece of granite with engraved letters and one with a simple carving in it, and a bucket of dust collected from these processes. We agreed to acknowledge their generosity in the exhibit.

Donations: Donors are different from sponsors in that their names are not used in conjunction with the exhibit. These are people who just want to help out. They get the benefit of a warm and fuzzy feeling as well as being able to take a tax deduction of their charitable donation. When you are advertising an upcoming exhibit in library public relations materials such as the website or newsletter, don't hesitate to mention that donations for the exhibit are welcome at any time and greatly appreciated. The library may have a general donation fund; use an exhibit or exhibits program as another incentive to get new donors and donations.

Grants: Grant money is most likely to come from a local source rather than a large national foundation or the federal government. This does not mean that no grant money is given from these larger entities, it's just not likely they will support a one-time or small exhibits program. The federal government's Institute of Museum and Library Services

Potential Exhibit Sponsors

(Include names of community members and businesses who express interest in sponsoring library exhibits (or hosting library book displays). Include their telephone numbers and a contact name, and any potential exhibit topics they might be interested in.)

_____

_____

_____

_____

_____

_____

_____

_____

_____

_____

_____

_____

_____

_____

_____

_____

_____

_____

_____

_____

_____

_____

does support exhibit projects that are unique in some way (see the details of a project they funded in chapter 11), but the grant process takes a long time. No matter where you apply for grants, do not count on the money; if this is the money you are relying on, don't start your exhibit until your grant application has been accepted. When looking into grants from local sources, beware of small grants with large administrative requirements; make sure the money is worth the extra work involved in applications and reports. Try these local organizations when looking for grant possibilities.[36]

- Civic groups, fraternal organizations, and women's groups
- State humanities or arts councils
- State historical societies
- State library councils
- State museums or state and regional museum associations

Record contact and grant information for these and other potential local sources of grants below.

1.6 Contracts

1.6.1 Determine If You Will Need Loan Agreements

If you are displaying items from outside the library, you will need to have a loan agreement with each lender or lending institution. If you are putting on a traveling exhibit, the exhibit vendor will provide you with a contract.

The same company giving us the granite agreed to loan us some of their hand-held, electric stone carving tools. We drafted a loan agreement to keep track of the tools.

1.6.2 Learn Lending Institution Requirements

Call the lending institution to ask about their requirements for display and conservation, insurance, and security. Work with the exhibit designer/developer to gather this information as they will need it, too — and they will be the ones determining which items will come to the library. It is important to know these things up front to be sure that you can handle the items safely and have budgeted appropriately. If they have loan contracts for you to sign, have them fax them over — they should include most of the information you need. Consider these things:

Display and conservation: Find out the requirements of display as soon as possible to make sure your library can meet them. If you cannot, you must not display the items. If the items have specific needs, the lending institution will most likely make this plain right from the start and insist on proof of the library's ability to meet them. They might require a facilities report as that proof (learn more about the facilities report in chapter 7). The exhibit designers will need to know the display requirements.

Insurance: The lending institution might require the library to get additional insurance to cover the value of the loaned items.

Local Sources of Grant Money

(List any local charities, foundations, or state or library organizations that offer grants for exhibit, educational, or library services. Include contact names and phone numbers, types of grant and amounts, application requirements and deadlines, and areas of interest.)

Security: The lending institution might require the library to have a certain level of security to ensure the safety of the loaned items.

Storage space: If the loaned items are arriving before the exhibit is ready to be put together, or being picked up sometime after the day the exhibit comes down, the library will need to store them somewhere. Make sure that you have an appropriate place that meets the handling requirements of the lending institution.[37]

Packing and shipping requirements: The lending institution might have specifications for how the materials must be packaged and shipped.

Responsibility for damage or loss: You will need to know (or perhaps negotiate) in what situations you could be held liable for damage to the exhibit, and whether there are limitations on your liability.

Loan fee: The lending institution might charge a fee for the loan of the materials.

1.6.3 Draft Loan Agreements

If you don't already have a generic loan agreement form create one now. The lender may have a contract that you must sign detailing the dates, costs, and handling requirements of the items for loan, but you will need a form to serve as a record of receipt and return of the items. Some lenders, particularly individuals rather than institutions, do not require a contract or loan agreement; they are happy to loan you items on the basis of a verbal agreement. For the library's protection, however, you should insist on one. The form need not be complicated. It should specify:

- The exhibit for which the items are being borrowed
- The borrower's name, address, phone, fax, e-mail, and agent or contact person
- The lender's name, address, phone, fax, e-mail, and agent or contact person
- A list of the items to be borrowed
- A description of each item, its dimensions (if needed for layout purposes) and its condition
- The value of each item
- Any special conditions of the loan and expectations for handling items
- The language by which the lender wants to be acknowledged
- The date the items will come to the library and the date the items must be removed/returned
- Who will be responsible for transporting the items to and from the library and how this shall occur

You should fill in all of the sections except the list of items (if it is not settled), and their descriptions and values. The lender will fill these sections in (or provide you with the information). In addition, the form should have a place for signatures indicating the receipt of the item(s) at the library and the return of the item(s) to the lender. (See the sample loan agreement form.)

Sample Loan Agreement Form

Granitetown Public Library

One Granitetown Way w Granitetown, Vermont 00000 w (000) 000–0000 w (000) 000–0000 (fax)

Loan Agreement Form

Lender_____ Contact person_____

Address/fax_____ Telephone_____

_____ E-mail_____

Exhibit_____ Contact person_____

Dates of loan: _____ to _____

Shipping/delivery responsibility:

Item	Condition	Dimensions	Value

Special conditions: (handling, packing, shipping
instructions, conservation, insurance, fees, etc.)

Credit line:

Date received_____ Signature of receiving party_____
Date returned_____ Signature of receiving party_____

1.7 Insurance

1.7.1 Additional Insurance

If you are displaying items from outside the library, depending on their value and the requirements of the lending institution, you may have to get additional insurance. Even if the lender does not require such insurance, you may choose to get it anyway. Traveling exhibits usually require insurance also. The lending institution will most likely have informed you of insurance requirements when you discussed contracts. If they didn't, however, make sure you find out now. Get a general idea of the amount for which the loaned items will need to be insured.

1.7.2 Insurance Company Details

Call the library's insurance company to find out what might be automatically included under the library's current policy. Ask them what steps you must take to purchase a rider to cover any items not already covered or needing additional coverage; typically you will simply write a letter including a description of the items, their value, and the dates of coverage. Giving them a general sense of the value of the items will enable them to estimate how much the rider will cost. If you are displaying the library's own items, be aware that on exhibit, they will be in a more precarious situation than when in their usual location. If they are particularly valuable, make sure your insurance policy covers them while on display. In addition, at this time, find out what to do if there is any damage: How do you make a claim? Will a representative of the insurance company need to inspect the damage? Should you take pictures now and after?[38] Keep your insurance company contact and exhibit-related information.

1.8 Security

1.8.1 Determine Security Needed

If you are borrowing items or exhibits from outside the library, find out from the lender what kind of security it requires. For your own exhibits, you probably have a pretty good idea of what kind of security an exhibit will need in your library — it depends on your community, the size of the library, the kind of exhibit, and where the exhibit is located. Levels of exhibit security range widely and include putting the exhibit within view of a regularly staffed desk, displaying signs that say "do not touch," displaying items under glass or behind a barrier (for instance, a rope or railing), putting items in locked and/or alarmed display cases, allowing people to enter the exhibit room by request only, posting signs saying the exhibit is being monitored, having a video camera monitoring the exhibit,[39] having a guard check on the exhibit periodically, having a guard stationed near the exhibit at all times. The key is to be realistic about the chance of vandalism or theft in your library and plan accordingly. Record exhibit-related security information.

The Library's Insurance Company Information

(Include the insurance company's name, address, and fax number; the name of the person in charge of the library's account and their phone number; and the process for getting additional insurance.

_____

_____

_____

_____

_____

_____

_____

_____

_____

_____

_____

_____

_____

_____

_____

_____

_____

_____

_____

_____

_____

_____

_____

1.9 Programming

1.9.1 Generate Ideas for Possible Programs

If the person handling the exhibit is not also taking care of the programming, there will need to be an exchange of information. Once the exhibit topic has been narrowed down and the big idea identified, the research about the topic should be shared and reviewed to get program ideas. Ask the exhibit person if he or she had any exhibit ideas that they ruled out because they would work better as a program. As you brainstorm ideas, conduct additional research as necessary to flesh them out.

There are many kinds of programs to consider including lectures, slide shows, book groups, story times, lap sits, discussion groups, after-school activities, interpretive tours of the exhibit, etc. You can plan new events in honor of the exhibit or use the exhibit topic as the inspiration for your monthly book group, weekly story time, daily after-school activity, quarterly lecture, or whatever your library's usual program is. There's no need to reinvent the wheel: link the exhibit with current library programming and take a look back at successful past programs to see if you can do something similar. This will increase the success of your programs by taking advantage of staff skills and loyal program audiences.[40] What you choose to do at your library should depend on your goals and the needs of your library visitors. A program that addresses a need or has a specific purpose will be the most successful.[41]

We had discarded the idea of allowing granite carving in the exhibit, but thought it would be a great opportunity for kids and adults alike, so planned a program instead. The program involved a number of local stone cutters demonstrating their carving methods (from letter engraving to bas relief to full-blown sculpture) with both manual and electric tools, in different kinds of stone. Parts of the program took place on the library lawn, and some in the art gallery. In addition to demonstrations, everyone present got an opportunity to try carving.

1.10 Publicity

1.10.1 Determine the Best Ways to Advertise

The many ways to advertise your exhibit and programs range from free to expensive, easy to involved. Here are some possibilities:

Library website: Your library website probably has a page for upcoming events. The exhibit and each of the associated programs should be listed on this page as soon as their dates are known. In addition, there may be an area of the website (the home page!) where a longer description of the exhibit and some pictures can be placed.

Library newsletter: The exhibit and each of the programs should be included in the library newsletter as upcoming events. You could also write an article about the

Security Concerns

(Include any security problems your library has had, any that you think could be a problem, and a list of the security measures that make the most sense for your library.)

_____

_____

_____

_____

_____

_____

_____

_____

_____

_____

_____

_____

_____

_____

_____

_____

_____

_____

_____

_____

_____

_____

_____

_____

_____

exhibit topic, do an interview with the exhibit team or related community members, or highlight library materials relating to the exhibit.

Brochures: Brochures describing the exhibit and its accompanying programs allow people to take the entire schedule home with them. They can be placed at the library's circulation desk, with the exhibit, in doctor's waiting rooms, or with local businesses or offices (especially those that have some connection to the exhibit).

Fliers/posters: Advertising posters, or fliers, can be placed in strategic locations to reach your intended audience. Community bulletin boards are located in libraries, schools and colleges, stores and businesses, town halls, grocery stores, information kiosks, and on the street, etc. Fliers can be made simply on letter-size paper (8½ × 11 inches) or printed outside the library for a fancier glossy, color look. Ask permission before posting them, but almost everyone will be willing to advertise library functions.

Community events calendars: Most daily and weekly newspapers have community events calendars which will advertise your exhibit and programs for free. Many towns also have community-based websites run by nonprofits that also have events calendars. And some public access cable stations show rotating lists of upcoming events on television. These are some of the easiest and best places to advertise. Each calendar will have its own deadline for inclusion.

Press releases: Press releases are short articles providing the basic details and related information about your exhibit and special programs. If they deem it worthy, some newspapers (especially local weeklies looking for filler) will reprint part or all of your press release. Others might add it to their community calendars or edit it to just a blurb. Check the newspapers' policies before sending them out.

Public service announcements: Public service announcements (PSAs) are read on the radio (and sometimes television). They are particularly common at college radio stations. Check the stations' policies before sending them out.

Letters to specific organizations or groups: If your exhibit topic might be of interest to the members of a local organization, write that organization a letter letting them know about it. Ask members to spread the word through their meetings and to mention the exhibit and programs in their newsletters or other publications and on their website. Consider fraternal organizations, social groups, social issue and political groups, clubs and hobby groups, historical societies, etc.

Mailing lists: You might have a list of people or businesses who have a specific interest in the library or the exhibit topic. Send a letter or postcard to them to let them know what is going on. Be discriminating with your direct mailings, too many can be expensive for the library and annoying for the recipients.

News coverage/news stories: If you have an event or exhibit of special interest, see if you can get news coverage of it by following up your press release with a phone call to see if any of the reporters are interested in doing a larger story. You could get news coverage in local radio, television, newspapers, magazines, or newsletters. Be sure to ask those places whose audience fits well with your exhibit's audience; you'll be more likely to get a story.[42]

Paid advertisements: If you have the money, you can always place advertisements in local radio, television, newspapers, magazines, or newsletters. When you are spend-

Local Places to Advertise

(Include daily and weekly newspapers, public access television, local television news, local radio stations, local colleges and schools, community organizations, community websites, community or neighborhood newsletters and groups, locations of popular community bulletin boards, etc. As you contact these places, record the name and number of each publicity contact person, fax and address, target audience, deadlines, and policies or requirements for press releases, public service announcements, etc.)

_____

_____

_____

_____

_____

_____

_____

_____

_____

_____

_____

_____

_____

_____

_____

_____

_____

_____

_____

_____

_____

_____

ing money, pay special attention to the target audience of the publication or station you want to advertise in: you want to reach the right group of people. Most publications and stations have data on their demographics, so ask before you buy.[43]

Which of these advertising methods you choose depends on what your exhibit or program is, how big it is, and how common it is. If you hold one major exhibit a year, you might want to pull out all the stops with paid advertisement and try to get it covered by the local television news. If you have story time every week, television will be overkill (and they're not going to care), but the local parents' newsletter will want to include it in their community calendar.

Your target audience will also affect how and where you choose to advertise. If you are hoping to attract new visitors to the library, you won't want to use only the library website, newsletter, and bulletin board to spread the word. If your programs are for teens or children, send letters to the appropriate local schools and teachers. If you're trying to attract teens, find out what places they frequent (cafés, clubs, stores, etc.) and ask these businesses to post fliers. If you want to lure college kids, post fliers around campus, get in the student newspaper's "upcoming events" column, and write a public service announcement for the student radio station. If your exhibit appeals in particular to people of certain interests or backgrounds, send letters to local groups or organizations that serve these people asking them to spread the word. If the exhibit is at a branch library, advertise it in the local neighborhood newsletter and send a letter about it to neighborhood groups and places of worship. Maintain a list of possible places to advertise.

1.10.2 Find Out Deadlines and Make a Timeline

Once you've decided how and where to advertise, find out the deadlines and make yourself a timeline to follow.

1.10.3 Decide Whether to Have an Opening Party

If this is a big exhibit or a particularly special event, you might want to consider having an opening day party or reception. These kinds of events can be very time- and money-consuming. You should have a reason for the party and specific goals in mind to make devoting the energy required worthwhile. If you want a program at the event, talk to the program people about what might be possible.

Part II — Development and Design

2.1 Taking Stock

2.1.1 Present the Idea

Everyone will want to hear the latest plan for the exhibit; it keeps the excitement up. Ask others for questions and comments about your idea. Pay attention to these: they can point to possible problems or areas of confusion in your exhibit or give you great ideas that you hadn't thought of before. The great thing about a team is you don't have to rely only on yourself. Even if you aren't working in a team, you should run your ideas past other people — it's never a good idea to rely on one mind alone.

2.1.2 Report on the Budget and Fund-raising

Give a brief report on the status of the budget and fund-raising activities. If there appear to be money problems, now is the time to talk about possible solutions.

2.1.3 Review and Update the Timeline

Everyone responsible for part of the exhibit process should get together and review the timeline to make sure that things are on schedule. Pay special attention to any tasks that rely on someone else's work: confirm that those involved are aware. If the timeline isn't complete because you were unsure of ordering lead times on materials or outsourced work or other important dates, fill these in now (you should have gotten estimates for these during the first part of the process). Then make sure that everyone understands these new deadlines, including those outside the library staff responsible for part of the exhibit process be they volunteer or paid service. It's a good idea to make a new copy of the timeline for each member of the exhibit team after it has been updated.

2.1.4 Discuss Problems and Rethink

If any problems have arisen, you must decide how to address them before you go any further in the exhibit process. Problems could include lack of money or unexpected expenses, inability to properly handle items you were hoping to borrow, longer than expected lead times on outsourced materials, a shortage of staff time because of the unexpected amount of time exhibit work takes or other library needs, and a whole host of other possibilities. You must solve your problem before moving on whether that means delaying the exhibit in order to raise more money or allow staff more time, scaling back your exhibit idea to fit the budget or the library's capabilities, or, in the worst-case scenario, scrapping the exhibit idea totally and starting again from scratch.

2.2 Making Exhibit Labels

Although we give an introduction to exhibit labels here, for those who make a lot of exhibits or want further discussion and examples of labels, we highly recommend Beverly Serrell's book *Exhibit Labels: An interpretive approach.*

2.2.1 Plan the Labels

Depending on what kind of exhibit you are making, you will use different kinds of labels. These may include:

Title: The title is likely to be the first thing people will see when they look at the exhibit and it is certainly what they will read and hear about in the publicity materials before they even get to the exhibit. Therefore, it should give some indication of the exhibit topic and should try to arouse curiosity.[44] It can be clever or cute, but make sure this doesn't obscure the meaning.

Cloudy and Colder
WEATHER IN VERMONT

This exhibit combines a catchy main title with an informative subtitle. It was created by applying vinyl lettering to a wall. Because the title is so large, a decorative typeface not appropriate for blocks of text could be used.

Introduction: If the exhibit is a display of objects or images, an introductory label can be used to give an overview of why they are on display, what is special about the objects and how they might be of interest to the visitor. A group of exhibits needs an introductory label to say how they relate. In a single hands-on exhibit, this label can be passed up in favor of a label with instructions and explanations.

Instruction: For a hands-on exhibit, a label with instructions about what to do or how to use it should be located *on* the interactive area or mechanism. Ideally, an exhibit's operation would be intuitive so such a label would be unnecessary, but usually, some clearly written steps are needed. A photograph or illustration of someone using the exhibit can complement the written instructions—enabling an even faster grasp of what to do.

This instruction label is designed so each instruction is right next to its corresponding control to maximize intuitive use of the exhibit. A main label provides more detailed instructions (e.g. "Push the start button," "Add or remove pegs.") and an explanation, but next to the controls single words and symbols are easier to read and understand than sentences.

For any display of objects in which touching is encouraged, a label indicating so is a good idea. Many people have learned not to touch and need a little encouragement.

Explanation: For a hands-on exhibit or any exhibit in which something happens or the user has an experience, you'll need a label to explain what's going on. This is a good place to try to relate what's happening to something that the visitor is already familiar with. It's also a good place to address the proverbial question, "So what?" If the visitor can relate the exhibit to his own life, it will have a stronger impact.

If a display of objects to be viewed is separated into groups, you can use these labels to explain what is significant about the groupings.

One end of the gear train* turns fast, but stops easily.
The other end moves slowly, but is hard to stop.

• Ask a friend to hold one handwheel still while you turn
the other one. Then trade places. Quite a difference!

It feels as if the gears add turning power in one direction,
and take it away in the other -- but they don't. The
amount of power at both ends of the gear train is the
same. It all came from your muscles.

The trick is that turning power is made up of two parts:
how hard you push, and how many turns of the handle
you make each minute. You can set up gears so that the
same amount of power creates a hard, slow push or a
weak, fast push.

Where to see this in action:
on your bike!

* a *gear train* is a series of connected gears

Here's an explanation of a label that plays many roles at once: title, instruction, and explanation. The first sentence in bold gives visitors a clue as to what to look for and is followed by an explicit instruction. The bulk of the label is used to explain the visitor's experience. Notice the image used on the label: it helps tie the exhibit experience to something the visitor is familiar with in real life.

Captions: Captions are labels that refer to a specific object or image on display. They describe something about the object that the visitor can see and explain its significance or put it in context. Captions are often the only labels people will read in an exhibit — and they will only read the captions of the objects that catch their eye. Because of this, each label must stand alone and be interesting and easy to read — or no more will be read.[45]

Identification: Identification labels simply tell what an object is and give basic information about it such as the maker, artist, title, material, date, scientific name, etc.

Images: In some cases, images are the objects being interpreted by the labels, but in other cases, images are used on labels as illustrations of what is written, or stand alone as their own label to support the big idea.

Directional and prohibitive signage: Directional signage tells people where to go. It may be a sign at the front of the library saying that an exhibit is downstairs, or a sign at the door of the exhibit room welcoming people to go inside.

Prohibitive signage tells them not to do something (touch the items, take pictures, eat or drink, etc.). Not all exhibits will need these kinds of signs, but you should evaluate whether they would help. (You can always make them after the exhibit has opened if you find there is a need you didn't anticipate.)

Sponsor/donation signs: These labels acknowledge sponsorship of the exhibit or donations of services and materials. They can stand alone or be included on the bottom

Harnessing the River

At first the belts and pulleys of machinery were turned directly by the river's flowing water. Later, when electricity came into use, the water's energy was used to produce hydroelectric power.

Dough mixing machines, Hanover Crackers, White River Junction, Vermont

DAM AND POWER HOUSE
HEIGHT 200 FT. CAPACITY OF RESERVOIR 18 BILLION GALLON FIFTEEN MILE FALLS LOWER DEVELOPMENT BARNET, VT.   MUNROE, N.H

Hydroelectric dam on the Connecticut River in Monroe, New Hampshire

This series of laminated labels includes an introduction of related images, scans of historical postcards, and captions describing those images. The point of the introduction label is made in only two sentences, and illustrated by the images included in the exhibit.

Fossils of an ancient fish
Bothriolepis (Bah' three oi e' pis)

Bothriolepis was an armored fish that lived 350 million years ago. These fossils show the hard, bony plates that covered its head and front fins. Its tail was bare. *Bothriolepis* probably crawled along the bottoms of lakes and rivers on its jointed fins, and lung-like pouches may have allowed it to breathe air when stranded on a muddy flat. These fossils are from Quebec.

top view

side view

of one of the main labels. See sample sponsor and donation signs in step 3.4.2.

You do not have to use all these kinds of labels. Identify and use only those your exhibit calls for. If the exhibit is small, you will be able to combine some of them onto one label (for instance, one label could have the title, an introduction and/or explanation, an image, and sponsor information).

Simple line drawings on this label help visitors to identify the fossil in the exhibit. Using illustrations is a great way to make an exhibit clearer and help get your message across. Notice the glare on this label. Exhibit lights can cause this glare just as the camera flash does. Be careful when you light your exhibit to avoid glare and laminate labels only when necessary.

Example Exhibit

We used almost all the kinds of labels in our exhibit. It began with a title. From there, the exhibit was split into two sections: the story of silicosis and working conditions and the story of the Brusa monument and the workers' fight for change. Each of these two sections had an introductory label. Each item or photograph within the exhibit had a caption briefly detailing its significance, and always trying to relate back to the overall idea of the exhibit. Basic instruction signs were used on the hands-on components of the exhibit. For example, the recorded histories were started by pressing a button, so we put a label by the buttons telling people to "Press here to start the story." The granite samples had a combination instruction and explanation sign: It asked visitors to touch the samples, then explained why they were different and how much dust was created to make them so. A similar sign was used by the mask, encouraging visitors to try it on and then explaining what it is used for. Finally, a donor sign was included to acknowledge the local company that provided parts of the exhibit.

Along with "Do not touch," this is one of the most common prohibitive labels. Here it is displayed on a movable stanchion to allow for the most effective placement. (Velcro on the bottom of the stanchion sticks to the carpet to help prevent accidents.) Prohibitive and directional signs can also be placed on walls and exhibit components, as long as visitors see them at the right time and place to get the message.

In the art exhibit we used only four kinds of labels: a title, a brief introduction for the entire exhibit, identification labels on each of the works, and prohibitive signage asking visitors not to touch the art work. We felt it was especially important to use such prohibitive signage in the art gallery since we had asked people to touch things on the history exhibit and didn't want them to be confused or to have any accidents occur.

2.2.2 Write the Labels (First Draft)

Without exhibit labels, a visitor may have no idea what the objects on display are, why they are important, how they relate to each other, and most importantly, how they relate to the visitor. They may have no idea how to use the exhibit, what is happening when they do, and why it matters that anything happens at all. They may get frustrated, annoyed, or just not care. Your goal with exhibit labels is to make the user's experience positive and meaningful. You want to answer the (usually) unspoken question, "So what?"

Before you begin writing your labels, remind yourself of the message you want visitors to take home with them. What are you trying to tell them? Everything you write should help make your point. You will be tempted to throw in any number of fascinating, but irrelevant facts about your subject; resist that urge. Include only information that supports the big idea. Visitors have only a certain amount of time to spend with the exhibit; they are not sitting down to read a book.

Keep your labels short and focused. Most people will want to read about the exhibit, but not if it's a chore.[46] Visitors are put off by anything that looks too long: keep your paragraphs short, the type size big, and restrict the amount of information you ask them to read. Remember that whatever you write in 12 point type will look even longer on a label in 20 point type. After you write your first draft, go back and remove every sentence and word that isn't necessary. It will be hard at first, but be brutal and slash away with that red pen. If you question whether something is needed, chop it out. As you evaluate your labels with the help of other people, you will recognize the point at which you have chopped too much and your point is lost, but this moment often comes after you've removed a surprising amount of text. Here are some more things to keep in mind as you write:

- Try to give the user something to think about or notice when they are looking at, touching, or manipulating the exhibit. You can even begin your sentence with the verb "Notice." Make sure that what you point out is something that visitors can see or experience for themselves. If they can't notice it or it doesn't match their experience with the exhibit, they can become frustrated, annoyed, or feel stupid.

One of our labels included two large photographs comparing the working conditions inside granite carving sheds before and after safety measures were installed. The earlier shed is filled with dust, the other has clear air. In the label we asked visitors to "Notice the different amounts of dust in these two photos of stone cutters at work." We identified the first photo as "The dusty working conditions of the 1930s when the average life span of a stone cutter was 42 years," and the second photo as "A 1950s workplace after stone-dust removal systems were finally required by law. Stone cutters lived longer because of the cleaner air."

- Try to relate the content of the exhibit to something that the visitors already know, something that is familiar to them in their own lives. Remember the question, "So what?"
- If you have instructions on your label, put them first, and make them stand out by setting them apart with a heading like "To try" or "Try this." Write them in the form of a list instead of a paragraph; it will make them easier to read and follow.
- Make every word count! Don't waste words on things people can see for themselves. For example, don't write "This beautiful book shows"; the visitor can see that it's beautiful. Choose words that are meaningful and help get your message across.[47]
- Pay attention to your writing style. Labels should be accessible to everyone who comes to the library. Your patrons vary in age, education, ability to read and understand English, cognitive functionality, and intellectual level. (This is not just a matter of children versus adults. Adults read English at varying levels of ability for all sorts of reasons: it's not their native language, they have a cognitive disability, they never learned very well, they were born deaf and learned it only as a second language, etc.) You want to reach as many people as possible. Keep your language simple so people don't have to struggle.
- Let each sentence express only one thought.[48]
- Keep sentence structure simple. (Avoid embedded phrases.)[49]
- Keep sentences short (no more than 25 words), but vary their lengths.[50]
- Use the active voice.
- Use everyday vocabulary. Always use the simplest word that is appropriate: for example, use understand instead of comprehend; use instead of utilize, etc. If you must use unfamiliar words (for instance technical terms), define them in parentheses or using the word "or" in the text.

  Serrell recommends a technique called "core editing" to allow the use of more sophisticated, colorful vocabulary without obscuring the label's meaning for those who don't understand certain words. After writing your label, cross out any difficult words and see if it still makes sense. If it does, you can leave the words in. If not, you'll need to rewrite. Through this process, you'll see that the nouns and verbs of your sentence should be of a basic vocabulary, but you can add some informative adjectives. Use these words only in if they provide additional information that supports but is not essential to everyone's understanding of the big idea.[51]
- Use humor and puns only if they do not obscure the meaning for those who don't "get" them.[52]

- If you do have a long section of text on a label (for instance, an introductory label) consider putting a two to three sentence summary statement in larger type at the beginning of the label. This will help you get your message across to visitors who are unable to read the entire label because of low-vision, unable to understand it because of cognitive disabilities, or simply unwilling to read more than 20 words. Make sure that your summary stays within the context of the exhibit by referring to what people can experience.
- Beware of using questions in your labels. You should only use questions that visitors would naturally ask themselves. Using questions that wouldn't occur to the visitors or that have only one answer which the visitors can't find through observation can insult their intelligence, make them feel stupid, bore them, or frustrate them. You can find out what kinds of questions visitors would ask themselves by observing and questioning them at the exhibit prototype.[53]
- Remember that your visitors will not always start reading at the "beginning." They may look at the last label first, they may look only at the captions, or they may pick and choose which labels to read at random. Try to write your labels so they stand alone and make sense without the other labels. Ask yourself whether people will get the big idea if they only read a few of the labels. A certain amount of repetition of important concepts is okay: it will give people more than one chance to get the point and your labels will reinforce one another.

We tried to reinforce our message that breathing in stone-dust caused workers to die by repeating it in several labels throughout the exhibit and using expressive label titles such as "Last Breath" and "Worked to Death."

The most important thing to keep in mind with labels is how much information you are providing. We will say it again: Your visitors can only take so much. Studies have repeatedly shown that visitors are more likely to read shorter labels.[54] If there is additional, fascinating information that you are dying to get across to your visitors but that doesn't quite warrant precious space on the labels, consider making "optional labels." These can be laminated and placed in a rack on a nearby wall or on the exhibit base. They will provide extra information for those visitors who want more without putting off those who are happy with what's already on display. You could also make handouts or brochures that visitors can take home.

2.2.3 Write Handouts

Writing, designing, and making "optional labels" or handouts will take extra time and money. Before you decide to do it, make sure there is a real need that the handout or "optional label" serves. Perhaps in your front-end evaluation, you found people are interested in a question or topic tangential to your big idea that would work better on a separate sheet. Maybe there is a newspaper or magazine article that links your exhibit topic to your local community. Maybe you'd like to suggest some additional activities that visitors can do with the exhibit. These are all good reasons to make a "label" that

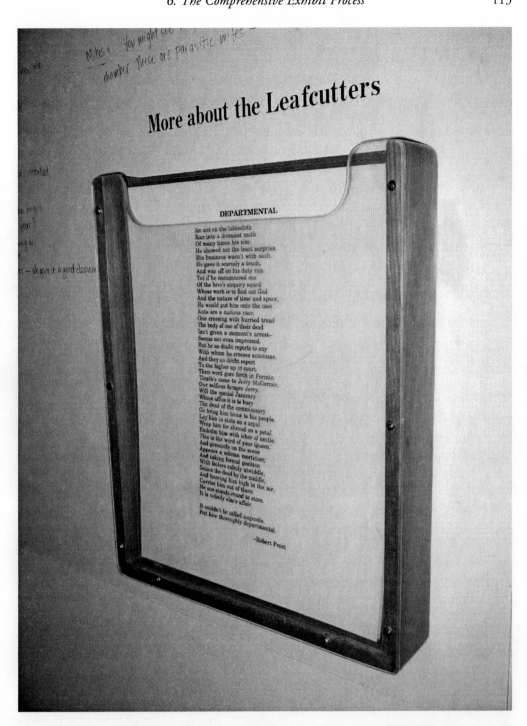

Extra information can be laminated in thick plastic and included in an exhibit as "optional labels" located in a box like this one mounted on a wall or exhibit. Include things like newspaper articles, poems, etc. Take-home handouts can also be offered in such boxes. This box was purpose built, but pre-made plexiglass displays for many different sized papers are available.

visitors can choose to pick up, or not. Take-home handouts are best used for information that the visitor can use later, rather than a recap of the exhibit information. Possible content includes a bibliography of library materials related to the exhibit topic, a listing of related community resources, or suggestions for activities related to the exhibit topic that visitors can do at home (or things to look for in the "real world").

In our exhibit, we included a handout for visitors to take on a trip to Hope Cemetery with them. It included a photo of the Brusa monument and a brief retelling of how he carved the tombstone for himself to make a statement when he was diagnosed with silicosis. The handout also included a map showing how to get to the cemetery from the library downtown and a list of other interesting tombstones in the cemetery. It was written and designed by a volunteer from the historical society and printed using the library's copy machine. We hoped that this would be a resource to encourage further exploration of the granite cutting history of Granitetown and one that people might share with their out-of-town guests and visitors.

2.2.4 Edit the Labels

Once you've written the copy for a set of labels that you are happy with, have some of the other library staff read them. Passing the label copy past other people can expose problems that you didn't notice: typos, grammatical and spelling errors, incomprehensible sentences, and in the worst of all cases, labels that make sense to no one but you. Ask your coworkers to point out areas of the label that confuse them or sentences that they don't think follow one another. Ask them to restate what you are trying to say in the labels to find out if your point is clear. It's important to keep in mind during this process that although something makes perfect sense to you, it might not to other people. When multiple people trip over, are confused or bothered by, misunderstand, or miss the point of a word, sentence, paragraph, or entire label, that's a sign it needs to be rewritten, no matter how much you like it.

Rewrite the labels to sort out the problems and check with staff again to see if they are any better. You are trying to get the best label copy you can that will require the least editing after you design it. If you hash out a lot of the problems now, it can save you time later, and give you a better product to test on the public. As you talk to your coworkers you will find that some are more willing than others to voice their opinions and speak candidly about what they don't understand. Cherish these people! They are a huge asset to the exhibit process.

2.2.5 Design the Labels

You've got your label copy, now it's time to stick it in a label. An attractive label will attract people. If a visitor is drawn to your label, she is more likely to read it. On the other hand, a cluttered, confusing design will discourage people from reading. We don't go into great detail here about design principles, because there are hundreds of books on design out there. (An excellent one for beginners is *The Non-designer's Design Book: Design and typographic principles for the visual novice* by Robin Williams. It gives simple, well-illustrated tips to help you create appealing pages.) What we do cover are the different label formats that affect your design, how the label's purpose and location affect the design, how to design for greatest label accessibility, and the use of images on labels.

The labels you can make at the library are limited in size by your printer. A standard laser printer can print on letter-sized (8½ × 11 inches) or legal-sized (8½ × 14 inches) paper. Some printers can print on ledger-sized paper (11 × 17 inches) and some can handle paper up to 18 inches wide and any length. You will have to design your labels accordingly — it's the rare label that looks classy when spliced. Your ability to design in color and include photographs in your labels is also limited by the capabilities of your printer. If you need larger labels or higher quality color images than you can make at the library, order them from a print shop. There are a multitude of professional printing processes and kinds of paper that allow you to create labels for virtually any use: floor labels, outdoor labels, labels with acrylic surfaces, labels printed on canvas, labels with adhesive backing, etc. In addition to labels, you can order vinyl letters. These are letters (or words or sentences) cut out of a thin, sticky-backed vinyl. They peel off together and stick onto a wall or case as one. (Then at the end of the exhibit, they peel off— if you've got fingernails.) They come in many colors, look very professional, and can be reasonable in price (especially if you buy from a large vendor). Very small letters cannot be cut (over 48 point is best), so they are best used for titles or large-lettered introductory labels.

The design of labels you make at the library can be done using word processing programs like Word or WordPerfect. If you plan to have your labels printed outside the library, however, you will have to use a graphics programs like Adobe Illustrator or Canvas. These programs are also better if you are working with images or color. They are much more powerful and much more fun than word processing, but they take some time to learn. Most print shops will accept Adobe Illustrator or Adobe PhotoShop files, but make sure you call for their specifications before you start designing. If your file does not meet their requirements, your time will have been wasted. In addition, they may have a requirement for the minimum resolution of images. For vinyl letters, you can create the design yourself and send in the file, or simply specify what you want (for example, you would choose a font and a color, and say you want the letters to be 2 inches high and the entire phrase shouldn't be more than 3 feet long).

Beware of designing in color: Things aren't always as they seem. Colors look different on the computer screen than when they are printed out and usually print out differently on different printers. This means that printing a test label at your library will not ensure that your label will look as you want when you send it out to be printed. Your best bet for getting the colors you want is to use a universal color palette such as Pantone. Choosing your colors from this palette and notifying the print shop of the choices will help them understand what you are looking for so they can make the best match. You can also have a proof printed to check the colors, but this adds to the cost.

Images and copyright: Using images in your labels can be attractive and support your big idea. Use them only when they support your text though, not just for the sake of having pictures. You can use photographs from stock photo agencies which cost money or from local archives (at historical societies, colleges, etc.) which usually cost no money (or just the price of printing). You can find images on the web of virtually anything. If you find something you like, contact the photographer. Some are professionals who charge varying amounts for the use of their images. Some are researchers or amateurs who are glad to allow free use. Either way, you must get copyright permission, and you will probably need to get a higher resolution file from the photographer as web files (usually 72 dpi) will not print well on your label. Government agencies have a large array of pictures all of which are available for use without permission. In addition to photographs, there is a ton of clip art available free or reasonably priced on the Web, on CD-ROMs, and in books. Clip art can be used without acknowledgement.

 Most of our images belonged to our own archive, but one belonged to the World Health Organization. We called them to ask for permission (which they gave without asking for payment). The copy of the picture on their website was of sufficient resolution for our label, so we did not have to ask them to send a higher quality picture.

Label purpose and location: Where the label will be and what its purpose is also affects its size and design. You don't want a caption label to be so large that it overwhelms the object it describes. You do want an introductory label to be large enough to catch the visitors attention and say "Read me before you read the others!" A title should stand out and pull the exhibit together. Consistency is important in label design and location both for an attractive exhibit and a functional one. Each kind of label should look like the others of its kind and be located predictably. For example, all caption labels should be cut to the same size; use the same color, typeface, type size, and design; and be placed in the same (or a similar) place relative to the object they describe. This consistency acts as a visual clue to help visitors understand the purpose of each label. It also aids in accessibility as it helps people with low vision locate labels without searching. For the same reasons, there should be enough difference in the design of each kind of label to easily distinguish them. At the same time, the designs should relate to each other to create a unified, attractive whole.

The type size used on a label depends in part on the label's location and purpose. Titles will be in the largest type size, introductory labels will come next, and captions will be the smallest. This doesn't mean that captions can be infinitely small; there is a limit. The smallest recommended type on a label is 20 points; 22 points is often better, and no type should be less than 18 points. People with low vision often have to get as close as 3 inches from the text of a label.[55] If you have to put a label in a place where this won't be possible, make the type larger to compensate. This means that captions located on the back wall of a case should be more than the minimum 20 points.

Labels should be installed in locations that allow for comfortable reading by both those standing and those using wheelchairs. The following guidelines will help you decide the best location and therefore design for the labels.[56]

- The viewing range for labels on a wall that accommodates both standing and seated readers comfortably is 48 to 61 inches from the floor.
- Labels on a wall placed lower than 48 inches from the floor should be tilted towards the reader at a 30 to 45 degree angle.
- Labels placed horizontally on a flat surface, shouldn't be above 36 inches from the floor. If they are, tilt them toward the reader.

Labels should be located closest to the part of the exhibit that they interpret. This means that instructions should be near the part of the exhibit to manipulate and a caption should be close to the object it describes. Explanations of a larger group of objects should be located relative to the group, and explanations of an activity or hands-on event should be located where the event takes place. People tend not to search for labels. If you place your label right where they are looking when they want information, they will be more likely to read it. Keep this in mind as you design the labels. Think about where they will go beforehand and size them accordingly. If there is only a 6 -by 7- inch space by the hands-on element, you'll want to try to get your label to fit there.

Label accessibility: The accessibility of your labels is one of the most important thing to keep in mind as you design them. If people can't read them, they won't. We've already discussed issues of accessibility under label writing and label location above. The following design factors contribute to the accessibility of labels, too.[57]

Typeface: Some typefaces are easier to read than others and certain kinds of formatting can decrease legibility. The overall goal is to use typefaces with easily distinguishable letters. Medium weight (regular) sans-serif or simple serif typefaces are best. Common examples include Arial, Helvetica, Times New Roman, Palatino. There are many others.

Avoid using script, light or black typefaces, narrow, condensed, or extended typefaces, typefaces with letters that touch each other, typefaces in which the stroke width varies or fades, and decorative typefaces. In addition, do not format large portions of text in boldface or all caps. Save these methods for highlighting information. You can also use underlining, larger type, or indentation to highlight information, but avoid using italics altogether.

These guidelines are especially important for blocks of text. You can be more creative with your titles — they have fewer words and are often larger — but you still want them to be legible.

Type size: As mentioned above, type should be no less than 20 points, but fonts vary in their size — 20 points for some will be too small. To check, measure an upper case letter; it should be ³⁄₁₆ to ¼ inch high. As already mentioned, the type size used in labels should increase as they get farther away from the visitor.

Script

Light

Black

Stroke width varies

Extended

Condensed

Narrow

Decorative

Typefaces in these styles should not be used for blocks of text; however, many of them can be used successfully for larger titles.

Character proportion: Character proportion is the height to width ratio of a letter. You might have played around with this in Word using "WordArt." With graphics programs you can change it even more dramatically. But as the ratio is exaggerated, the letters become less recognizable. It can be fun to play with character proportion in titles, but make sure you don't stretch the letters too far.

Granitetown Public Library

Granitetown Public Library

Granitetown Public Library

This shows exaggerated character widths. The first line of text is the original size and shape of the typeface. The second line has been stretched out and the third line condensed. Notice that the letters have changed shape, not just size or spacing. Character height as well as width can be adjusted.

Letter and line spacing: Regular spacing and predictability of line location is important for people with low vision. Paragraphs should be left justified with a ragged right margin in order to make finding the beginning of the next line easier. Do not fully justify your text: the spacing between words and letters becomes irregular.

Lines should not be too long: as their length increases, it becomes harder to find the beginning of the next line. An average of 45 to 50 characters is best. If your labels are large enough that the lines become longer than this, break the paragraph into columns. For the same reason, do not use a hyphen to break a word at the end of a line.

Come see *Deadly Dust*, a new exhibit the Granitetown Public Library.

Come see *Deadly Dust*, a new exhibit

the Granitetown Public Library.

Come see *Deadly Dust*, a new exhibit
the Granitetown Public Library.

These sentences have different leading, or line spacing. The first sentence shows the typeface's original leading. This should be used in label text as it has been designed for readability. In the second sentence the leading has been increased and in the third sentence, it has been decreased. Both of these result in decreased readability when applied to entire paragraphs.

Leading is the space between lines. It is measured from the bottom of one line to the bottom of the next. It should be 20 to 30 percent greater than the type size used. Most typefaces are preset within this range. If your lines are long, the leading should be closer to the high end of this range.

Kerning is the space between letters. Using graphics programs it can be adjusted to squeeze your words together or space them out, but avoid this — most typefaces are already spaced for best legibility.

Although a double space after a period is no longer standard, some people feel it increases the legibility of a paragraph in labels.

Color contrast and glare: Letters should be in high contrast to their background.

Granitetown Public Library

Granitetown Public Library

Granitetown Public Library

The kerning, or spacing between letters, is different on these three phrases. The first line shows the original kerning of the typeface. This should be used in labels for best readability. In the second line, kerning has been increased and in the third line, it has been decreased. Notice how the letters in the third line have been condensed so much they touch each other. This provides terrible readability. Increased kerning, while no good for paragraphs, can often have a classy effect in large titles.

Combinations like black on white, white on black, white on dark charcoal, white on navy blue, navy blue on cream work well. Combinations like white on light gray, cream on pale blue, pale blue on medium blue, and even red on white are more difficult to read. Make sure you choose a very light color and a dark color. When in doubt, step one of your colors up or down a notch to increase the contrast.

If you use color-coding on a label, make sure the code can be read by another method (such as shapes or numbers) also so it is accessible to those who are color-blind.

Never place text over a patterned background or a picture. It doesn't matter how cute an idea it is or how classy you think it will look, it will not be easily read by anyone, low vision or not.

In our example exhibit, we were very excited to print some of our labels on paper with a granite-look background. When we printed samples, however, we noticed that our staff members held the labels within inches of their face to read. We realized that although the patterned background added a meaningful design element to our exhibit, it was making the labels unreadable. We switched to a very pale gray paper, reminiscent of the color of the local granite, but without the texture, as a compromise.

Labels with glossy surfaces can cause light to reflect. This glare often makes the labels unreadable. This is most likely to occur with laminated labels or labels behind glass. If you are ordering your labels from outside the museum, request a matte or eggshell laminate. If you are laminating labels at the library, set the lighting on the exhibit so that it doesn't reflect on the labels.

2.2.6 Prototype and Edit the Labels

You now have your first set of labels as you would like to see them in the exhibit. Again, run them past some of the other staff. Ask them what they think of the design and whether they find any of the labels confusing or hard to read. Edit as necessary until you are satisfied they are the best they can be. Then print out fresh, draft copies. These should not be laminated or mounted yet — they must still be evaluated on the exhibit.

2.3 Prototype and Evaluate the Exhibit

2.3.1 Create an Accurate Exhibit Prototype

It's time to make a fairly accurate prototype of your exhibit. You'll be testing this one on the library staff first, then on the general public, so it should be as close to what you actually want to put on the floor as possible in terms of content and design. Gather the items you are going to display or the hands-on elements you have already proto-typed. If the items are being borrowed and you don't have them yet, use pictures of them.[58] If pictures aren't available, get the dimensions and substitute a cardboard or paper cutout of the appropriate size and shape. If you are planning to have anything (cases or labels, etc.) made outside the library, this is the time to evaluate and finalize their design before ordering. In your prototype, you should substitute the closest pos-sible recreation of the item to determine its success. (For a cabinet or case, you might use a regular table as your base, recreating the design using cardboard and duct tape — or even plexiglass. In the case of a large-format label, you can print out your design in black and white on the library's regular printer and tape the 8½ × 11 sheets together to form the big label.)

Using the display items or hands-on elements, your exhibit labels, and your revised exhibit design which came out of your first round of prototyping, put your exhibit together in it's planned location (without worrying about any of the decorative details for now). If you have the actual base or table on which the exhibit will be displayed, that's great; if not, use something similar in size and shape.

To create an exhibit prototype, we had to choose which sections of our recorded interviews with stone cutters should be included for visitors to listen to. We picked the parts we thought were most representative of the big idea as well as being interesting and poignant. In some cases, there were too many memories we thought were good to fit in the exhibit, so we pro-totyped them all to choose the best for the final exhibit.

2.3.2 Evaluate the Prototype

Take a look at your exhibit. Does it look as you planned? Does it make sense to you? Do you think the big idea is clear? Look back at the characteristics of an ideal exhibit in step 1.2.4. How does your exhibit measure up? Has it met these criteria? Make any adjustments you deem necessary, then it's time to evaluate with the help of the other library staff and the public. The goal of this kind of evaluation is to find the parts of your exhibit that aren't working quite right and improve them, as well as those that work well, so you can keep, or even emphasize, them. As you evaluate, keep in mind that you are testing your exhibit, not the visitor. Most people will think there is something wrong with them if they can't understand the exhibit — reassure them that their confusion reflects on the exhibit, not on them. You are attempting to find out the answers to these questions:

- Do people notice that there is something to look at?
- Do people understand what to do at the exhibit (look, touch, play with, etc.)?
- If it's a hands-on exhibit, do people understand how to use it?
- Is the exhibit accessible? (There is more detailed discussion of what to look for below.)
- Do people understand what they are looking at?
- Are people reading the labels?
- Does the label copy make sense to people?
- Are people making a connection between the labels and the items they are viewing or what they are doing?
- What message are people "taking home?" Is it the message you were aiming for?
- Do people enjoy the exhibit?
- Do people feel spending time at the exhibit was worthwhile?
- Is the exhibit prompting discussion or interaction between visitors?

You can find the answers to these questions directly by conducting evaluative interviews with people and indirectly by observing their behavior or through a combination of these two approaches. Start your evaluation with members of the library staff to try to fix any major glitches before you talk to the public. Take notes as you observe and talk to people — after a certain number of people all the comments begin to blur in your mind. Writing down what people say and do will help you keep track of where the trouble areas in the exhibit are. Write down even comments that appear to be unhelpful — you will often find that they become more meaningful in light of what other people say later.

Observation: If your prototype is finished enough to put on the floor and leave for the public to view, you can start your evaluation by lurking inconspicuously in a corner and watching what they do with it. You might be surprised at how much you can find out just by observing. Pay attention to how much they read, how long they spend at the exhibit, what parts they spend the longest time at, if they look confused or frustrated at any point, if they touch when they aren't supposed to (or don't touch when they are supposed to), how close they get to the labels, and any other telling behavior. If they are with a friend, listen to what they say to each other about the exhibit — you often hear more honest opinions when they don't know you are listening! Once they've looked at the exhibit, you can approach them to ask questions if you like.

If your prototype is a little "rustic," you can still use the observation approach. Stand by the exhibit and invite visitors to look at it as they pass. Tell them you are working on it and you would like to know what they think. If they are interested, let them approach the exhibit without giving them any directions as to what they should look at or do. Just observe what they do once they are there. If it is a hands-on exhibit, you might find they look to you for assistance immediately. Prompt them to read the label (which should have instructions), but tell them no more at first. This way you will get the best idea of how they would manage the exhibit on their own. As they use or look at the exhibit, they might ask you questions. Their questions can tell you things such as: the information they want is missing; they are not reading the labels or they are not understanding what they read; they are confused about a specific area, idea, mechanism, or the exhibit overall; they have completely missed the point you were trying to make. After you give people a chance to look at or use the prototype, you can move on to asking them questions.

Interviewing: Observation can take you only so far, and to get a good sense of what message people are taking away from the exhibit, you have to talk to them. The key to this kind of interviewing is not to make the visitors feel like they are being tested, but rather to help them understand that you are the one being tested; if they don't get the exhibit it's not their fault, it's your fault. Many people are shy about questions, but there are ways to get helpful answers without making them feel bad. The kinds of questions you ask will affect how they feel and how candid they are with their answers. The following tips will help you start out, but evaluative interviewing is something that you will get a feel for as you do more of it.

Avoid asking visitors direct, factual questions about what they learned in the exhibit: it will feel like a test to them, and you won't find out what you need to. Instead, ask questions that try to get to their understanding of the big idea. Answers to questions like "What do you think this exhibit is about?" and "Do you think _____ is important? Why?" will begin to tell you what people are taking away with them. If you phrase questions in terms of what people think, they'll be less likely to feel there is one right answer and therefore, more willing to talk. Other questions about the exhibit that can work well include[59]:

- What do you want to know more about?
- Is there anything that confused or frustrated you?
- If you were going to tell a friend about this exhibit, how would you describe what it's about?

(This is a way to see if your message is getting across without putting pressure on the visitor.)

- What do you think about the labels? Was there anything that didn't make sense?

(Here you will want to ask further questions to see if they have an understanding of instructions, content, graphics, and flow of ideas, especially in areas you think might be tricky.)

- Do you see connections between these images and the exhibit? Do they help you understand the exhibit?
- What's your favorite part of the exhibit?

If there are any areas of the exhibit you are particularly worried about, ask visitors questions specifically about those areas. Also ask direct questions when you are trying to determine what information is "common knowledge," so you know what needs explanation and what doesn't (for instance, whether people know what a specific word means or understand how two things are related). If people seem uncomfortable with your questions, let them know that the "test" is for you, not them, and that you need help in making the exhibit work. If they continue to be uncomfortable, by all means, thank them for their time and let them go.

 When in doubt about which stone cutter memories to use in our final exhibit recording, we asked our visitors which they liked best. You can also do this with label copy (e.g., which of these two sentences or paragraphs is easiest to read? Which makes the most sense to you?) It's often easier for people to indicate what works by choosing between two things rather than evaluating one.

The number of people you have to talk to or observe using the exhibit isn't set in stone; it's really a matter of judgment. Sometimes watching four people will make it clear that there's a problem in a specific area; sometimes you'll talk to ten or more before you decide that things need to be revamped — or that they are okay. Major problems often become apparent quickly. There's no sense in beating your head against the wall asking more people — you'll know when there's a problem. It's necessary to bury your ego during this type of evaluation. It can be hard to accept that there is a problem with your exhibit (your baby!), especially when whatever it is makes perfect sense to you. When this is the case, there is a tendency to think that the problem lies not with the exhibit, but with the public. Don't fool yourself. When evaluation with multiple people turns up a problem, it's not their fault. Don't try to hang on to things that don't work because you like them; it will be the downfall of your exhibit. It's easier for you to change a problem than to fight it, and you will end up with a more successful exhibit if you do.

2.3.3 Adjust the Exhibit as Necessary and Re-evaluate

When you have discovered a problem with the exhibit, stop your evaluation. Make a change in the exhibit to fix the problem, then continue your evaluation with the new and improved prototype. If you are lucky, and the fix is something small like rearranging the labels you can do it in a short time while the prototype is on the floor. If it is a larger problem, you will have to take the current prototype off the floor and go back to the drawing board. Each time your evaluation turns up a problem, fix it by rearranging, rewriting, redesigning, or rethinking, and start the evaluations again. The idea is that you improve bit by bit until you have an effective exhibit. It's very important to evaluate each change you make though. As we've said before, you never know what that perfect idea in *your* head is going to do in everyone else's.

2.3.4 Consider Safety

Even worse than people not getting the big idea is people getting hurt, so check the exhibit for safety concerns as you evaluate it. This is especially important in a library where children might be without their parents or where parents might be keeping only a casual eye on their children. Look for these things:

Choking hazards: Any small parts, whether they are items on display, interactive elements, or pieces of the exhibit that can accidentally come off, are potential choking hazards for children under the age of 3. Small items on display should be in a case where they can't be touched (for their safety as well as a child's). Exhibits should be fabricated in a safe manner so small pieces (screws, plugs, etc.) do not come off. All hands-on elements should be tested in a choke test cylinder to determine if they are small enough to be a hazard. Choke test cylinders can be purchased for about three dollars from any store that sells child safety products.

Cane or bump hazards[60]: Some people who are blind use a cane for finding their way. Objects whose lower edge is above 27 inches from the floor are not cane-detectable. Check your tables, exhibit cases, and barriers to make sure that they measure up. (If table legs are close together, the height is less important because the legs will be detectable.) In particular take a look at anything (objects or cases) mounted on a wall — if it extends more than four inches, its lower edge must be less than 27 inches from the floor so it is detectable. If it is not, you can lower it or place something beneath it on the floor to act as a warning. Obviously canes are also unable to detect low hanging ceilings and things that hang from the ceiling. Anything hanging lower than 80 inches from the floor can be a head bump hazard. Check the area above and around the exhibit for such hazards — they might include hanging items for display (works of art or objects), hanging decorations, or sloped ceilings (for instance under a stairwell). For hanging items, you can either move them or place a barrier around them on the floor. Ceilings will need a barrier (or case, bench, etc.) below them to act as a warning. Finally, look at the natural route by and around the exhibit; there should be nothing (chairs, a bench, the exhibit itself) that sticks out into or obstructs this path.

Moving parts: Moving parts are a special safety concern. The parts should not move fast enough or be strong enough to hurt someone if they put their hand (or other body part) in the way. They should not be able to catch on people's clothing (for instance a sleeve or pocket). There should be nowhere for fingers to get pinched or jammed if inserted where they shouldn't be. Remember that tabletops are level with many children's heads; moving parts should not have any risk of sticking a child in the eye, or catching their lip or nose.

Electrical cords: If your exhibit is plugged in (for a computer, lighting, etc.), the electrical cord should be taped down along the floor so it isn't a tripping hazard.

Exposed wiring and hot light bulbs: Make sure any part that a visitor can touch is safe. All wiring and electrical mechanisms should be appropriately wrapped, grounded, and locked away in an untouchable area. Try to use 12-volt wiring for any controls visitors touch. Light bulbs should not be within touching range or should be heat shielded.

Sharp angles or edges: Check your table or exhibit case for any sharp edges or points that could cut skin, catch and rip clothing, or poke a child's eye. Feel the underside of the table and the legs too, as children might be down at this level. Sand any problem areas smooth.

2.3.5 Reconsider Accessibility

We've talked about the accessibility of the exhibit content, the label text and design, and some of the physical issues and barriers to think about. Now, with your prototype, it's time to evaluate how well you've addressed these issues. When you are evaluating the accessibility of your exhibit, it's a great help to have advisors. If you don't have the disability that you are considering as you design, there is only so much you can do. In the end, advice from people with disabilities is the most valuable tool for designing accessible exhibits. (Read more about getting accessibility advisors in chapter 9.) With the help of your advisors and the accessibility checklist below review the following areas of your exhibit[61]:

Exhibit content: Is the exhibit content available through more than one sense and to more than one intellectual level? Does the exhibit show bias towards or against any group?

Items and labels on display: Are all items and labels visible to both standing and seated visitors?

Label text and design: Is the big idea communicated clearly to those with difficulty reading English or seeing? Does the overall design of the labels facilitate people's understanding of how to use them and the exhibit?

Hands-on elements: Can hands-on elements and interactive devices be reached by someone seated? Can they be manipulated without much force and with a closed fist?

Circulation route: Is there enough room to circulate around the exhibit? Is the circulation route obstructed by anything? Is the circulation route around the exhibit clear?

Lighting: Is the exhibit lit adequately? Does each individual label have enough light on it? Do shadows or glare affect the visibility of the objects or labels?

2.3.6 Confirm Conservation

Confirm with this prototype that all the necessary conservation measures are working and in order. This includes double-checking that:

- The level and type of light is appropriate.
- The humidity and temperature controls are working.
- Items placed together in cases can safely co-exist.
- Any mounts or stands used to display items are covered or painted in materials that are safe for the items. Any painted items have had enough time since painting to fully dry and off-gas.
- Measures have been taken to prevent infestation.

2.3.7 Prototype Lighting

If you are adding additional lighting, try it out now. If you decided against additional lighting during your preliminary prototype, take a second look now that you have the labels and objects for display. Check with other people to see if they think there is enough light on them. (Think about those with low vision when you think about lighting.)

Accessibility Checklist

(Adapted from the Smithsonian Institution Accessibility Program Exhibition Accessibility Checklist. Related measurements are located in step 1.3.3.)

Content

- Message is conveyed aurally, tactually, and visually.
- Exhibit provides multiple levels of intellectual access.
- Objects on display are visible to someone who is short or seated.

Labels

- Labels are in a readable type face and type size.
- Text contrasts sufficiently with the background of the label and is not printed over patterns or pictures.
- Labels are located where everyone can see them.
- Labels are located in predicable locations, close to the objects they describe.
- Label text is concise.

Furniture

- Furniture color contrasts with nearby floor and wall color.
- Cases, barriers, tables, etc. are positioned so route is clear and predictable.
- The route between exhibits is wide enough and there is plenty of room in front of exhibits.
- Cases, railings, barriers, tables, etc. can be detected by a cane and there are no head-bump hazards.

Lighting

- Circulation route and labels are adequately lit.
- Light is evenly spread (no objects in shadow or dark exhibits).
- Visitor doesn't block light and cast a shadow on the label or object being viewed.
- Glare on labels, cases, and objects is minimized.

Hands-on components

- There is knee clearance under a hands-on exhibit for someone in a wheelchair.
- Hands-on components are reachable by someone who is short or seated.
- Controls are easy to use and don't take much pressure.
- Controls and buttons are large.
- Instructions for use are easy to understand.

2.4 Finalize the Exhibit Design

2.4.1 Check In with Administration About Budget

Before you finalize the exhibit design and place any orders, double check that the original budget is still accurate. If fund-raising is not going well, you may have to re-think your plan.

2.4.2 Finalize the List if Items to Be Displayed

During the prototyping process, you have decided which items you plan to display. Make a list of these final choices (with identifying marks or numbers) with their dimensions. Note which items are being borrowed.

2.4.3 Finalize Design and Layout

Once you've gotten to the point in prototyping where the responses to the exhibit are mostly positive people seem to understand the exhibit and how to use it, finalize your design by creating a scale drawing of the layout. Your drawing doesn't have to be fancy, but in order for you or someone else to recreate the design, it should be to scale. If you are displaying items on a wall, draw the layout as you look at it from the front, showing width and height. If your items are all on one level in a case, draw the layout as you look at it from above, showing width and depth. If your display has both height and depth, you will need to draw two layouts: views from the front and from the top.

You'll need graph paper, a tape measure, and a pencil (with eraser!). You can draw to scale using the squares on the graph paper, or an architect's three-sided ruler. If you are using graph paper, assign a number of squares per inch as your scale (e.g., 4 squares = 1 foot) and convert your measurements to those squares. Alternatively, use an architect's ruler to convert your measurements to whatever scale you choose (e.g., ⅛ inch = 1 foot). Whichever way you choose, write your scale on your drawing so you can translate it when you install the exhibit. Once you know the scale, draw the outer dimensions of the case or table on your graph paper. Then take the dimensions of each item or label and its measurements from the edge of the table, case, or wall. Scale these measurements down and draw them in the appropriate place. Make sure you label them.

2.4.4 Order Items Being Made Outside the Library

Having prototyped your exhibit to within an inch of its life, you are now ready to commit to your designs and order the labels or other items you need to have made elsewhere. Call the vendor to confirm what information they need to complete the order, how they will accept payment (will they bill you, must you apply for an account, can you give them a purchase number, do they need a check in advance, can you use a credit card, etc.), and when the order will be complete. When you send, e-mail, or fax the order, reiterate the date by which you need the work delivered and request that they fax or e-mail an official price quote for your approval before they fill the order. When the quote comes through, check that it is within the range of their original estimate and fax it back with approval immediately.

Although we were displaying photographs and labels on the wall, we needed special mounts for some of our artifacts. We got together with our fabrication volunteer and went over the plans for each piece and let him know the date by which we needed them. In particular we needed a base that would hold our granite samples and include a special area to hold the "touching dust," dust collected from the carving of the granite. The dust couldn't be out in the open for fear its container would tip over or visitors would throw it about. It needed to be enclosed, yet still be accessible. Our solution was to build a plexiglass cube to cover a dish of the dust. In the front of the cube would be a hole through which visitors could reach. We were worried that this system would not hold up, so we created a prototype and left it in the library lobby with a label to see how it would last. The prototyping process taught us that the system worked adequately as long as the dish holding the dust was anchored and not movable.

2.4.5 Finalize List of Collection Connection Materials

Make your final choices of what you will display with the exhibit. If you want to get items through interlibrary loan, call the libraries and discuss it with them. Purchase any items you are adding to the collection.

2.5 Funding

2.5.1 Monitor the Budget

Collect receipts and estimates of future expenses, donated materials or services, and staff time from everyone working on the exhibit and check them against the original budget to make sure things are on track. Also check if the remaining items on the budget are still going to be spent. You should know pretty early if your plans are completely impractical, and the 15 percent contingency you allotted should cover the rest.

Especially if you are new at exhibits, it's important to pay attention to the number of staff hours you are putting in. Do they match your original estimates, or is everything taking more time than you thought? Although there is little you can do about this in the middle of the exhibit process, other than try to cut back your time, this information will be valuable when making estimates for your next exhibit. After a few, you will have developed a pretty accurate sense of how much time is needed and therefore, what kinds of exhibits the library is capable of making.

2.5.2 Continue Fund-raising Efforts

If you are fund-raising, tally how much money you have taken in so far and decide if you need to continue. If you haven't been fund-raising but find you have a budget shortfall, you better start.

2.6 Contracts

2.6.1 Have Loan Agreement Forms Filled Out and Signed

Get the final list of items to be borrowed from your colleague working on the exhibit. Send the loan agreement forms to the lender to fill out or get the information about the items from them. Make sure that they understand when the items must be at the library and when they must be removed and that everyone knows who is responsible for doing this. If they are filling out the forms, give them a date by which you'd like the forms returned. This date should be well before the items arrive giving you time to trouble-shoot any problems or confusion that arises. You will need the information for insurance purposes and the exhibit designers might need the dimensions of the items for layout purposes. You might want to make a note on your calendar to prompt them halfway to your deadline to make sure the forms come in. When they do come in, double check that all the information is there. If necessary, send the appropriate information to those handling exhibit design.

2.7 Insurance

2.7.1 Determine the Value of Items to Be Borrowed

Get the final list of items to be borrowed and their values from the loan agreement forms. If the lender does not require you to have additional insurance, the total value of the items will allow you to decide whether the library wants to get extra insurance anyway.

2.7.2 Send Letter to Insurance Company

If you need additional insurance, send or fax a letter to your insurance company requesting a rider. Include a list of the items being insured and their values. With most insurance companies, this should be done at least two weeks before the items arrive at the library, so don't be alarmed if you haven't gotten the list of items finished yet — depending on your schedule, this can be completed in Part III of the exhibit process. Some lenders, however, particularly those of traveling exhibits, will require earlier proof of insurance.

2.8 Security

2.8.1 Arrange for Appropriate Security

You should have already decided what kind of security measures are necessary in your library. Now is the time to make them happen. This could mean having cases fitted with locks, buying or making a system of stanchions to be used as a barrier, installing a video camera, making signs that say the area is being monitored, making room for the exhibit near one of the regularly staffed desks, making a sign inviting people to ask at the front desk if they want to be let into the exhibit hall, or notifying the existing library security personnel of the exhibit dates and location and working out a system of checks. If you have an exhibit that is a security concern, let the local police know when it will be at the library so they will be prepared — and so they can drop by periodically if they feel a police presence should be felt.

2.9 Programming

2.9.1 Finalize Program Ideas

Talk to those who will be involved in the programming about your ideas. This includes library staff who will be running the programs, volunteers, and outside experts or community members who might give a talk or show slides. If everyone needed for a program is available and interested, write up a short description of the program. The description should include:

- Program title
- Type of program (and target audience and age group if necessary)
- Date and time (including indication of setup and cleanup time)
- Location
- Staff responsible for running program
- Nonemployees involved in program (with contact information)
- Cost to library (including cost of materials, refreshments, guest speakers, equipment, staff time, etc.)
- List of materials and equipment needed and the schedule for procuring them
- Description of the program

2.9.2 Reserve Staff and Location for Each Program and Date

Give a copy of the description of each program to the staff responsible. Send a letter confirming the date and time to anyone involved who is not library staff. If necessary at your library, reserve the space needed for the program.

2.9.3 Draw Up a Schedule and Give to Publicity

Give a copy of the description of each program to the publicity person. She will need the title, date and time, and description of the program to plan the publicity.

2.10 Publicity

2.10.1 Get General Blurb About Exhibit from Exhibits Staff

Get the details of the exhibit from your colleagues working on the exhibit. You will need this to help you write the copy for the publicity materials. It should include the title, dates, opening event date, a description of the exhibit theme, what kind of exhibit it is, who the audience is, and what kinds of things visitors can expect to see or do at the exhibit. It's especially important to figure out "what the big deal is." What is exciting about this exhibit? Why would someone want to see it? Is there something special about it?

2.10.2 Add Programs to the Timeline

At this stage the programming person should give you a list and description of all the programs being planned in conjunction with the exhibit. Decide where best to advertise these programs and add them to your publicity timeline.

2.10.3 Confirm Basic Information

There is certain information you must include in whatever methods of publicity you use. Whether you are writing a press release, designing a poster, creating a web page, or adding an event to the community calendar, use the following checklist to make sure you have included all the necessary information.[62]

- Title of exhibit or program
- Date and time (for exhibit include opening and closing date)
- Location
- Description of the program or exhibit
- Audience/age (especially for programs aimed at children or seniors)
- Cost (if any)
- Registration required, requested, recommended, or not required
- Telephone number for more information
- Sponsor (if any)

2.10.4 Put the Exhibit on the Website and in the Newsletter

All exhibits and programs should be included on the library's website and in its newsletter. These are the first and easiest places to advertise and will let your current visitors know what to look forward to. As soon as you know the dates of the exhibit and programs, put them on the library events web page. If you don't know the exact dates of the exhibit yet, you can still mention somewhere on the website that it is being planned. If the exhibit is a display of objects, you can include a picture of one as a taste of what's to come. If you are hosting a traveling exhibit, pictures often come with the publicity package and you can show one with your description of the exhibit.

Each newsletter published during the duration of the exhibit should advertise it. If you have time, the newsletter published before the opening of the exhibit should advertise its coming. Think about including articles relating to the exhibit: they can foster interest and enthusiasm.

2.10.5 Write Press Releases and Public Service Announcements

Both press releases and public service announcements have a specific format. Ideally they should be no more than one page. Press releases should answer the five W's: who? what? when? where? and why? Like a newspaper article, they can include quotations and other supplementary information but put the most important information at the beginning in the first paragraph. They should include a contact name and telephone number and a release date to indicate when the information can be announced.[63]

Public service announcements are measured in the number of seconds it takes to read them out loud. They are usually not more than 30 seconds, so are often shorter than a press release and contain just the basic information, written in a catchy way. They should include a contact name and telephone number, and the date after which they should no longer be read.[64]

2.10.6 Meet Deadlines for Community Events Calendars

Send information about the exhibit and each program to the community events calendars according to your timeline. You can usually send press releases in order to get on the calendar. If there are programs you are not writing press releases for, a simple letter with the details will suffice. The online calendars usually have a web-based form you can fill out.

2.10.7 Design Fliers and Brochures

You can make individual fliers for the exhibit and each program that will go up at separate times, or you can design one flier that describes the exhibit and each of the programs that goes with it. Which you choose to do depends on the number of programs, whether the target audiences for your programs differ widely, how much time you want to spend delivering fliers, and how much money you want to spend creating them. A flier with the exhibit and multiple programs will usually have to be larger than the standard letter-sized page (8½ × 11 inches). A legal-size page (8½ × 14 inches) might work, but ledger-size (11 × 17 inches) is probably better. Many libraries won't have a printer that can accommodate ledger-sized paper, so those fliers will need to be printed out-of-house. If you are unsure of your ability to design an attractive poster, look around for volunteers. Try local art schools students (high school and college) and graphic designers to see if anyone might be interested in joining the team.

Brochures should include information about both the exhibit and the programs: it is the complete package in a handy portable form. Think about where you might offer it besides at the library and call those places to see if they are interested. Brochures should be available throughout the life of the exhibit.

2.10.8 Distribute Fliers and Brochures

If your timeline says it's time for the fliers to go up and brochures to go out, send them to the appropriate people and businesses or walk them around town yourself. If you are sending them, include a quick note asking for the fliers to be posted. If you are walking them around, be sure to ask permission before posting them.

2.10.9 Design Ads and Submit Them

If you are paying for an advertisement, you might also want to pay a graphic designer to make sure it looks fabulous. If you plan to do it yourself, talk with the graphics department at the publication to get their requirements for the file. In addition, make sure you are clear about the cost and the deadline.

2.10.10 Write Letters to Community Groups and Mailing List

Research community groups that might take an interest in the exhibit topic. Write them a letter with the details of the exhibit and its programs (include a brochure or the press release) asking them to spread the word. The sooner you do this, the more people they will be able to reach and the more likely you are to get the exhibit in their newsletter. Compile a mailing list of individuals or businesses who might have a specific interest in the exhibit. Send them a postcard or letter to let them know about it.

We asked the local unions, art guild, historical society, and Italian-American society to spread the word to their members.

2.11 Opening Event

2.11.1 Plan the Details of the Event

If you are having an opening party or event for the exhibit, organize all the details now. Think about the following things. The answer to each question will depend on the goals of your party.

- Will the event be open to the public or by invitation only? If it is open to the public, advertise it along with the exhibit using the methods already discussed. Otherwise, develop the guest list now. Make sure to include donors or sponsors of the exhibit and staff and volunteers who have worked on the exhibit. Depending on the goals of your party, you might also want to invite the library board and members of city government, and to notify the press.
- Who is the audience? Is it for children and families, donors, important people, etc.? Your answer will affect the rest of your planning.
- What kind of event will it be? It could range from a program to a casual get-together to a fancy party. If it is a program, or a party with an optional program, talk to the program person now to find out what might be possible.
- What time will the event be held? It could be in the morning, afternoon, or evening, or at lunch or dinner time. If it is not open to the public, it makes sense to have it outside library operating hours or in a separate room (remember, though, that the event is about the exhibit, so you might want to keep it in the exhibit room).
- Will there be food or drink? If you decide to have refreshments, how complete will they be and who will provide them? They can be as simple as the library purchasing soda and chips, or as complicated and expensive as having a dinner buffet catered. Remember that if your exhibit is at all vulnerable to pests, it should not be exposed to food and drink.
- Will there be enough parking to accommodate the number of people you are expecting to attend the event?
- Who will work at the party? Which library staff or volunteers will help set up, clean up, and take care of any party jobs? Will there be outside presenters to arrange?

- Will there be decorations? There could be flowers, balloons, banners, party favors, and any number of other decorations.
- Will any equipment be needed (for instance, an audio system or LCD display)? Does the library have this equipment or will it be rented? Who will set up the equipment?
- Will you make nametags for the guests? Or perhaps there will be guest book.
- Will you display sponsor or donor information somewhere besides the exhibit label (for instance on a prominent sign set up specially for the event, etc.)?

We decided to hold an opening event for our exhibit as a way to show our library's connection to and commitment to our community, since the exhibit is a celebration of our community. It was open to the public, but invitations were sent out specifically to potential donors, the mayor, city counselors, our exhibit volunteers, and the local newspaper. It was a joint opening for *Deadly Dust* and the art show of local stone cutters' sculpture, to lure those interested in both history and art. We didn't have much in our budget for such an event, so we limited the refreshments to sodas and punch and held the event at happy hour. We planned a short speech of introduction and thanks by the library director, and asked one of our community members, a retired stone cutter, to share some of his memories. The rest of the time was for exhibit viewing and schmoozing.

2.11.2 Design or Purchase Invitations for Opening Event

If your opening event will be by invitation, determine when you will need to send the invitations out and design and fabricate or purchase them in time. Remember to run your invitation copy past the publicity checklist to make sure all the necessary information is included.

Part III — The Fabrication

3.1 Taking Stock

3.1.1 Give Status Report on Exhibit, Programs, Publicity, Budget, etc.

At this point, the programming person can give a full report on the programs that have been designed to accompany the exhibit, the exhibit person can share the finalized design of the exhibit, and the publicity person can show brochures, fliers, or other press materials that are being sent out. Everyone will like to know that the other areas of the project are coming along. This is the time to tell each other about any extraordinary happenings, strokes of good luck or insight, major setbacks, or minor problems. It's also a good time to bring up anything you have questions about or need advice on as you have a captive audience (What do you think of the design of this flier? Can you read the lettering on this label? Which of these objects do you prefer? etc.)

3.1.2 Review Timeline

Look over the schedule to make sure that things are on track and as a reminder of tasks to come. As always, take this time when everyone is together to pay special attention to those jobs that rely on the completion of another job — make sure the other job is completed or going to be completed as scheduled.

3.1.3 Raise (and Deal with) Any Problems

If there are any major setbacks or minor problems (as opposed to all those strokes of good luck!) now is the time to discuss how best to deal with them.

3.2 Exhibit Fabrication

3.2.1 Identify and Buy Materials Needed for Final Labels and Exhibit

Compare your original materials list to your final exhibit design. Delete and add materials as appropriate, always thinking about how much of each item you will need. Depending on the exhibit your list will include materials needed for these things.

- Labels (e.g., card stock, foam core, laminating film, X-acto knives, straight edges, cutting surface)
- Decorative touches (e.g., paper, paint, textiles, props)
- Mounts and supports (e.g., acrylic bases, wood, frames)
- Lighting (e.g., lights, lightbulbs, filters)
- Exhibit bases, cases, and panels (e.g., wood, glass, locks, Formica)
- Interactive devices
- Electrical components
- Computer components
- Finishing (e.g., paint, brushes, textiles)
- Equipment (e.g., power and hand tools, thermohygrometer, tape measure, stapler)
- Fasteners (e.g., nails and screws, wire, hinges, adhesives, Velcro, double-sided tape)

When you've completed the list, gather the items from library supplies or buy them.

 We bought a quality playback device and headphones with which to play our recorded stone cutter memories.

3.2.2 Fabricate the Exhibit

You've got all your materials and equipment in order, so you're ready to fabricate the exhibit. Depending on your exhibit, fabrication could vary from covering your bulletin board with paper or the bottom of your case with cloth; to building small mounts for objects, an exhibit base or table, a glass case, or some upright exhibit panels; to fabricating a series of hands-on elements out of plumbing pipes. Because there are so many possibilities, we won't go into many fabrication details here. The following books, however, contain exhibit fabrication and installation information from discussions of tools and fasteners to patterns for cases and mounts.

- *Good Show!: A practical guide for temporary exhibitions, 2nd edition* by Lothar Witteborg for the Smithsonian Institution Traveling Exhibition Service discusses the tools and materials used in exhibit construction, has extensive information on exhibit fabrication, and many tips on installation and lighting.
- *Exhibit Mounts on a Budget* and *Electrifying Exhibits: Low-voltage techniques*, technical leaflets produced by the American Association of State and Local History, are available for purchase at www.aaslh.org/leaflets.htm.
- *Book Displays: A library exhibits handbook* by Anne Tedeschi (Highsmith) has a few pages on making book and document supports.
- *Help for the Small Museum: Handbook of exhibit ideas and methods, 2nd edition* by Arminta Neal has designs for many styles of exhibit cases and panels as well as instructions on making plexiglass cubes and wiring case lighting.

In addition, these tips might come in handy:

- Wrap any stable container in paper or cloth to make an attractive mount — you won't have to build your own.
- Cover panels with felt or other Velcro-ready cloth (test them at the fabric store) to make mounting labels easy. (Paint adhesive all over the panels before you attach the cloth or it will wrinkle. If they carry very little weight, you can just wrap and staple them.)
- Sheetrock screws are handy, but ugly. Use them with special snap-on plastic caps or finishing washers to dress them up.
- Be careful when using fish line to hang heavy objects; it slips easily on itself, stretches, and as you maneuver it back and forth to get the object level, you can abrade it.
- When displaying books, you must give them adequate support. Displaying them upright puts stress on their spine, so whenever possible, lay them horizontally or at a gentle angle. When displayed open, do not lay them out flat, but create an angled base out of foam core to fully support the book. If the pages won't stay open, wrap strips of polyester film around each side of the book.[65]
- Let paint dry for several days before you put any real objects on or against it. Paint stays soft for a long time and can stick to objects.

3.2.3 Confirm That Outside Orders Are on Schedule

If you have ordered any items from outside the library or are having anything made by volunteers, call the vendor or volunteer a few weeks before the installation day to make sure that things are on schedule and that the item(s) will be delivered on the date you agreed.

3.2.4 Fabricate the Labels

There are four kinds of label that are easy to make with a few simple materials: laminated labels, foamcore labels, dry mounted labels, and plain or unmounted labels. The first three of these methods will permanently affect your label. Do not use them with original pictures or documents — mount only copies or scans in order to preserve the originals. To make any of these kinds of label, you will need these tools:

Computer and printer: Whichever kind of label you choose, make them with a computer. There's no excuse in this day and age for handwritten labels: they are unnecessarily amateurish and very bad for accessibility (although large title letters cut out of paper can look great if done well). You can use a color printer, but if your labels are just text, there's no need; black and white prints out clear and looks classy. Make sure the printer toner is fresh or your letters will come out faded.

Paper: If you are making laminated labels or unmounted labels, use card stock instead of regular weight paper. It's thickness will prevent the label fastener (tape, Velcro, etc. or a dark wall) from showing through and the label from curling. Foam core and dry mounted labels can be made with regular paper. The papers come in a variety of shades from white, to cream, to "parchment" to lightly speckled in case you want a look that goes with your exhibit. (You can often buy them at your local photocopy shop.) If you are printing color pictures or photographs, use photo paper; regular paper absorbs the ink, making the colors look dull. You can also print labels on clear adhesive label sheets to stick to light colored walls.

We scanned our archive photos into the computer, cleaned them up using Adobe Photoshop, and printed out fresh copies on photo-quality paper to make into labels. This way we kept the working copies in the archive, were able to add captions to the photos or put them into larger labels, change their size, and permanently mount them. To get great prints of photos, you have to scan them at the right resolution, make contrast and other adjustments as necessary, and resize them appropriately if needed. The adjustments are quite basic. If you don't know how to do them, check with the rest of the library staff to see if anyone can teach you, consult a book on scanning and digital imaging, or take a basic class.

Utility knife with extra blades (or push up, snap off ones)

Metal ruler (15 inches, 24 inches if you are working with 11 × 17 inch paper): This will be used as a straight edge to cut against, as well as a measuring tool. You can buy one at a local art supplies store. Make sure to get one with a cork back as it will help prevent slipping when you cut.

Cutting mat (not hard plastic): You can purchase self healing cutting mats at art supply or craft stores. If you can't afford a cutting mat, you can cut on any piece of plastic that isn't too hard (for instance a computer chair rolling pad will work as it is a bit soft, but a piece of plexiglass won't work — the grooves you create in hard plastic will trip up your knife.)

Scissors

Pencils (and a good eraser)

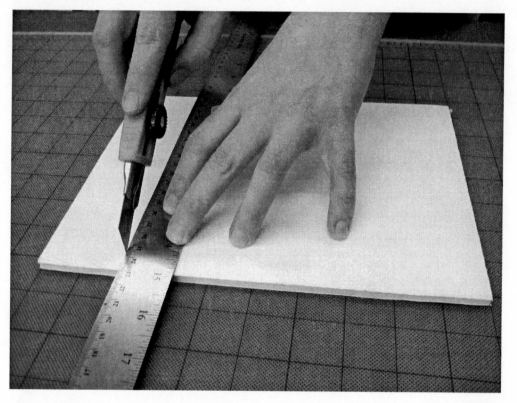

The basic tools of label fabrication being used on a piece of foam core: a cutting mat, a cork-backed ruler, a sharp utility knife, and a steady hand.

Laminated labels: Laminated labels are the simplest to make and the longest lasting (as they have protection from visitors' fingers). Any permanent label that can be touched by the public should be laminated, however, short-term exhibits may get away with labels that aren't laminated and labels that are behind glass do not have to be laminated. In addition to the tools listed above, you will need a laminator and some laminating film. (These can be bought at office supply stores.) If you don't want to buy a laminator you can have lamination done at photocopy shops, but it won't take too many exhibits before the laminator pays for itself. (It's also useful for creating library signs unrelated to the exhibit.)

Laminating film comes in pouches and rolls at varying thicknesses (from 3 mil to 10 mil). The pouches are easiest to use. You just slip your label inside, run through the heated laminator and voila, a stiff label ready to be mounted (or trimmed). The pouches come in letter, legal, and ledger paper sizes. If your label is exactly this size, you won't have to trim — there will already be a perfect ¼ inch margin with rounded corners. If your label is smaller, trim it to size, laminate it, and then trim the lamination to leave a margin. You can leave no margin if you prefer that look, but the edges won't be protected, potentially decreasing the life of the label.

The simple process of making a laminated label: insert the label into a laminating sleeve and run through a heated laminator.

Ten mil pouches make a very stiff label that doesn't flop at all when held up. You should use them for any supplemental labels that visitors pick up to look at. They are the most expensive, and sometimes hard to find in stores (but can be ordered by mail). If your labels are only going to be up for a few months you might try 7 mil pouches instead. Rolls of laminating film tend to be thin (3 or 5 mil). Use this thickness of lamination only on labels that will be mounted on another stiff surface. To use rolls, cut a piece of film, fold it over your label (making a pouch), and run it through the laminator. Because the film from a roll is thin and doesn't lie flat there is a tendency to get wrinkles. You can avoid this with practice, but mistakes are common.

Foam core labels: For foam core labels you will need sheets of foam core and a brayer (like a rolling pin with a handle — a 6 inch one is a good size for labels), both available at art stores. Foam core typically comes in black or white. The white foam core can be bought with an adhesive side which makes label making fast and easy. (It comes with regular, full strength adhesive or repositionable adhesive. We recommend the regular adhesive — it sticks forever at the slightest touch, whether to your label or your arm! This is preferable to the easier-to-work-with repositionable adhesive from which your labels or pictures peel up within hours.)

To make your labels, cut (with a sharp utility knife) a piece of foam core slightly larger than your label, peel off the backing, put your label on it (without getting any bubbles), and run the brayer over it (from the center out) to make sure it's stuck down all over. Then trim the excess foam core (using the metal ruler and your utility knife). When you trim foam core it is very important to use a sharp, clean blade; a dull or sticky blade will pull the foam out of the core creating an unattractive, jagged edge. For perfectly smooth edges on labels, change your blade regularly. If you can't find the adhesive-backed foam core, you can spray the backs of your labels with spray adhesive and stick them to regular foam core. Then use the brayer and trim as before.

The easiest way to make foam core labels is to use this pre-sticky foam core: just peel off the backing, smooth your label down, and trim.

Foam core works especially well for pictures you want to stand out as it gives them a three-dimensional quality: trim the background out of a picture and the building, object, or person in the foreground will pop right out. Foam core labels have the paper surface of the paper you printed on. To give them a fancier look laminate the paper label with the thinnest laminating film (roll film works well) before putting them on the foam core. When your labels are complete, be careful with them — foam core corners bash in very easily. These labels are fragile and can easily be damaged by people touching them. Laminating will protect the surface of the label, but the foam itself can still be dented.

Dry mounted labels: Dry mounting labels allows you to add some color to your exhibit. The process requires a few more steps than laminated and foam core labels, but the results can look quite nice. To dry mount, you need a dry mounting press which is a large and heavy machine that heats. Your library might not want to purchase one of these as you will get more use out of a lamination machine, but it's possible that a local school or organization has one that you could use. In addition to the press, you will need mat board (it comes in hundreds of colors) or stiff colored paper (do not use ordinary construction paper as it fades), dry mounting sheets (which adhere when heated), and a tacking iron (or regular iron that isn't used for anything else). All of these supplies can be bought at an art store.

To dry mount a label, trim a piece of dry mounting sheet to the same size as the label and tack it to the middle of the back of the label (using the iron) leaving the corners flopping free. Trim a piece of mat board larger than your label to provide a color margin. Center your label on the mat board and one by one, peel up the corners of the label while leaving the dry mounting sheet flat and tack the sheet to the mat board. Your label is now tacked in a couple places to the mat board backing. Make sure it is centered and put it in the heated dry mounting press for the appropriate length of time (the machine will have instructions). Your label will be permanently mounted with a color border.

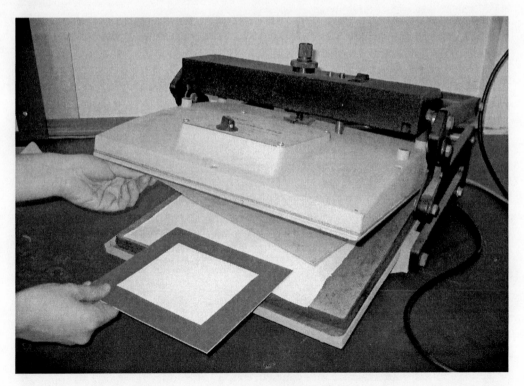

A dry mounting press enables you to mount your labels with borders. Your labels will have a classy, traditional look and you can choose from a thousand colors of mat board.

Plain or unmounted labels: If your labels will be located behind glass and therefore not touched, they do not need to be mounted. You can simply print them on card stock, cut to size, and place, tape, or pin them in the case. It is not necessary to laminate them for protection although you might choose to mount them for design reasons. Another method is to print your label on clear adhesive label sheets which can be adhered to light colored walls or cases. For short-term exhibits, as most library exhibits will be, these do not even need to be behind glass. Some brands of label, however, will require the use of alcohol or acetone to remove the leftover adhesive when the label is peeled off.

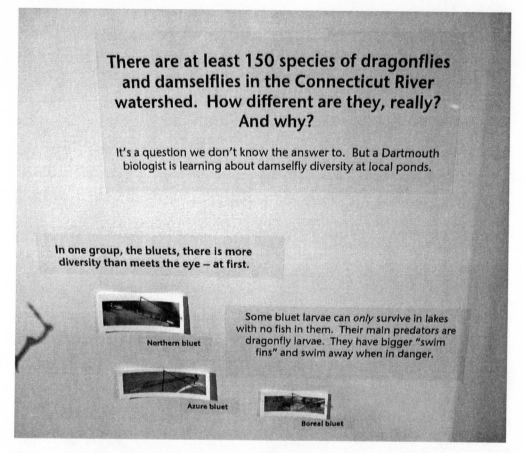

There are at least 150 species of dragonflies and damselflies in the Connecticut River watershed. How different are they, really? And why?

It's a question we don't know the answer to. But a Dartmouth biologist is learning about damselfly diversity at local ponds.

In one group, the bluets, there is more diversity than meets the eye — at first.

Northern bluet

Some bluet larvae can *only* survive in lakes with no fish in them. Their main predators are dragonfly larvae. They have bigger "swim fins" and swim away when in danger.

Azure bluet

Boreal bluet

There are two kinds of labels behind the glass of this case. The text is printed on clear full-sheet labels that stick to the case backing and allow the paint color to show through. The pictures are printed on photo paper and pinned to the case backing.

3.3 Prepare for Exhibit Installation

3.3.1 Make a Plan for Installation

How detailed your installation plan is depends on the size of your exhibit and the number of things to install. If you are filling one small case with items, all you will need are your supplies, your scale layout, yourself, and a little time. If you are hanging 25 works of art in the community room, you will need all of that and a little more time.

Or you could get a helper to cut back the time. If you are installing large pieces, you will definitely need a helper. For a traveling exhibition with multiple exhibit components, you may need an entire day and a gang of helpers. Decide now what time and help you will need. There is nothing worse than facing a huge job alone. And it always ends up being a bigger job than you thought.

3.3.2 Arrange Help for the Installation

If you've decided that you will need helpers for the installation, round them up now. Even if you need only one other person to assist you for 15 minutes, plan it with them now (and ask them to schedule a half hour!).

3.3.3 Gather Installation Supplies

Before the installation day, identify all the supplies you will need and gather them in one place. You will need the drawing(s) you made of the exhibit layout and depending on what you are installing, you might need any of the following:

- Picture hangers
- Butterfly clips
- String
- Picture wire
- Fishing line
- Double-sided tape (carpet)
- Velcro
- Pins (insect, map, or silk)
- Hammer
- Screwdriver/drill and screws
- Wire cutters or pliers
- Scissors
- Level (a small, 8 or 9 inch level is very helpful)
- Tape measure
- Masking tape
- Ladder or stepstool
- Soft cloth (and cleaner if safe)
- A trolley/book cart to put it all on
- Mounts, stands for the objects
- Decorative materials and props
- White cotton gloves

3.3.4 Gather Collection Connection Materials

In preparation for installation of the exhibit, take the materials you are planning to display with the exhibit off the shelves or order them through interlibrary loan. Mark their records to indicate that they will be on display (in case anyone is looking for them). If they will circulate, mark their records to indicate to the library staff that they are to be reshelved with the exhibit books, not in their regular location.

3.3.5 Make a Bibliography of Collection Connection Materials

If you haven't already, think about creating a bibliography handout that people can take away from the exhibit. This would be especially helpful for visitors if the materials you display are not for circulation. It can also be passed out at programs. The bibliography could include only those materials on display, additional related materials from your library's collection that didn't make the display, and/or other books available from other local libraries in a consortium or through interlibrary loan. Like any bibliography, this one can be divided by kind of material or audience.

3.3.6 Make Notes of Maintenance Procedures and Conservation Checks

If the exhibit has any interactive devices, moving parts, or hands-on elements, it will have to be checked regularly (daily) to make sure that everything is working and as it should be. If it has delicate items on display, the temperature and humidity may have to be monitored. All exhibits have to be cleaned regularly, particularly those mounted behind glass. Write up the necessary daily procedures and who is responsible for them. In addition to detailing how often checks should occur, include any specific instructions (e.g., whether special cleaning solutions are to be used, what to do if the temperature or humidity is off, how to fix such-and-such when it breaks, whether and how to turn the computer on every morning and off every evening, etc.). If multiple people are responsible, make sure each knows what she must do. Include a plan for the days that those responsible don't work and a back-up plan for days that they are out unexpectedly.

3.4 Funding

3.4.1 Begin to Wrap Up Fund-raising

You have until the exhibit opens to continue fund-raising for it. Now is the time to start wrapping up what you have started. If you have contacts and possibilities that don't look like they will come through this time, start to think about next time and whether they would like to be involved in the next exhibit.

3.4.2 Arrange for Sponsor Sign

If you have a sponsor(s), talk to whomever is making the labels about creating an appropriate sponsorship sign. If you have two sponsors, make sure that the sign copy indicates they are equal in rank, unless one gave more money, in which case it should distinguish between them (first billing and a larger type size can make it clear). It is nice to put the sponsor's logo on the acknowledgement, but beware: logos can cost a lot of time. The digital file provided by the sponsor may not be of a high enough quality to look good on the sign. Fixing it up might be possible, but can take a long time — even for someone who is experienced at computer graphics. It's best to avoid such time traps — you can end up spending the sponsorship money on making the sponsorship sign! You'll find some sample signs below.

3.5 Contracts

3.5.1 Make Sure That Loan Agreement Forms Are Completed

Make sure the loan agreement forms for all the items being borrowed have been turned in and are complete. Reconfirm the details of item arrival with the lenders and the conditions of treatment with the library staff and anyone else who will be involved in putting the exhibit together.

This exhibit has been made possible by
the generous support of Gray Granite Quarries.

**The tools and granite
on display in *Deadly Dust*
have been generously provided
by Gray Granite Quarries.**

**The Granitetown Public Library
would like to thank
Gary G. Garfield
for his invaluable assistance
in the creation of *Deadly Dust*.**

3.6 Insurance

3.6.1 Confirm the Insurance Rider

If your insurance company has not sent a confirmation letter or insurance certificate, call them to confirm that the rider is in place for the dates that the loaned materials will be at the library. If you have not sent the letter requesting the insurance rider yet, fax it now. Then mark your calendar for a week from now to confirm the rider is in place.

3.7 Security

3.7.1 Confirm Security

Confirm that whatever security measures have been decided on are in place.

3.8 Programming

3.8.1 Collect Materials Needed for Each Program

Using your program descriptions, compile a list of all the supplies that will need to be purchased. If it is appropriate to purchase all the materials now, do so. If it makes more sense to purchase each program's materials before that program, mark your calendar to remind yourself when to get them.

3.8.2 Confirm with Volunteers and Staff

Make a call to all outside volunteers and staff a couple weeks before each program to confirm the date and time and any materials or equipment needed. Mark your calendar now to remind you when to make these calls for each program.

3.9 Publicity

3.9.1 Look for Earliest Publicity Efforts

As you send out publicity information to the media, check to see that it is appearing where it should be. Check the community calendars, look for your advertisements, ask around if people have seen posters, check local media for evidence of press releases being used, etc. Double check all of these places for the accuracy of the information. If you find errors, contact the publication or station immediately.

3.9.2 Continue Meeting Publicity Deadlines

Continue to follow your timeline and send out publicity information as necessary.

3.9.3 Follow Up with a Call About News Coverage

If you have sent press releases about an important exhibit, event, or program that might warrant news coverage, follow the release up with a phone call to the publication or station. Know when deadlines are and don't call right before them because no one will have time to talk to you; when you do call, be prepared to offer additional information.[66]

3.10 Opening Event

3.10.1 Send Invitations for Event

If you haven't already, send the invitations for the opening event.

3.10.2 Buy Materials Needed for Event

Purchase all materials needed for the opening event.

3.10.3 Confirm Staff and Volunteers for Event

Confirm the date, time, and duties with all library staff, volunteers, and outside presenters who have committed to working the event. If you need more help for certain jobs, arrange that help now.

3.10.4 Confirm Outside Hires for Event

Confirm with outside businesses everything that is being provided for the event including, catering, flowers, equipment, etc

Part IV — Installation Until Deinstallation

4.1 Taking Stock

4.1.1 Review and Deal with Any Last-minute Needs or Questions

It's the end of the line for planning and preparation, so now's the time to sort out any last minute crises or questions.

4.1.2 Review Final Section of Timeline

The job doesn't end when the exhibit opens. If the timeline ends with the installation, add the additional jobs that still need to be taken care of (programming, publicity, maintenance, evaluation and documentation, and deinstallation). Make sure that everyone knows what is expected of them during the installation and over the life of the exhibit.

4.1.3 Evaluate the Exhibit Making Process as a Group

Take the time as a team to evaluate the exhibit process (this does not have to be done before the installation). You can have a discussion (in which someone takes notes), all fill out a survey, or have each member of the team write a synopsis of their experience and what they think went right or wrong. However you choose to do it, keep a record and try to extract some tips for improving things with the next exhibit. Keep these areas in mind as you evaluate:

Staff time: Did you correctly estimate the amount needed for each job? In which areas were your estimates least accurate?

Budget: Was your budget enough? What were fund-raising efforts like? Can you continue to make exhibits you like on this kind of budget?

Outside vendors, workers, and volunteers: Was working with outside people a success? Were any vendors bad to work with? Did you have enough volunteers? Were they a true help?

Team meetings: Was your schedule of team meetings helpful? Were there too many? Not enough? How well did the team work together?

4.2 Exhibit Installation

4.2.1 Prepare the Exhibit Area or Case

Before installing the exhibit clean the case or exhibit area. If you are installing objects that have conservation needs, make sure any cleaning solutions you use are safe. If they are not, just dry dust and vacuum.[67]

4.2.2 Check Borrowed Items Carefully

Sign and date the loan agreement forms as items arrive. If there are multiple items listed on one form, check that each item has arrived. Look each borrowed item or traveling exhibit component over carefully as they are removed from their packing. Report any blemishes or problems to the lender in a condition report. The lending institution may provide such a report to you which you can use as a checklist to evaluate the condition of the items. This form may include the following information about each item[68]:

- Title
- Creator
- Dimensions
- Note of damage or special condition
- Page opening permitted (if a book)
- Language for acknowledgement of lender
- Conservation recommendations
- Specifications for display (mounts, appropriate materials, light level, etc.)
- Packing requirements
- Special handling requirements

4.2.3 Install Items and Labels

Take all the installation tools you've gathered, the labels, and the objects or exhibit components to install to the room or area for installation. If you are installing during library open hours and using tools or delicate objects, you may want to rope your area off to avoid mishaps with visitors. If necessary, wear white cotton gloves to protect delicate items and keep fingerprints off the inside of glass cases.

There are a number of ways to install labels:

Double-sided tape: Carpet tape works well, but beware of using tape on painted walls — it can peel off the paint when removed. Put the tape in the corners of the labels so they don't peel up when people touch them (but if your labels are laminated, don't let the tape show through the border.) When you remove tape, use Goo-gone or acetone to soften the adhesive before you pull, then more Goo-gone and a razor blade to scrape off whatever is left.

Velcro: You can use the hook Velcro with adhesive on the back to put your labels onto certain cloth surfaces. If you don't have cloth surfaces, you can put up strips of loop Velcro (it also comes with adhesive on the back). Like tape, these will have to be taken down when the exhibit is done. This would be a good system for an exhibit area that has changing labels but a similar design (the loop Velcro could stay up). Velcro works well for labels you might want to put up again.

Stands: Labels standing on a shelf or table can be propped up with a stand. If the exhibit can be touched, the label will need to be anchored in some way, but inside a case or behind a barrier, a simple stand can display your label nicely. You can make a stand by taping a triangle of foam core onto the back of the label or with a piece of thick, bendable wire. Bend both ends of the wire into a hook. Tape one hook flat onto the back of the label. Bend the wire at the base of the label and use the other hook as the prop. With this method, you can easily adjust the angle of the label. If your labels are small enough, you can use jumbo paper clips for this purpose (by pulling one side away from the other). These stands should be used only where they are not visible from behind.

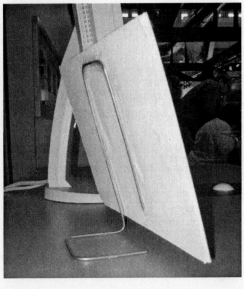

Above and right: This simple stand allows a foam core label to be propped on an exhibit table or inside a case.

Pins: If the backing of your exhibit is made of the right material, you can use pins to put up your labels. Avoid pushpins; they'll make your exhibit look too much like a bulletin board or office. Instead buy insect, map, or silk pins. They have a much classier look to them. If you like pinning, but your case doesn't have pinnable walls, you can create them by painting or wrapping sheets of ½ inch thick pinnable board and screwing them to the solid case backing.[69]

Nails: You can get short brass nails with nice round heads and hammer them into place.

Butterfly clips: For a certain look, you can clip the top of your label with a butterfly clip and hook one of its arms over a nail or pushpin.

4.2.4 Fix Lighting

Once the exhibit is up, adjust the lighting so that everything is appropriately lit. Labels should be evenly lit over the entire surface (with 100 to 300 lux). No shadows should be cast on them from nearby objects or the reader's head.

4.2.5 Clean Up

When you're done with the installation, clean up. Clean the glass on the cases, vacuum if you've been drilling or making other debris, put away all your tools and un-rope the area.

4.2.6 Feed Volunteers and Staff

Okay, you don't have to feed volunteers and staff, but if you have a long installation, providing lunch is a good way of keeping up morale. And food is likely to influence their answer when you ask them to come back to help with the deinstallation.

4.3 During Exhibit

4.3.1 Perform Exhibit Maintenance

Follow the written instructions that have already been made to maintain the exhibit. The following things should be done:

Check for problems: Check the exhibit daily to see if anything is wrong. Look for things that are broken, missing, or moved. Check that all the lights are working, and all the labels are in place. If there are any problems, fix them immediately (preferably before the library opens to the public).

Clean exhibit regularly: Clean the exhibit regularly with the appropriate materials. Any glass cases or barriers that can get smudges should be cleaned daily.

We had a dust-filtering mask that visitors could try on and a pair of headphones. Every day, we wiped them down with rubbing alcohol. In addition, we checked our bowl of granite "touching dust" every day. It usually needed to be replenished or cleaned up every few days.

Make conservation checks: If the items on display are dependent on certain conservation measures, check daily to see that they are being met. If the person responsible for this isn't in, someone else must do it. Make sure they know what to do if there is a problem.

4.3.2 Evaluate the Exhibit

Now that the exhibit is up, you will have a chance to watch people use it. In spite of all your hard work and prototyping, additional problems with the labels, lighting, or other parts of the exhibit may become apparent. Pay attention to how people are using the exhibit and make changes as necessary.

We placed a label asking people to touch the stone and dust samples on the wall next to them. We found nothing wrong with this during prototyping, but once the exhibit was up, people didn't seem to be touching the samples. We thought they probably were missing the labels, so we moved them to sit just below the samples on the stands holding them, tilted up. This worked; people began noticing the labels and touching the samples. Perhaps during prototyping, we were inadvertently prompting the visitors to touch, so we didn't get a chance to see how the label worked.

It's also time to conduct summative evaluation through visitor interviews, surveys, or observation to find out how successful the exhibit is at its intended goals. Through observation you can find out how much time people are spending at the exhibit, whether they are reading the labels, which labels they are reading, which parts of the exhibit seem to be the most popular, and whether the exhibit is prompting interaction among visitors. Interviews and surveys can offer valuable feedback about what visitors are getting out of the exhibit and whether they consider it a worthwhile attraction.

Be careful as you write your evaluation questions; you need to evaluate the right things and keep your original goals in mind. As we discussed earlier, exhibits educate less by imparting hard information or transmitting specific content than by "generating enthusiasm, challenging opinions, affecting attitudes, arousing interest, raising awareness of specific issues, or generating deep emotional responses"[70] and helping people make connections to their own lives and things they already know. Therefore, fact-based questions that focus on what information visitors have retained may show that the exhibit has failed, even if it has been a success. Using open-ended questions that get at what connections people have made or what emotional responses they have had can give you a better sense of how your exhibit truly succeeded or failed. Raphling and Serrell designed a questionnaire that asked "visitors to briefly tell in their own words what they think the purpose of the exhibition is, and to write about something they didn't know or never realized before, and what they were reminded of in the exhibition."[71]

By analyzing the data collected you can draw some generalizations about the most effective exhibit elements and approaches to providing information to help you when creating your next exhibit. Write a short report or simply make notes on the successes of the exhibit and the areas that needed improving and the implications for future exhibits.

4.3.3 Evaluate Collection Connection Materials

During your exhibit evaluation, include questions and observations about the use of the collection connection materials. At the end of the exhibit period, if your circulation system allows, print a report of the use of the collection connection materials. This report should be included in the file documenting the exhibit. It will enable a comparison to the circulation statistics of those materials during ordinary times, giving you one potential measure of the success of your exhibit. In addition, evaluating the success of the materials you chose can help you choose which materials to display with the next exhibit.

4.3.4 Document the Exhibit

It's important to document the exhibit for a number of reasons. Your exhibits reflect well on the library (what a wonderful thing you are offering your community and patrons). Documentation will come in handy for future public relations and fund-raising materials and the library's annual report. It will also help you negotiate for continued or additional funding for future exhibits. In addition, keeping a record of your exhibits will prevent you from repeating the same topics down the road and from dealing with vendors who were less than satisfactory.

Take photographs of the exhibit (alone and with visitors using it). In addition, collect testimonials of visitors; save any letters regarding the exhibit (positive and negative); if possible, collect statistics on the number of visitors; keep all receipts for work done on the exhibit from outside vendors (and notes about the quality); keep a list of all items displayed; and make a record of all exhibit details (paint or Formica colors, manufacturer of lights and filters or other special items, photographer and copyright permission for images used, etc.).[72] Although it's not necessary to keep the labels after the exhibit if you feel they will not come in handy, do keep a copy of any brochures, advertisements, fliers, and handouts that were created for the exhibit and its publicity. Include any news stories published about the exhibit. Keep a documentation file for each exhibit you do. Include all these things plus the evaluation reports about the exhibit, the budget, the security, the programs, and the publicity.

4.4 Exhibit Deinstallation

4.4.1 Confirm Deinstallation Volunteers/Staff

A week before the last day of the exhibit, confirm any volunteers or staff who agreed to help with the take-down.

4.4.2 Take Down the Exhibit

Take all the precautions taking down the exhibit that you did when putting it up. If you take the exhibit down during library open hours, rope off the area you are working in to avoid accidents with visitors. If you're displaying delicate items, have their containers and packing materials present before you remove them from the exhibit. If necessary, wear cotton gloves when handling the items.

4.4.3 Return Display Items to the Appropriate Place

If the library is responsible for returning borrowed items to the lender, try to do this as soon as the exhibition has been taken down. You do not want borrowed items waiting around — it's asking for trouble. Dealing with these items should be your first priority. If they cannot go back on the day the exhibit is taken down, store them in a safe place. Whether you are shipping the items or taking them back yourself, you cannot be too careful in packing and moving them. There is nothing worse than breaking or damaging a precious object because of carelessness — especially one belonging to another institution and entrusted to your care.

4.4.4 Take Down Collection Connection Materials

Return the collection connection materials to their usual shelf locations or to their lending libraries. Remember to remove any exhibit related instructions you made in their record.

4.4.5 Clean Up

Once all the delicate objects are removed from the exhibit area, clean up. Spackle and repaint any holes in the walls. Wipe down the cases, vacuum, and put away your supplies. Store any decorative materials that might be used again.

4.5 Funding

4.5.1 Make Sure Fund-raising Money Has Come In

Confirm that all promised donations and sponsorships money have been received by the library. If they haven't, gently request the money through a phone call followed up by a letter.

4.5.2 Write Thank You Notes to Donors or Sponsors

If you have received donations of money, materials, or services or exhibit sponsorships, write a thank you note to those individuals and businesses for their support. Be sure to invite them (and their employees) to come see the exhibit.

4.5.3 Reconcile Budget and Write a Brief Report

Collect the final receipts and tallies of expenditures, donations, and staff time and reconcile the budget. Write a report indicating areas that were under- or overestimated and what fund-raising efforts were the most successful. Accurate records of how much money and time was spent on an exhibit will help in planning future exhibits. This report should be included in the exhibit documentation file.

4.6 Contracts

4.6.1 Confirm Arrangements with Lenders

A few weeks before the deinstallation of the exhibit, call the owners of display items to confirm the collection or delivery arrangements. (This information should be on the loan agreement forms.)

4.6.2 Oversee the Departure of Loaned Items

When the exhibit has ended, note the return (whether by delivery or pick-up) of each item on the loan agreement forms. Indicate the date returned and make sure you get the signature of the representative of the lending institution who received them.

4.7 Security

4.7.1 Evaluate Security Success

Write a short report indicating any problems or successes with the exhibit security. You can use this information to plan your security for future exhibits. For instance, if the locks on your display case failed, you will want to get them fixed or replaced with a better system. If someone broke the glass or stole an object, you might consider having a human presence in the exhibit room in future. This report should be included in the exhibit documentation file.

4.8 Programming

4.8.1 Hold Programs

At each program, talk about the exhibit, how the program relates to it, and show the collection connection materials and offer participants copies of the bibliography handout.

4.8.2 Evaluate Each Program

After each program, write a short report or make notes about how it went. Include the number of participants as well as a qualitative judgment about its success. If it's a new kind of program you might want to ask the participants what they thought: Did they like it? Would they come again to a similar program? Is there anyway it could be improved? Is there something else they would have liked to do? Consider especially how well the program worked with the exhibit: Did it complement it? Did it raise people's awareness of the exhibit? Did it supplement or expand their knowledge of the exhibit topic? Did it answer their questions about the exhibit? Did it encourage their curiosity and foster their interest? Include in your report any telling comments, positive or negative, that you noticed program participants making about the exhibit (or the program). A copy of the evaluation of each program should be included in the file documenting the exhibit.

4.9 Publicity During Exhibit

4.9.1 Hold Event

Use the opening event to publicize the exhibit program overall, to thank donors and sponsors, and to network for future exhibit and donor opportunities. And have fun!

4.9.2 Maintain Publicity

Continue to follow your publicity timeline. Don't forget that although much of the exhibit publicity will have already gone out, the programs may still need individual information to be sent out at the right times. In addition, if the exhibit is proving highly successful, you might want to create an additional press release indicating this, highlighting the number of visitors and their responses to the exhibit.

4.9.3 Update Website with Pictures of Exhibit

Now that the exhibit is up and running, take some pictures of people using or looking at it. Add these to the section of the website that talks about it (make sure you get permission from anyone in the photos). You can do the same for the programs as they happen. Find out what people are saying about them and add some quotations with the pictures.

4.9.4 Continue to Watch for Evidence of Publicity

As you look for the publicity you have worked so hard to create, collect it. Clip your advertisements, blurbs and press releases, any articles written about the exhibit and programs. These items, along with sample fliers, brochures, and invitations, should go in the file documenting the exhibit.

4.10 Publicity After Exhibit

4.10.1 Make Sure Exhibit Comes Off Any Continuously Running Calendars

If the exhibit information has been on community events calendars for an extended period, make sure that it comes off when the exhibit ends. Even if the blurb specifies an ending date for the exhibit, if a visitor doesn't notice it and comes to see the exhibit, they could be angry or disappointed. It is usually unnecessary to go around to take down posters as they tend to get covered up with more recent happenings.

4.10.2 Take Exhibit Off Website

When the exhibit is over, remove it from the website. You could fill the space with a teaser about the next exhibit if one is already being planned.

4.10.3 Document and Evaluate Publicity Efforts

Write a brief report detailing how you publicized the exhibit and each of its programs. Evaluate how well each of the methods worked; if they reached your target audience; which ones were worth the effort; whether there are other methods you should try; what problems there were; what serendipitous events affected publicity and attendance; what you will do differently next time; what you will do the same.[73] This report and copies of the publicity materials should be included in the exhibit documentation file.

7

Traveling Exhibits

In this chapter, we review the benefits of traveling exhibits and the ways in which they differ from regular exhibits. A modified exhibit process is presented to address the specific requirements of hosting traveling exhibits and to draw attention to those areas of work that potentially require more time. Within the process, we address administrative issues, costs, the traveling exhibit contract, and the facilities report. Finally, we suggest places to look for traveling exhibits.

What Is a Traveling Exhibit?

A traveling exhibition or exhibit is a prefabricated, full-scale exhibit designed to be transported to different exhibit venues all over the country (and in some cases around the world). When a library rents a traveling exhibit, they will receive a complete package including objects to be displayed, cases or panels on which to display, interpretive labels, and sometimes hands-on components, computers, audiovisual equipment, and lighting.

There are many different kinds of traveling exhibits. They can range from an exhibit of photographs that take up 25 running feet along one wall to an exhibit of life-size dinosaur skeletons taking up a 10,000-square-foot gallery. Accordingly, their prices range from free to tens of thousands of dollars. Their topics vary; you can rent exhibits about science, history, anthropology, art, literature, popular culture, regional issues, geography, sports-every topic imaginable. You can also find a style of exhibit to suit any need whether it be two-dimensional or three-dimensional, for children or adults, hands-on or hands-off, stuffed animals or living animals, pictures or sounds, color or black and white, education or entertainment, etc.

Why Have a Traveling Exhibit?

Traveling exhibits enable libraries to bring a multitude of different subjects and experiences to their visitors, many of which they would not be able to create on their own. Changing exhibits brought in from outside can be a big draw for visitors, both regular patrons and nonusers. It's a chance to bring new people into the library, give them a great experience, show them what else is available, and get them hooked so they return to use other library resources. By regularly introducing new topics through traveling exhibits, libraries give themselves an opportunity showcase their own related materials, potentially increasing access to and interest in the collection.

Traveling exhibits can work especially well for libraries with limited or no exhibit experience. They allow the inclusion of exhibits in the library for a minimum amount of input. The time, staff, and money involved is typically more structured and easily planned for than in the creation of an exhibit from scratch. The product has a professional feel, without the need for exhibit professionals on the library staff. And for those libraries who are hoping to create their own exhibits, traveling exhibits are the perfect way to get ideas, learn about how exhibits work, decide the kind of exhibits they like, and find out how to design an exhibit that engages people.

Traveling exhibits might not be appropriate for every library though. They need a certain amount of space in which to be set up. While there are exhibits that are very small or designed specifically for mounting only on walls, there are some libraries that could not even accommodate this. The cost of traveling exhibits vary-while there are inexpensive and even free exhibits available, many have a significant rental fee. You can tailor a homemade exhibit on any topic to fit your budget, but are limited in traveling exhibits by the pre-set fee. Finally, traveling exhibit topics cannot be focused on your library patrons specifically, the way a homemade exhibit topic could be. They are designed with the general public in mind. While this means that a traveling exhibit should be designed to be of interest to your library's public, certain local topics close to your community's heart can only be addressed by an exhibit you design.

How the Process Works

The traveling exhibit process differs somewhat from the exhibit process we have discussed so far; more work is required in some areas and less in others. The bulk of the work when making your own exhibit is designing and testing it. Obviously, when hosting a traveling exhibit, you don't have to worry about this kind of work; you are renting an exhibit that has gone through these processes. With a traveling exhibit as with any loan, however, you will spend more of your time dealing with administrative arrangements such as contracts, insurance, shipping, and security, and installing and deinstalling the exhibit. The process of hosting traveling exhibits is detailed, step-by-step, below.

Initial Planning Stage

Research Exhibits (and Choose Exhibit)

The kind of exhibit you host depends on a number of factors. You can limit the amount of time you spend researching available exhibits by determining your needs and setting criteria up front. Before you start researching exhibits, consider these things:

Exhibit goals and your target audience (see the Taking Stock section of Part I of Chapter 6): What you want your exhibit to accomplish for you library will influence what kind of traveling exhibit you consider. You might be looking for an exhibit to attract families, to educate about books, to encourage reading, or simply to attract as many people as possible. There is a wide variety of traveling exhibits available and not all will accomplish your goals.

Size of venue: Determine how much space you have to display an exhibit. An exhibit needs a certain amount of space to be attractive and accessible, and to allow comfortable movement around its components and prevent damage or injury. One of the basic pieces of information about the exhibit is how many square feet (for a three dimensional exhibit) or how many running feet (for a two dimensional exhibit on a wall) it needs. Whether you have one exhibit room or gallery or a less well-defined space, you need to measure the square or running footage. An exhibit doesn't have to be in a room; it can be installed in an open space, even a oddly shaped open space, as long as there is enough room and the exhibit is versatile in its design. Sometimes, there is scope for rearranging pieces or leaving certain components out of the display to save space. Some exhibits are designed in two versions, a smaller one and a larger one, priced accordingly. Some exhibits are designed to be anywhere from 500 to 10,000 square feet depending on which components the borrowing institution chooses to include.

Exhibits sometimes have requirements for ceiling height, door width, or elevator size in order to fit the exhibit components. Knowing your library's measurements in advance and being aware that this can be an issue can prevent a disaster in which you can't get the exhibit you rented into your building. In addition, the shipping crates of an exhibit must be stored somewhere during the life of the exhibit. Determine how much space the library has to keep these. If you have no space, you will have to factor in the cost of renting a storage space.

Budget: As already mentioned the price of traveling exhibits varies from nothing too astronomical. You will be able to rule out many exhibits right off the bat by determining your budget, just be sure that you factor in all the costs of the exhibit, not just the rental fee (see more about this below). Some exhibits have price scales that depend on the annual visitation statistics or budget of the borrowing institution, and some exhibits can vary in size and are priced accordingly.

Style of exhibit and suitability for venue: The style of your institution will influence the exhibit you choose. You could choose an exhibit that has flashing lights, loud noises, and moving parts or one that has artifacts sitting behind glass in dim light with a strict "no touch" policy. You could choose an exhibit of silent, flat photographs of flowers that hang on the wall or one of silent, flat posters of optical illusions that hang on the wall and cause visitor to loudly exclaim "wow." You could choose one of these or all of these;

it depends solely on what you feel is appropriate for your institution and its available exhibit space.

Determine Cost of Exhibit

Costs of traveling exhibits can be initially deceiving. It's easy to think of the rental fee as the whole deal, however, there are a number of additional costs to consider. Even those exhibits that are "free" have costs associated with them. In addition to the rental fee, your budget for a traveling exhibit must include the following:

Insurance: Most lending institutions require proof of insurance for the exhibit. They will tell you the amount of insurance needed, and your insurance agent can tell you how much this will cost.

Labor and equipment for installation and maintenance: Putting up a traveling exhibit takes time and manpower. Even the smallest two-dimensional exhibit will take two people to set up and large exhibits will take many more. Sometimes the lending institution sends someone with the exhibit to help with installation and train docents or staff. Even if they don't send someone, they will be able to give you an accurate estimate of how long it will take to set up the exhibit and how many people are needed. Although the exhibit will come with all the pieces necessary to put it together, you will need to provide the appropriate equipment with which to do it. This may include basic tools such as an electric drill, level, hammer, screwdriver, etc. and can include more serious equipment such as a dolly or forklift to move crates.

Shipping: Typically, the borrowing institution is responsible for shipping the exhibit one way-often to the next venue. Some lending institutions will arrange the shipping and bill you, but sometimes you arrange it and pay the shipper directly. Either way, you need to determine up front how much it will cost; given the size of some of these exhibits it can be a significant amount. If the lending institution arranges the shipping, ask them for an estimate-if they have shipped it often, they will give you a pretty accurate figure. If you have to plan the shipping and you don't have a company that the library regularly works with for such matters, ask the exhibit company if they recommend any national shipping companies. If not, call a local museum that hosts traveling exhibits and ask who they recommend.

Packing crate storage: The crates in which the exhibit arrived must be stored during the life of the exhibit. If the library does not have space for this, you will have to rent storage and move the crates to it.

Publicity: The cost of publicity for a traveling exhibit can be similar to that of an exhibit made in-house. Although some materials such as posters and press releases may come with the exhibit, decreasing the amount of time spent preparing materials, you still have to factor in the cost of postage, hosting an opening event, and staff time spent organizing and sending out publicity materials.

Programming: Some traveling exhibits come with pre-planned programs, cutting down on the preparation time, but you will still need to factor in materials and staff time. If you simply topically link your regular programming with the exhibit, you won't have to spend additional money.

Check Exhibit Schedule

Most exhibits are on a scheduled traveling itinerary, renting in set time slots for the next few years. Typically, large, national exhibits rent for three or more months while smaller or local exhibits rent for four to six weeks. Check the schedule to see which slots remain open for booking. Exhibits can book up years in advance, so long-term planning is crucial. If the entire schedule for the exhibit you want is booked, ask if they will extend the life of the exhibit. Often, an exhibit will keep traveling beyond the current itinerary (although sometimes the price goes up at that point).

Determine Suitability of Exhibit

Once you've decided an exhibit might be right for you library, ask some questions about it. In addition to the dates and rental fee and associated costs, find out if your facility meets the handling requirements of the exhibit. You need to know whether the exhibit has special requirements for:

- Space (exhibit size and layout, height of ceilings)
- Electricity (access from above, from below, certain number of outlets, etc.)
- Crates (are your doors, elevators, hallways big enough; will you need a forklift)
- Shipping (what kind of receiving area is needed-loading dock, driving accommodation for truck of certain size, etc.)
- Environmental controls (climate control, air quality system)
- Security
- Modular wall partition/panel system (allows walls to easily be put in place and exhibit components to be attached to a ceiling grid)
- Lighting

See the sample facilities report questions in the Booking the Exhibit section that follows to get an idea of what you might need to know about your own institution.

Booking the Exhibit

Book Exhibit

Once you have determined that you want and can manage the exhibit, book it tentatively by phone with the lending institution. They may ask you to fill out a facilities report and will send you the contract to review and sign.

Complete Facilities Report

As mentioned above, your facilities must meet certain standards for each exhibit. The lending institution may require a facilities report that will tell them about your library. They will typically provide the form, but if you have a standard one already filled out, they might accept it. The facilities report may ask for the following details:

Institution and staff
- Name of institution
- Address and contact information
- Kind of institution
- Name and contact of person directing exhibit
- Name and contact of person responsible for receiving and installing exhibit

Building specifications
- Floor plan of building
- Date built
- Building materials (brick, wood, stone, concrete, glass, steel, etc.)
- Number of floors and access (stairs, elevator, etc.)
- Food policy (is eating/drinking allowed in exhibit space, storage space, exhibit preparation areas, or receiving area)
- Pest control (routine inspection or extermination)

Receiving and handling
- Facilities (loading door, loading ramp, loading dock-covered, dimensions)
- Equipment (forklift, pallet jack, dollies, etc.)
- Maximum dimensions and weight of crates that can be accommodated (through doors, elevator, hallways, etc.)
- Number of staff available for unloading and installing exhibit
- Qualifications of staff in handling exhibits
- Volunteers (do they handle objects)

Exhibit space
- Kind of space (room, series of rooms, open)
- Size (floor space, wall length, ceiling height)
- Other uses (lobby, lounge, hallway, cafe, classroom, reception area, etc.)
- Water fixtures (plumbing, sprinkler systems, water fountains)
- Is there a modular wall partition/panel system
- Type of lighting used (daylight, incandescent, fluorescent, UV filtered)
- Are light and UV meters used?

Security
- Security guards (how many, how trained, what schedule, when library's closed?)
- Electronic security system (what kinds, where does it sound?)
- Exhibit space (can it be locked, how can windows or door to outside be secured?)
- Installation/deinstallation (how is access restricted?)

Environmental control
- Kind of temperature control (24-hour centralized system, window air conditioning units, portable heaters, fans, none, etc.)
- Kind of humidity control (24-hour centralized system, portable humidifiers or dehumidifiers, none, etc.)

- Is temperature and humidity monitored?
- Range of temperatures and humidity in exhibit and storage space
- Central air filtering system

Fire protection
- Fire/smoke detection alarm system (how is it activated, where does it sound?)
- Fire fighting equipment (sprinkler system, fire hose cabinet, fire extinguishers, etc.)
- Nearest fire hydrant and fire department

Insurance
- Insurance company
- Agent's name
- Address and contact information
- Kinds of coverage and exclusions
- Limit of liability

Read and Sign Contract

When you receive the contract, read it carefully before signing. If there is anything you don't like the sound of, don't hesitate to contact the lending institute and negotiate. They may agree to changes and send you out a fresh, revised copy to sign. The contract is not set in stone ... until you sign it. You should expect to see the following information in the contract.

Booking dates: This may include both the dates the exhibit will be displayed as well as the delivery and pickup dates.

Cost of exhibit and payment schedule: Typically, the lending institution will require a deposit (often 25 percent) to be returned with the contract. The remainder of the fee will be due by a certain date before the delivery of the exhibit.

Insurance amount and deadline: The amount the borrowing institution must insure the exhibit for will be stated. In addition, a deadline will be provided by which the lending institution expects a certificate of proof of insurance.

Display condition requirements: Expectations will be stated for the amount of space, lighting, environmental controls, janitorial services, and security of the exhibit.

Handling requirements: This can include expectations about packing and unpacking, evaluation of exhibit condition, and procedures for dealing with damage or repair.

Shipping: The contract will give the date the exhibit will be picked up, or the date by which it must be at next venue. It will indicate who is responsible for arranging this shipping, how payment will be handled, and whether there are any special requirements. You may want to be sure that the venue you are shipping to is not in China. Some contracts specify that the lending institution is only responsible for the cost of shipping within the 48 contiguous United States (shipping to Hawaii, Alaska, or internationally to Canada can be extra expensive).

Credit language: It will specify any language acknowledging the exhibit creators, funders or sponsors, and participating organizations that must be used in all publicity and publications.

Pay Deposit (25 Percent)

Once you are satisfied with the contract, return it with your deposit payment.

Before the Exhibit Arrives

Receive Advance Materials

Traveling exhibits frequently come with a lot of documentation. Much of it will be sent before the exhibit arrives (one to two months) to assist you in your planning and promotion. There may be materials for the exhibit team, the public relations department, and the educators or programming team. Such materials might include:

Materials for the exhibit team
- Installation and deinstallation guide
- List of crates and contents (including weights and dimensions)
- Care and maintenance guidelines
- Object checklist
- List of exhibit components with dimensions
- Curatorial information
- Initial and final condition reports
- Evaluation forms

Materials for public relations
- Photos
- Press releases
- Posters
- Brochures
- Catalogues
- Advice on promotion of exhibit and hosting of special events

Educational materials
- Program and community outreach ideas
- Completely designed programs and materials
- Training manuals for exhibit docents
- Curriculum guides and other teacher materials
- Family or student guides
- Audiovisual programs
- Bibliographies
- Handouts of further information for visitors to take home

Get Insurance

Write to your insurance agent requesting the additional insurance and a certificate of proof. Specify the amount, the dates needed, and the reason, including the name and details of the exhibit and lending institution. Send a copy (or have your insurance agent send) of the certificate to the lending institution by the deadline.

Pay Remainder of Rental Fee

Take note of the deadline for the balance of the rental fee so you can pay in time.

Arrange Outgoing Shipping

Contact local shipping companies as soon as you can to make sure you are able to book one that can deliver the exhibit to the next venue on time. You will want to find out from the company what day they need to pick up to deliver to the next venue on the appropriate date. The pick up date could influence your schedule for deinstallation. It is crucial that you ship the exhibit to the right place at the right time or you may be liable for the rental fee of the next venue in addition to your own.

Plan Collection Connection Display

As mentioned, a traveling exhibit can be a great opportunity to show your visitors what's in your collection. Take some time to think about what you might display with the exhibit. The materials can be available for circulation to take advantage of the interest and enthusiasm generated by the exhibit. A bookcase, table, or display shelf could easily be added to any traveling exhibit.

Design the Exhibit Layout

Traveling exhibits often can be set up in many different ways within one space. In order to install the exhibit, you have to know where things go. The best way to figure out how an exhibit will fit in your space is to play with small-scale cutouts of each exhibit component on a scale drawing of your exhibit space. Find a floor plan of your library showing the exhibit space, or draw a scale drawing of it. (A scale of ¼ inch or 3⁄16 inch to 1 foot works well.) Make some photocopies. The lending institution should have provided you with the dimensions of each exhibit component. Using an architect's ruler draw each exhibit component to the scale of your exhibit space and cut them out. You know have a set of tiny flat exhibits that you can shuffle around on the "floor" of your exhibit space to see how they best fit.

When making the exhibit layout, it's important to leave enough space around each exhibit component. There should be about five feet between each to create an accessible, comfortable, and attractive exhibit. Also consider the flow of traffic and the intellectual flow of the exhibit. Ask yourself how people will approach the exhibit, how they might walk through it, and how the components interrelate (Is there an introductory exhibit? Can the components go anywhere or do some need to be next to each other?). And don't forget about lighting the exhibit. Will your layout take advantage of your lighting capabilities or will you need to add additional lights? If you are adding a display of collection connection materials, be sure to include that in your layout design. When you have settled on a design, tape the components in place so you have a "map" during installation.

Plan the Installation

One of the largest jobs in a traveling exhibit is installing (and deinstalling) it. Depending on the size of the exhibit you will need from two to 10 or more people. Volunteers can be a great help for this kind of work. In addition to the exhibit layout, you need to determine:

- Who will work
- How long it will take (and therefore when you will start to open on time)
- How to prepare the exhibit space (clean, paint walls a new color, etc.)
- What kinds of tools and equipment will be needed (see "Prepare for installation" in the Exhibit section of Part III of Chapter 6).

Plan Programming

Using the advanced materials that come with the exhibit, plan your programming. You can simply add a couple of the planned programs to your programming, design your own programs just for the exhibit, or modify some of your programs (book discussions, story times, lectures) to link to the traveling exhibit's theme.

Plan and Execute Publicity

In addition to creating a publicity plan as you would for any exhibit (see the Publicity section of Part I of Chapter 6), think seriously about an opening reception. Traveling exhibits can make a big splash. The professional feel about them can do wonders for the library image at a party.

Upon Receipt of the Exhibit

Unpack Exhibit and Complete Condition Report

When you receive the exhibit, examine all crates for signs of damage. The lending institution will most likely have provided you with a condition report. You should record any damage to the crates before unpacking, then indicate the condition of each item as you unpack. Do not unpack the exhibit until you are ready to set it up; don't take any additional risks by leaving items lying around waiting to be damaged. When you are ready to unpack and install the exhibit, close or rope off the area you are working in to prevent library patrons from getting too close and damaging or being damaged by the exhibit. You may need to unpack the crates in a particular order. Instructions should come with the exhibit if this is the case. After completing the condition report, send it back to the lending institution, reporting any problems or areas that are broken, missing, or damaged. If there is major damage, call them to discuss it immediately.

Install Exhibit

Using the installation guides, install the exhibit. Installation might involve putting together major exhibit components (tables or counters, cases or walls, hands-on components), arranging items in cases, hanging framed pictures, putting together electrical or electronic components, and trying out the exhibit components to make sure everything works. The level of detail in the installation instructions will depend on the complexity of the exhibit. Hanging framed pictures will be pretty straightforward, instructions concentrating on display order and matching the label to its piece. Hands-on exhibit components made of many different parts or cases that need to be assembled will likely have every piece labeled and referred to in step-by-step instructions, perhaps with illustrative pictures.

Store Crates

When installation is complete, put everything away, store the crates, and clean the exhibit for its opening day.

During the Life of the Exhibit

Host Opening Event

Maintain Exhibit

Like any exhibit, this one will need to be checked for problems such as damage, broken hands-on elements, or burned-out light bulbs as well as cleaned regularly. If you find things broken or damaged, fix only what you can using the guides from the lending institution. If there are major problems or damage, call them immediately. Do not fix anything beyond basic maintenance that you have not been authorized to fix. They may have specific ways of dealing with certain problems and you wouldn't want to harm anything further or be held liable for damage. When there is a problem, the lending institution may be able to send replacements, give you instructions on how to fix something, or send some one out to fix it. Alternatively, there may be nothing that can be done and you will have to take that component away for the remainder of the exhibit.

Conduct Related Programming

Complete Final Condition Report

Just before take down, complete the final condition report provided by the lending institution and return it to them. Be sure to include information about loss or damage. If there is any major loss or damage, you should call them before you repack the exhibit.

After the Exhibit Period Is Over

Take Down and Repack Exhibit

Clean the exhibit before you take it down. Repack it using the guidelines sent by the lending institution.

Ship the Exhibit

Prepare the exhibit to reship in time for its pick up date to go to the next venue or back to the lending institution.

Evaluate Exhibit

Most lending institutions require an evaluation of the exhibit. This evaluation can occur through a written survey provided with the exhibit materials, a telephone interview, or an online form. Often, they request samples of the press coverage of the exhibit.

Where to Look for Traveling Exhibits

Traveling exhibits are available nationally and locally. State organizations tend to create exhibits on locally relevant topics that can be especially appealing to your audience. Many also create exhibits with universal themes however, and while some reserve their exhibits for rental within their state, others rent nationwide. The following state organizations often create traveling exhibits, many small and affordable.

- State humanities councils
- State arts councils
- State historical societies
- State museums
- State libraries
- State or regional museum associations

Nationally, many large and some smaller museums offer traveling exhibits. The following places are just some of the many options.

American Library Association
Public Programs Office
50 E. Huron St.
Chicago, IL 60611
(312) 280-5054
www.ala.org/ala/ppo/currentprograms/currentpublic.htm
Offers exhibits on topics varying from libraries and books to math and science to history and culture.

Association of Science-Technology Centers
Exhibition Services
1025 Vermont Avenue NW, Suite 500
Washington, DC 20005-6310
(202) 783-7200
www.astc.org/exhibitions/index.htm
Offers science-related, hands-on exhibits created by a number of different museums.

The Bell Museum of Natural History
10 Church St. SE
Minneapolis, MN 55455
(612) 624-2357
www.bellmuseum.org/travel_exhibits.html
    Relatively small, inexpensive exhibits about the natural world and ecological issues.

Blair-Murrah Exhibitions
Sibley, MO 64088
(816) 249-9400
www.blair-murrah.org
    More than 80 traveling exhibits on art and architecture, botany, political history, and science and industry.

George Eastman House
International Museum of Photography and Film
900 East Ave.
Rochester, NY 14607
(585) 271-3361
www.eastmanhouse.org/inc/exhibitions/traveling.asp
    Large and small exhibits of photography of all types on all topics. Many require high levels of environmental controls and security, but some exhibits have a print version without such restrictions.

Oregon Museum of Science and Industry
OMSI Traveling Exhibits
1945 SE Water Ave.
Portland, OR 97214
(503) 797-4659
www.omsi.edu/store/traveling/
    Hands-on exhibits about science and math ranging from 400 to 6,000 square feet.

Smithsonian Institution Traveling Exhibition Service
PO Box 37012
1100 Jefferson Drive SW, Suite 3146
Washington, DC 20013-7012
(202) 633-3168
www.sites.si.edu
    The largest traveling exhibit program in the country offering more than 50 exhibitions of artifacts from the Smithsonian's collections on topics ranging from art to history and culture to science and natural history. The Smithsonian prints a nice glossy catalog providing details of exhibits.

    Find more traveling exhibits through a subscription to the Traveling Exhibition Database maintained by Informal Learning Experiences, Inc. at www.informallearning. com; at the traveling exhibits section of MuseumsUSA at www.museumsusa.org; or in the *Guide to Organizers of Traveling Exhibitions* edited by Shirley Reiff Howarth and published by the Humanities Exchange, Inc.

8

Hands-on Exhibits

Providing hands-on experiences can be a successful exhibit strategy. In this chapter, we discuss how hands-on components can improve an exhibit and review special issues surrounding hands-on exhibits such as navigation, exploration, labeling, and prototyping.

What Is a Hands-on Exhibit?

A hands-on exhibit can be defined as any exhibit that asks to be touched or manipulated by the user. Also known as interactive exhibits, they require the visitor to take some sort of action to experience the exhibit. Exhibits can be entirely interactive, or offer hands-on components as just one way to convey the exhibit's message. Everyone is probably familiar with the kinds of hands-on exhibits at science museums. In these exhibits, the visitor manipulates some aspect of the exhibit and watches what happens. What takes place is the exhibit message and is typically interpreted with a label. There are two basic kinds of these exhibits: the demonstration and the open-ended exhibit. In a demonstration, typically, there is one way for a visitor to manipulate an exhibit (push a button, lift a lever, etc.) and the resulting effect is the same each time. An open-ended exhibit, on the other hand, allows a visitor to explore an exhibit, choosing to manipulate it differently each time and being rewarded with changing outcomes.

These typical interactive exhibits are not the only way to take advantage of the benefits of hands-on learning, however. There are many ways to incorporate hands-on experiences in exhibits as a means of supplementing the message. For example, in an exhibit of paintings that cannot be touched by visitors, information about the different textures of various painting techniques could be conveyed using sample touchable canvases to complement text labels. In the example exhibit described throughout Chapter

6, hands-on elements such as touchable samples of granite and a mask to try on were used to supplement historical artifacts and photos. An exhibit about animal ecology might include samples of various hides or teeth to touch and compare. An exhibit about arctic explorers could have a set of winter gear including snowsuit, hat, and gloves to try on. An exhibit about firefighters could have a sample hose to pick up that would be weighted to give a sense of how heavy it is when water flows through it. You might ask visitors a question about themselves in relation to the exhibit and allow them to write and post their thoughts (more about this kind of interactive element later). Using any of these methods can increase an exhibit's ability to engage its audience and help them understand its message.

Why Have a Hands-on Exhibit?

There are a number of reasons to have hands-on elements in your exhibits. People like to do things. Hands-on elements can make an exhibit more appealing, increasing the number of patrons who will look at it and therefore the potential number of people you can reach. They can increase accessibility, offering different kinds of experiences besides reading and looking (for more about accessibility, see "Think about accessibility" in the Exhibit section of Part I of Chapter 6). Perhaps most importantly, they can aid in meeting the exhibit's objectives whether those objectives are to learn something, to feel a certain way, of to take a certain action. As almost everyone knows, people learn more by doing something than by seeing or being told something. Hands-on components encourage visitors to do something, to get involved with the exhibit actively rather than simply viewing it passively. An active experience is more likely to stay with a visitor, giving them the opportunity to make connections between the experience and other things they know, whether in that moment or later on in life. Passive experiences can be enjoyable in the moment, but they often don't have as much staying power and don't prompt as involved a thought process as active experiences. Another benefit of this type of active experience is that it makes the exhibit, in part, about the visitor, a topic they are always interested in. The experience can prompt them to make decisions, try out different things, ask questions, feel emotion, remember something, or compare something they don't know to something they do know, all processes that are based on themselves.

Using the previously mentioned example of allowing visitors to write and post their thoughts, we'll describe the expanded learning opportunities provided by hands-on exhibit elements. Imagine a station with little sheets of paper some pencils and a bulletin board asking a question about the exhibit prompting the visitor to write an answer and post it. The question is an open-ended one that asks the visitor to think about themselves in relation to the exhibit, for example, how they would react to or change something, whether they have memories of an event or time, how something makes them feel, if they are reminded of anything, whether they have a favorite (book, etc.). It can be directly related to one of the exhibit objectives. It could also ask them to draw a picture about something instead of writing.

A few interesting things happen with this kind of exhibit component. It instantly brings into the exhibit that thing which visitors find most fascinating and delightful in all the world: themselves. When you ask people to think about themselves in regards to the exhibit, you take advantage of their inherent interest and encourage an engagement with the exhibit topic that might not have otherwise occurred. Once they're thinking about the exhibit topic in relation to their own lives, their chances of making connections between what's in the exhibit and what they already know have dramatically increased. If they make a connection, they are more likely to walk away with something-your exhibit has helped them build knowledge. The other thing that happens can be quite amazing: what visitors write can affect the experiences of other visitors. Often, thoughts are added to your exhibit that you never would have been able to come up with initially. They can be insightful, funny, touching, shocking, honest, and meaningful to both you and future visitors. We remember seeing an exhibit about communication that asked people if they kept a secret. Reading the hand-written responses tacked to a bulletin board was an overwhelming experience. That exhibit burned in our minds information that will last years, and adds to our ability to create knowledge.

While hands-on exhibits can have many of the wonderful effects described above, not all hands-on opportunities further the goals of your exhibit. Just because an exhibit component is interactive, doesn't mean it expands the experience of the visitor. Hands-on components must be designed carefully to create an experience that prompts new thought processes in the visitors' minds. Imagine an exhibit that allows visitors to touch an animal hide. The fur might feel nice, but unless your exhibit guides the experience, it won't be meaningful to the visitors-they might come away from the exhibit thinking not much more than, "Wow, I'd like a coat made out of that!" "To have these exhibits really work you need to have some "minds on" planning or outcomes for the exhibit activity" meaning that the visitor needs to be actively thinking about the exhibit in a focused way as they use it.[1] Your job as exhibit designer is to focus their thinking.

Another exhibit strategy that is "interactive" but doesn't necessarily contribute to learning is the flip or spin label. A flip label provides extra information or the answer to a question underneath-the visitor must lift the label to find it. A spin label is a box that turns to show different labels on each side. Just because a visitor has to manipulate a label doesn't make this the kind of "hands-on" experience that improves your exhibit. Often the information not immediately visible on these labels stays that way-visitors don't bother flipping or spinning. While kids like to do stuff like this, it's not the kind of "play" that helps get your exhibit message across. Don't rule out this kind of label completely, but be aware of its shortcomings.

How the Process Works

A hands-on exhibit can be made using the exhibit process that we've discussed in detail. When planning a hands-on exhibit, you should keep in mind the characteristics of successful exhibit (step 1.2.4 in Chapter 6). These characteristics are as important for hands-on exhibits as for other exhibits: the exhibit should promote thought, focus on the visitor experience, encourage interaction, include real things or phenomena, and be accessible and have wide interest. There are a couple additional things that are particularly important for hands-on exhibits: navigation and exploration.

In a typical exhibit, visitors know what to do: They come in, they look at what is on display and they read labels about it. A hands-on exhibit is not so predictable. There is any number of things the visitor might be asked to do: Touch, manipulate, play, talk, listen, move their body, try things on, etc. People fear the unknown. When a visitor doesn't know what to do, they will feel hesitant and uncomfortable and will want to retreat to a familiar place, away from the exhibit. So it is crucial in a hands-on exhibit to make it as easy as possible for the visitor to use the exhibit successfully. They want to know what to do and they don't want to have trouble or stumble when trying to do it.

Ideally, an exhibit would be so easy to use that a visitor would be able to interact with it intuitively. Often, this is not the case. Instead, the visitor needs clear instructions on what to do. These instructions must come in a label. They should be one of the first things on the label and should be written and designed to make them easy to read. Consider writing them in numbered or bulleted steps rather than a paragraph. One of the best ways to let people know how to use an exhibit is to provide an illustration of someone doing the steps. In many cases a visitor can look at a picture and instantly know what to do with an exhibit, while even one or two sentences of instruction can be confusing. Often, visitors take a trial and error approach to using an exhibit rather than bothering to read instructions. A picture increases their chance of success by making the instructions easier. Illustrations can be in the form of drawings or photographs. Photographs are easiest (unless you have an artist on staff) but a good, simple line drawing can make a point instantly clear and is sometimes easier to see on the label. Some exhibit instructions are particularly hard to articulate with words. As soon as you start getting bogged down trying to write your instructions, think about using an illustration instead (or in addition). It's very important to get the exhibit navigation right because a visitor who fails make an exhibit work "will at best, think it is a confusing exhibit, and at worst, will think that they are stupid for not being able to figure it out."[2] Either way, they will swear off the exhibit and your chance to get your message across will be gone.

A hands-on exhibit can invite exploration or not. An exhibit that has more than one outcome, allows the visitor to make changes, prompts them to ask questions or form ideas that they can test, or allows them to discover things for themselves will be most successful.[3] By being open-ended, such an exhibit encourages visitors to think, question, make connections with what they know, and discover, all part of the process of learning that you are hoping will happen in an exhibit. Alternatively, an exhibit can be "closed." Demonstrations are often this way: No matter what you do with them, only one thing happens. Other than reading an explanation of that thing, there is nowhere else to go with this exhibit. It's a one-hit wonder. Successful exhibits make visitors want to come back to them to try out something new.

How a visitor explores an exhibit and what they get out of it depends, in part, on the exhibit's labels. Labels for hands-on exhibits are unique because they require instructions as well as an explanation of what happens. A common method splits hands-on labels into these two parts: the first says, "Try this:" or "To do:" followed by instructions and things to notice and the second says, "What's happening?" or "What's going on?" followed by an explanation. A newer technique is to ask a question that includes elements of both instruction and explanation. Such questions invite the visitor to use the exhibit by asking something they can find out only by using it. To be successful, there are four important elements in this one question: it brings up the concept of the exhibit, it indicates what action to take in the exhibit, it says where this action should happen, and it points out what to notice in order to answer the question.[4] It's important to keep in mind that the question being asked here is one that visitors can answer themselves by using the exhibit, not just by reading a label. "The concept brought up in the question encourages the visitor to use the interactive device, and using it answers the question."[5] This learning-by-doing approach turns out to be successful: a study by Borun and Adams found that such labels improved visitors' understanding of exhibits dramatically.[6]

Placement of labels also affects the success of hands-on exhibits. Instructions that refer to specific parts of the exhibit should be located close to those parts. Explanations about what's happening in an exhibit should be located close to the event. Visitors will not search for words to read. They will read what their eyes fall upon. Always consider where a visitor looks as they are using an exhibit and place labels accordingly.

So how can you tell whether visitors can and want to navigate and explore your exhibit and how well your labels work? You prototype. A hands-on exhibit that hasn't been tested is a guaranteed failure. When testing these kinds of exhibits, focus your questioning on three issues: can the visitor navigate the exhibit; do they understand the content; and what is their experience like? The first is simplest. You will be able to tell just by observing if visitors are having trouble using the exhibit. In interviews, you can ask them questions like "Can you show me how this works?"[7] Whether they understand the content of an exhibit is a much more complicated question. Watch them to see what they do with the exhibit. Do they try different things out? Are they talking to their friends or family about it? Interview them to find out if the exhibit is raising questions for them and if they are making any connections to things they already know. Make sure that all the words in the labels are clear and ask them to explain to you in their own words what is happening in the exhibit or to summarize the label; this will give you a sense of whether the exhibit idea is getting across or getting lost. Last, but not least, find out if they enjoyed the exhibit experience. Did they like it? Would they come back to it? Would they tell friends about it? Why did they like it? (Or what about it didn't they like and how would they change it?)

Hands-on exhibits have some special characteristics that must be considered when planning for them. They get used in ways other exhibits don't. They are touched, turned, tossed, smelled, pulled, pushed, yanked, banged, and worse. They must be designed to stand up to this kind of "abuse" and fabricated with quality, durable materials. Any movable part must be secure and all removable parts must be anchored so they can't be removed. These exhibits also need more maintenance than most. All exhibits require cleaning, but those exhibits that people are supposed to touch will get dirty faster. In addition, movable or touchable parts will wear out or break. They need to be replaced or repaired as soon as this happens and every time it happens. This requires regular monitoring and extra funds.

Libraries should also consider what kind of hands-on exhibit is right for them. The activity involved in a hands-on activity can be excited and loud. Often, people will work together using the exhibit and talk or laugh out loud. Sometimes the exhibit itself makes noise. These kinds of hands-on elements might be too disruptive for some libraries. Safety is also an issue with hands-on exhibits. With movable parts and things to touch, there is more opportunity for injury. Exhibits must be designed to minimize dangers. Even so, libraries will have to decide what level of risk they are willing to take. (See the "Consider safety" step in the Exhibits section of Part II of Chapter 6 for more about exhibit safety.)

Where to Look for Hands-on Exhibits

A number of traveling exhibits are designed with hands-on elements, particularly those on science-related topics. The Association of Science-Technology Centers offers many such exhibits (see Chapter 7 for their contact information). If you are interested in creating your own hands-on exhibits, consult the following books for ideas.

Make an Interactive Science Museum: Hands-On Exhibits by Robert Gardner (TAB Books).

Simple instructions to enable students and teachers to build their own hands-on science exhibits. Includes ideas for puzzles, optical illusions, long-term exhibits where visitors need to check in periodically, hands-on exploration exhibits on electricity, and more.

Magic Wand and Other Bright Experiments on Light and Color; Cheshire Cat and Other Eye-Popping Experiments on How We See the World; and *Spinning Blackboard and Other Dynamic Experiments on Force and Motion* by Paul Doherty and others at the Exploratorium.

Three books in the Exploratorium Science Snackbook Series that provide instructions on creating scaled-down science-museum exhibits.

Exploratorium Cookbooks I, II, and III by the Exploratorium.

Construction manuals for over 200 science exhibits created by the Exploratorium.

User-Friendly: Hands-On Exhibits That Work by Jeff Kennedy (Association of Science-Technology Centers).

Cheapbook: A Compendium of Inexpensive Exhibit Ideas (and *Cheapbook 2* and *3* by Paul Orselli (Association of Science-Technology Centers).

A collection of inexpensive exhibit ideas for exhibit developers on a tight budget. The book provides construction tips and exhibit schematics.

While all of these resources focus on science exhibits, there's no reason that hands-on elements can't be used in exhibits on other topics. In fact, they should be, so use your imagination and think of new ways to create interactive experiences in all your exhibits. Observing and reading about interactive science exhibits, will help you start to recognize the different philosophies behind them and apply these philosophies to all your exhibits.

9

The Exhibit Program

Once you get the hang of creating or hosting exhibits at your library, you may want to consider developing a more formal exhibit program. Or perhaps your library has had exhibits haphazardly for years, but would prefer a more methodical approach. Using this book as a record about your library is a good start to establishing such an approach. Fill in the areas provided for exhibit-related information about your library including community interests, vendors, volunteers, exhibit spaces, funding sources, insurance and security, and publicity opportunities. The book will become a unique resource for your library, to be used not only by the current exhibit coordinators, but by future ones. This book is only the first step in establishing an exhibit program, however. In this chapter we discuss many other considerations of such a program.

Dedicated Staff

If your need or desire for exhibits has grown to the point where you are considering implementing an exhibit program, you probably have employees whose responsibility it is to create the exhibits. When creating an exhibit program, the library needs to formally recognize the work that goes into planning and creating exhibits. This recognition should occur in the form of appropriate job titles and descriptions. In libraries today, exhibit work falls under any number of job titles from adult programming to reference librarian to marketing, but rarely under a title that describes what it truly is. Whether your library creates new job titles or just rewrites job descriptions depends on its attitudes, needs, and administration. We would suggest, however, that the creation of a job title shows that an institution values the work in question. When responsibilities are tacked onto unrelated job titles, the work can often be seen as secondary, getting pushed aside when other, more typical library tasks loom large. As you've seen from this book, a lot of creative, skilled, and hard work goes into exhibits; that work and the people who do it deserve to be recognized.

If your library is typical, the employees who work on exhibits do so as only one part of their duties; that is, they do not work full-time on exhibits. This does not mean they can't have a job title related to exhibits. If an employee spends a quarter of her work week on exhibits, she could be a quarter time "Exhibits Curator" and three-quarter time Reference Librarian. If she is currently the director of the Adult Programs department, but half of her time is spent on exhibits, perhaps the department should be renamed to Adult Programs and Exhibits. Potential job titles include "Display Coordinator," "Exhibits Curator," or "Exhibits Librarian."[1]

Think also about the possibility of co-coordinators. Exhibits can benefit from a team approach. Brazer and Wyman[2] say that in their exhibit work, "our two heads are better than one philosophy has paid off any number of times." Perhaps you have one FTE worth of exhibit work at your library. Instead of creating one full-time position, consider splitting the job. Even if you have only a few hours a week of exhibit work, if you have two staff members interested in taking it on, let them work together on it: Your exhibits will surely benefit as a result. The next step in establishing exhibit duties as a regular part of library staff time is providing professional development opportunities. Allowing those employees who work on exhibits to get trained in exhibit skills the same way they get more traditional library training is imperative if the library values exhibits as one of its services.

Exhibit Policies

An exhibit program calls for a formal library exhibit policy or library display policy. If your library has been having exhibits for a while, you may have already written one, or at least the beginning of one. You will, at least, know some of the things to include in it. Before beginning or revising an exhibit policy, however, be sure to read the American Library Association's interpretation of the Library Bill of Rights for "Exhibit Spaces and Bulletin Boards" available at www.ala.org/ala/oif/statementspols/statementsif/interpretations/exhibitspaces.htm. This interpretation states that a library must "endeavor to present a broad spectrum of opinion and a variety of viewpoints" in its exhibits and "should not shrink from developing exhibits because of controversial content or because of the beliefs or affiliations of those whose work is represented."[3]

An exhibit policy might address any or all of the following, depending on the needs of your library and the kinds of exhibits you have.

- The purpose of having exhibits or a description of how exhibits help fulfill the library's overall mission.
- The spaces in your library available for exhibits.
- The duration and frequency of exhibits.
- The responsibility for exhibits.

Does the library accept exhibits from outside organizations or do they only display their own work? If they display their own work, who in the library are the decision-makers regarding that work?

- The procedures for reconsideration of exhibits (including an Exhibits Challenge Form).

Your library may restrict its exhibits to those made or booked by library staff, but many libraries accept exhibits from outside organizations. If this is the case, your policy should have a special section specifically detailing what will be allowed. These rules might include the following and should be applied equally to all organizations and individuals requesting exhibit space.

- The criteria for exhibits.

What exhibit themes and purposes are acceptable? For instance, you might specify educational, recreational, cultural, intellectual, civic, charitable, commercial, historical, artistic, political, religious, informational, regional, local, etc.

- The exhibit application and scheduling procedures (including an Exhibit Application Form like the sample that follows).
- The rules or guidelines for exhibits

What is the duration of exhibits? How often can an organization have exhibits? Who is liable for damage and insurance? What kind of security will be provided? Who is responsible for installation and deinstallation and when must these events occur? Who is responsible for exhibit labels? Are there required labels (titles, name of organization, etc.)? Who will conduct publicity? Are special events, opening receptions, and sales of exhibit items permitted? Does the library take a certain percentage commission on sales?

Statements indicating that the library does not endorse the viewpoints presented by the exhibits and/or that the library reserves the right to refuse any exhibit application.

Funding

One exhibit can be funded by a grant, by a sponsorship, or by "borrowing" from other areas of the library budget, but regular exhibits need regular, consistent funding. To establish an exhibit program, you must dedicate part of your budget to it. Of course this doesn't mean that you should stop making efforts to get grants and sponsorships; a budget can always be supplemented. In fact, you may find that with an established exhibit program, people are more likely to want to give you money. When you can demonstrate past successes, a level of exhibit expertise, and a positive audience and community response, more grant opportunities will be within your reach, and sponsorships will be especially desirable to local businesses.

Sample Exhibit Application Form

Name/Organization _____

Contact person _____ **Telephone** _____

Address _____

E-mail _____

Description of exhibit (title/subject, purpose, things to be exhibited, space requirements)

_____

_____

_____

_____

_____

Preferred date of exhibit: _____ to _____

Preferred location of exhibit: (circle one)

lobby glass cases   art gallery
circulation desk display shelves   children's room glass case

Signature _____ **Date** _____

****

LIBRARY USE ONLY

Application approved: (circle one)   yes   no

If exhibit not approved, reason _____

Date of exhibit: _____ to _____

Location of exhibit: _____

Date to install _____ Date to deinstall _____

Authorized Signature _____ Date _____

When you are comfortable with your exhibit staff and program, you may want to consider creative, innovative exhibit projects like the library-museum partnership described in Chapter 11. Projects like this are excellent candidates for grant money. When looking for exhibit sponsors, send a letter to the local chamber of commerce asking the members to spread the word that sponsorships are a possibility-you might even have businesses approach you!

Exhibit Schedules

The nature of an exhibit program is that your library has multiple exhibits. For your program to work, these exhibits must be scheduled. In order for it to work well, they must be scheduled intentionally, with a design and some forethought. The key is to maintain a balance of exhibit topics and audiences.[4] If you had an exhibit of untouchable objects aimed at adults in the spring, try a hands-on exhibit that will attract kids in the summer. After a traveling exhibit about a universal topic, create an exhibit with specific local appeal. Follow an art exhibit with an exhibit about science. After a professional art show, let the local high school kids show their stuff. You get the idea-mix it up! Libraries with multiple exhibit spaces should also attempt to balance the exhibits they have up at the same time. For example, try not to show three exhibits of books at once. If your library chooses to only display books, choose varying topics: You could have a show of books on fashion next to one of books on industrial history. Or relate your topics in a funny or unusual way: a show of books on fashion next to one of books on bird plumage! Finally, make sure that you do not use exhibit topics too frequently: let them fade out of your patrons' minds before repeating them.[5] When you do revisit topics, come at them from a new angle each time.

An exhibit schedule can affect your publicity and programming methods. When the exhibit schedule is planned far enough in advance, you can create a webpage or brochure detailing the upcoming exhibits. It could be a brochure of the year to come or one of what's on offer for a specific season. It should be arranged by the date of the exhibits and include exhibit titles and descriptions as well as locations (within the library) and dates. For those exhibits with set opening and closing dates, include them; for those that are not yet set, just provide a general month or season (e.g., December 2005 or summer 2006).

For the programming department or the individual librarians who do programs, an advanced exhibit schedule can be a boon. Not only can special programs be planned for specific exhibits, but regular library programs can be linked to upcoming exhibits. With a long-term exhibit schedule, it is easy to come up with program topics. For instance, the library's weekly story time might focus on books with bridges during July, the first month of the traveling exhibit about bridges in the main exhibit hall; in August, when a smaller display of bird's nests is made in the lobby exhibit cases, it might include books about birds. Another great example is a program that many libraries have: book discussions. Often books are chosen months in advance to allow patrons plenty of time to borrow and read them. If an exhibit schedule has been established, the exhibit topics can be taken into account when choosing books for the discussions. The advantage of relating your programming to your exhibits is twofold. First, it acts as free publicity: Those in the program become interested in the exhibit, those who like the exhibit, want to participate in the related programs. Second, and most importantly, it furthers the educational goals of the library by "cross-fertilizing" patrons' minds. The exhibit and the program reinforce each other, patrons are given multiple ways to learn about and make connections with the message of the exhibit.

Accessibility

As we've already discussed in the chapters on the exhibit process, accessibility is something to strive for in every exhibit. The best way to create an accessible exhibit is to work with people who have personal experience with disabilities. The guidelines we've discussed in previous chapters are a great help and should always be consulted, but they can never replace the firsthand knowledge of a person with a disability. These advisors can tell you best what they need in an exhibit. If you make many exhibits, you will benefit from developing relationships with such individuals who are willing to come to the library to test your exhibits. When looking for accessibility advisors, try to find people with a variety of disabilities: wheelchair users, people who are blind, people who are deaf or hard of hearing, people with motor difficulties, and people who have learning disabilities. People with the same kind of disability often have different needs. The more advice you get, the more equipped you'll be to make decisions, so if you know more than one person with a specific kind of disability, talk to both of them. Sometimes people with different disabilities have conflicting needs. Getting an accessibility committee together can give you a variety of perspectives and help you decide the best course of action.

There are a number of professional accessibility consultants. If you are building a large exhibit, it is worth hiring someone to advise you. However, there are many people willing to provide volunteer help. At the library, you already have a great link to the community: maybe there are current library patrons who you could approach. If not, you can look for contacts in the following places:[6]

- Offices for students with disabilities at local colleges and universities
- Local or state service organizations (VSA, United Way, veterans, etc.)
- Independent living centers
- State government (e.g. division of the blind and visually impaired)
- Schools for the deaf or blind
- Parent training and information centers for parents of children who are disabled

You can find contact information for the kinds of organizations listed above in the state resources section of the National Dissemination Center for Children with Disabilities website at www.nichcy.org/states.htm.[7]

Documentation and Evaluation

As your exhibit program grows, so will your exhibit knowledge. "Each year you think of something better or quicker or easier, or a more profound or more exotic way of putting your exhibits together."[8] Through constant evaluation, both formal and informal, you determine which things worked in your exhibit and which need to change. Documenting this evaluation helps that change actually take place. Documenting an exhibit cements in your mind what you did and how you did it. It gives you a moment to reflect on your evaluation and make decisions about next time. Then it lets you look back over the exhibit information to remind yourself of those decisions.

There are a host of other reasons to document your exhibits besides just getting better. The primary reasons relate to public relations and fund-raising. As we already discussed, if you can prove that you have a successful exhibit program, it will work in your favor. If you bring glory to the library, you help secure both its place and your program. So make sure you have a good record of that glory. Documenting exhibits will allow you to include a section in the library's annual report about the year's exhibits paying special attention to positive statistics such as number of visitors and positive statements such as visitor testimonials. The library will be able to tout the exhibit program as yet another of its wonderful services to the community. You will be able to competitively apply for grants, successfully solicit sponsorships, and lobby for budget increases for the exhibit program.

Documenting your exhibits can help you grow your program in another way, too. Start a web page of all your past exhibits. Describe each exhibit and include a photo or two. This will do two things: provide inspiration and lure people in. Just imagine a web page with all your exhibits on it. After your first exhibit, you have a list of one. After a year, you'll have five or six (or ten or 12). In a few years, there will be so many that you'll have to reorganize the information for better access. With one click of the mouse you'll be able to see your progress and get nostalgic for all your old favorites (and you will have favorites!). But it won't be just you admiring your work and getting new ideas. The world at large will be watching and they just might want to get involved with such a fun-looking program.[9] If you include your name and contact information on the page, people might give you suggestions, offer their services, bring you collections, and help out in any way they can. They might even help you come up with new exhibit ideas.

New Exhibit Ideas

When you're having regular exhibits, you need a lot of exhibit themes. The exhibit web page we recommend above is going to come in handy as a lure for ideas when your well starts running dry. Obviously you can (and will) draw inspiration from your library's collection, but when you feel you need something new to help the brainstorming, cultivating outside resources is the way to go. Look in your community for potential exhibit ideas or people who might have exhibit ideas: organizations, groups, and clubs, collectors, artists, professors and teachers, students (of all ages), and museums or historical societies.[10] These groups and individuals can help you think of new and exciting exhibit topics as well as topics unique to your community. They might even be able to help you make the exhibits. Whenever you get new ideas, add them to your list in the Exhibits section of Part I of Chapter 6.

Exhibits by Outside Organizations

Whether to allow community groups or members to create exhibits is a decision every library has to make. One of the main advantages of this exhibit strategy is the variety of exhibit topics, many of which are highly related to the community and therefore of great interest. In addition, letting others create exhibits takes some of the pressure off the library staff and budget. Many libraries open their exhibit spaces up to community organizations for these reasons. Some devote one or more of their exhibit cases to such exhibits. Others rely entirely on exhibits by outside organizations and their exhibit program consists solely of managing these exhibits. Allowing exhibits by and about the community can help establish the library as a community center and bring the community into the library. There are risks, however. When outsiders make your exhibits, you relinquish quality control. Do not be surprised if some exhibits look sloppy and are not up to library standards. You also run the risk of exhibits that do not show up or show up at the wrong time when you rely on others to meet deadlines. In this situation, the mistakes of others can reflect poorly on the library.

There are ways to take advantage of outside exhibits while avoiding some of the problems: work with an organization or individual rather than relinquishing full responsibility for an exhibit. This kind of collaboration can take two forms. The library staff and a group or individual can truly work together, taking equitable roles in interpreting materials, designing and building the exhibit, writing and testing labels, etc. Alternatively, the library staff can take the primary role in developing and designing the exhibit while the group or individual simply provides a collection or topic idea and acts as an "expert" advisor for the exhibit interpretation. A library need not choose one of these strategies: It can use whichever best fits a situation. Both strategies allow the library to have exhibits on a variety of topics, while maintaining a certain quality and having more control over the process. An added benefit is the relationships the library can build with members of the community through this kind of collaboration. Working with many different people to put on exhibits about things they (and others) care about is a great way to develop a network of library supporters.

Whether you let outside groups make their own exhibits, work with them to make exhibits, or make exhibits about them or their collections yourself, you will need to have a policy indicating the kinds of exhibits appropriate for the library, how they are scheduled, and guidelines dictating their creation. This policy should include an exhibit proposal or application form for the public to fill out to request an exhibit. See the sample exhibit application form and policies in the Exhibit Policies section of this chapter. Such a form can be adapted for use by groups or individuals wanting to make their own exhibit, wanting to work with the library to make an exhibit, or wanting to lend collections with which the library can make an exhibit.

Challenges to Exhibits

Every library with exhibits should be prepared to deal with challenges to those exhibits just as they would challenges to their collection. Most likely you already have in place a reconsideration of materials policy that includes procedures and an official reconsideration form. Depending on the extent of your exhibit program, you may choose to write a similar policy to deal with exhibits or simply treat them as yet another part of the collection and add them to your existing policy. If you add them to your existing policy, take a look at your request for reconsideration form and make sure the questions asked make sense when applied to an exhibit. If they don't, revise the wording of the form or create a separate one to be used for exhibits. Those libraries that have adopted the ALA's Library Bill of Rights "should not censor or remove an exhibit because some members of the community may disagree with its content."[11] Keep in mind also that the removal of exhibits often pits community groups against each other and attracts the press like a moth to a flame, not necessarily with a positive result.

10

Cataloguing Library Exhibits and Exhibit Objects

During planning, thought should be given to after the exhibition has ended and it is time to de-install the exhibit. What will become of the exhibit and its objects? What will become of the knowledge and effort that went into assembling the exhibit? Perhaps it will be beneficial if not necessary to catalogue, for later reference, exhibits, exhibit documentation files (see chapter 6, part 4.3.3), and exhibit production notes.

Some items in the exhibit may have come from the library's collection and will be returned during de-installation. Is there a need to record the selected items as a group under the exhibit's subject or topic, perhaps with an annotation about why these items were selected for this exhibit (and perhaps why other items were excluded)?

Some items may have been borrowed from sources outside the library's collection and will be returned during de-installation. Is there a need to record the source of these items and stipulations for borrowing them, perhaps with an annotation about other items related to the subject of the exhibit that were available from this source but were not selected for this particular exhibition? Are there items from other sources that were not used in this exhibit that might be used in a future exhibit on the same or a related topic?

Some items or constructions may have been produced for the exhibit and merit storing for future use; some may have been produced in collaboration and might be stored at a partner institution. It will be useful to catalogue these rather than rely upon memory to recall their existence, characteristics, and location. Some items or sections of the exhibit may need to be discarded although their memory (through photographs, plans, notes) would be useful to retain for future use or reference.

We are suggesting that when libraries set about with a planned exhibit program, some cataloguing of the themes, sub-themes, objects, and production notes is in order.

The catalogue may be an index file on the director's desk or an electronic database accessible by library staff; we will suggest a way to keep a catalogue using a three-ring notebook system. But maintaining some useful catalogue will facilitate reuse of objects, reconstruction of exhibits, and retention of knowledge.

This is not a chapter on cataloguing library collections or on cataloguing museum collections. This is a chapter on common sense cataloguing of exhibits and the exhibit process in order to promote, within and among libraries, the reuse and sharing of exhibits, exhibit objects, and exhibit know-how. Exhibit objects that will become part of the library's collection should be catalogued according to current library policy. Those interested in cataloguing of museum object are referred to *Cataloguing Cultural Objects: A Guide to Describing Cultural Works and Their Images*[1] and to the bibliography for books by Blackaby and Greeno (Chenhall's System for classifying man-made objects); Stuckert (cataloguing from scratch); and Swidler et al. (registration methods). The purpose of this chapter is to demonstrate how to catalogue exhibits and exhibit documentation.

Dividing into Reasonable Units

Exhibits can be a bit like silverware, there are basic units or objects (fork, spoon) and conceptual units (place setting, serving pieces, floral patterns), determined by functional use or purpose or common theme, that permit one to efficiently and effectively package or describe the assortment of items as a unit. In considering future access to and storage of an exhibit, we need to identify single items and groups of thematic items that might be reused in future exhibits. We will want to catalogue basic units (objects) and conceptual units (groups of items) as well as the full exhibit. Once we have broken the exhibit into basic and conceptual units we can plan how to store each savable portion that the library will keep and document other portions so they can be retained in the library's collective memory.

In thinking beyond the exhibit and its de-installation, we want to consider whether the exhibit as a whole or in part or as individual objects has a use beyond the current exhibit. If this is a complex exhibit with sub-topics or other distinct divisions, could any of the subdivisions stand as a smaller exhibit itself? Could any of the subdivisions become part of another larger future exhibit? Are there objects that might be used in a future exhibit the library is planning? Are there details of planning that need to be remembered, such as the source of objects or materials or information? Are there craft or trades people the library may want to contact again? For the newly acquired items the library will retain, what space and handling is required for storage? Are there plans or requests for the exhibit or portions/objects of the exhibit to travel to other locations for display? These are kinds of information that we recommend you record in an exhibits catalogue or record.

Let's consider an example. An exhibit on flight is planned. To call attention to the exhibit, a display of three paper kites, an elaborate dragon kite, and a doll of Icarus with spread wings will be suspended around the exhibit title "Walking on the wind." An exhibit table will hold an interactive model that demonstrates the principles of aerodynamics. A display case will house photographs of landmark aircraft, including the *Spruce Goose*. As a backdrop and to tie the three distinct areas together, a folding screen will be painted to resemble a pale blue sky with clouds. Five main conceptual units are identified as having potential future use: kites; Icarus; aerodynamics, planes; and sky. In addition, one kite (dragon kite) and one plane (*Spruce Goose*) are identified as objects that merit separate identification for use in planned future exhibits on the Chinese New Year and on Howard Hughes. In thinking through de-installation, the sky-background is a unit that can be folded flat and stored within the library; a number of potential uses have been identified and an easy to access storage location is desirable. Three kites are inexpensive paper and will be discarded; one kite is a very fancy Chinese dragon borrowed from the collection of a local resident and will be returned; however, it will be borrowed again for a display about the Chinese New Year; an entry will be made for the collection of Chinese artifacts and specific items or kinds of items will be listed in the description. Icarus is a 12-inch hand puppet found by chance in the basement in a crumbling cardboard box along with puppets and dolls resembling various book and folktale characters. The puppets and dolls will be cleaned and stored more appropriately. Icarus will be used again in connection with an exhibit on mythology; it is decided to catalogue the collection of mythological characters and list the individual dolls and puppets, including Icarus, in the description. The model of aerodynamics principles was constructed in collaboration with the local high school physics teacher; the model will be stored at the high school and will be available for use by area teachers, schools and libraries. The photographs of airplanes will be returned to library files but an exhibit on Howard Hughes is planned that will include the photograph of the *Spruce Goose* so a notation is placed in the Hughes exhibit planning documentation and with the photograph about the location of the photograph and its inclusion in the future exhibit.

Classifying and Cataloguing

When something is saved for later retrieval, it must be properly described, catalogued, and stored, otherwise it risks being obscured and becoming effectively lost. The exhibit itself and elements of it will warrant being described, catalogued and added to the collective memory of the library. Each exhibit should be documented (notes and photographs) and filed under the subject or topic of the exhibit. And, as we have mentioned, portions of an exhibit, or individual objects in an exhibit, may also merit separate classification. Access to the stored description will be through the topical or subject label we give to the exhibit, exhibit part, or exhibit object. We will discuss for just a moment what it is that is being catalogued and then the naming of the classified objects, groups, or ideas.

What are you cataloguing? Let's consider a grouping of four-inch-high furniture pieces: a desk, a chair, and a table. Is it doll furniture? Is it a 3-D model (versus 2-D photograph) of specific furniture? Are the items meant to represent that kind of object (a typical table, desk, chair) or grouping (furniture) or to represent a period of design (Queen Anne) or perhaps to say something about the person who owned or used the original (Benjamin Franklin's desk)? You need to understand what you are cataloguing before you can know how it should be catalogued.

What is it called? Access to the stored items or information will be through the category or proper names assigned to them. Consider, for example, the framed photograph of a cat taken by an unknown photographer and titled "Kitty." We could label this "photograph (cat)" or "cat (photograph)" or "animal, feline, photograph of" or "Kitty." We may decide more than one label would be needed to service the different purposes this object might serve: depictions of a cat; photographs of pets; photograph of the library's mascot. We want the topical or subject heading to be the most specific term that encompasses the entire essence or theme of the object or group or idea that we wish to recall. When more than one heading is needed, we will want to choose one as the main heading which will be used for entering a description of the item; the other headings will then reference the main heading, for example: "photograph (cat) *see* cat (photograph)."

Making a Catalogue in a Binder

Each exhibit or each exhibit unit or exhibit object that is being catalogued is recorded on a separate page. At the top of the page, record the topic or subject label or name. (For entries other than the main entry, record only the cross-reference, for example "feline, *see* cat.") On the main entry sheet or card, record the vital information about the object or unit or exhibit. This should include:

Category information
> Object name or subject of the unit
> Reference to other units of similar topic
> Larger unit(s) this is part of

Unit information
> Type of work
> Title, if applicable
> Classification
> Description of the unit
> Parts of this unit
> Bibliographic reference, if appropriate
> Size
> Materials and techniques

Source information
> Donor/date
> Owner/contact information/date/conditions of loan
> Reference number
> Location information
> Loaned to/date: (including contact information and conditions of loan)

Loan information
    Loaned to/contact information/date [to be] removed
    Conditions/expected return date/date returned

Other notations

You should design an organized format for the information and use this format consistently throughout the entries; this will facilitate finding information in each entry. Pages should be ordered alphabetically by subject headings. If a computer is being used to generate the pages, a template or master file can be created and then copied, completed, and printed as needed. If hand entry is being used, it may be desirable to have a form created and duplicated. An index of subject headings should be created and placed at the beginning of the notebook; be sure to include any "see" or "see also" notations with the subject heading. When looking for materials, ideas or associated ideas, the index will be quicker to browse than each page. For more extensive catalogues, A-Z index dividers would be a helpful addition.

Exhibits as Learning Objects

Now that we have considered the de-installed exhibit in terms of future reuse, we want to introduce the concept of learning objects and apply this to exhibits; that is, we want to consider exhibits as learning objects.

A learning object, according to the Institute of Electrical and Electronic Engineers' (IEEE) Learning Technology Standards Committee (LTSC), is "any entity, digital or non-digital, which can be used, re-used or referenced during technology supported learning." Technology supported learning includes interactive learning environments and collaborative learning environments in addition to electronic systems such as computer-based training, intelligent computer-aided instruction, and distance learning. Learning objects can include multimedia content, instructional content, persons, organizations, or events.[2] While some definitions seem to limit learning objects to digital resources, the IEEE definitions seem to accommodate nondigital exhibits without much stretching or modification.

The Wisconsin Online Resource Center, a partnership among the 16 Wisconsin Technical Colleges and funded through the U.S. Department of Education's Fund for the Improvement of Post-Secondary Education (FIPSE) and the National Science Foundation (NSF), defines learning objects as a "new way of thinking about learning content."[3] Learning objects, according to the Resource Center, typically require from two to 15 minutes to complete, are self-contained, and can be combined into larger collections of content. Learning objects can be interactive, "requiring the visitor to view, listen, respond, or interact with the content in some way" or noninteractive, such as reading text; and reusable or disposable ("may expire as new information and knowledge changes the content").[4]

In Chapter 3 we established the educational role of exhibits and use of exhibits as teaching tools. Some exhibits can be considered a collection of self-contained learning units (or collection of smaller, single goal exhibits). Other exhibits in their entirety may constitute a self-contained learning unit. We believe these teaching exhibits can be learning objects or reusable learning units. Exhibits as learning objects are one way to provide informal library, bibliographic, and information literacy instruction that is flexible to patron learning styles and time availability. We will want to catalogue these sharable teaching exhibits or learning objects and create an index that will facilitate finding and sharing them.

The Wisconsin Online Resource Center gives us a model for creating a Web-based *Exhibits as Learning Objects* index and repository. The title of the exhibit, its creator and institution, date submitted to the repository, description of the learning unit, and visual documentation (digital photographs or digital exhibit).[5] The resource center also provides links to reviews of each learning object. For example:

Subject: Information problem-solving
Title: Tackling Information Tasks: Planning the Task
Author: Creator's Name
Library: Local City Public Library   **Date:**1/30/2005
Description: The visitor selects a common information problem and uses a problem-solving approach to define the task and determine the best of a range of sources for the information desired. First in a series of four exhibits: Planning the Task, Locating Information Sources, Synthesizing Information to Fulfill the Task, Evaluating the Sources and the Product. A related series, "Constructing an Information Resource Guide," introduces visitors to various kinds of information resources found in the library.

View this object   Read reviews (6)

The purpose of this chapter has been to introduce the benefit if not need to catalogue exhibits, reusable portions of them, and exhibit production notes.

The beginning of this chapter discussed the need to catalogue exhibits as a resource to benefit the planning of future exhibits in the library. Chapter 6 (4.3.3) discusses keeping a documentation file as a record for each exhibit. The exhibits catalogue should index the exhibit documentation file in addition to the exhibit itself.

The concluding portion of this chapter discussed cataloguing and sharing exhibits that are used particularly to teach library and information skills. In Chapter 2 we expressed our belief that in the future of exhibits will gain increasing recognition of effective educational tools for teaching and learning, including for bibliographic and information literacy instruction. We have applied the concept of learning objects to exhibits used as teaching or educational tools and have suggested a mechanism for sharing these exhibits learning objects and their design.

11

Examples of Exhibits
in Libraries

"Centennial History Project"

The "Centennial History Project" is a series of exhibits celebrating history and diversity created by the East Chicago Public Library and its community.

The desire to show off a wealth of fascinating items not usually available for browsing makes exhibits a common practice in archives and special collections. Some libraries don't settle for showing what's in their collection though, they get the whole community involved. In 1989, as part of a "Centennial History Project" to build its local collections, the East Chicago Public Library of East Chicago, Indiana, began soliciting its community for materials that illustrate its diverse history. With these materials the library created exhibits celebrating the history of the many ethnic groups comprising the community. The "Centennial History Project" exhibits proved to be such a great success that the program still exists and the library continues to create such exhibits today. Gloria Dosen, the administrator of the East Chicago Room, told us about their exhibit process.

Planning

The goal of the overall "Centennial History Project" was to preserve East Chicago's heritage for scholars and local residents. The exhibits' role in this overarching goal was to keep alive this heritage by telling East Chicago's unique story of industry and ethnicity to new generations. Due to its nature, much of this history was not recorded through typical means such as books, so exhibits were used as a special strategy to bring it to light for all to see.

The initial force leading to the development of the exhibits was the impending demolition of a local Lithuanian church and school. Community members approached the library hoping it would be interested in helping preserve the story of the Lithuanian community. In a perfect example of "knowing your audience," the library took notice of the level of interest this demolition generated in the community and decided to work with it. East Chicago has a very diverse population, driven by over a century of immigration from many different countries. Since the community seemed interested in the history of its people, the library saw a perfect opportunity for an exhibit series focusing on the different immigrant or ethnic groups and their arrival, way of life, and contribution to the community. Such exhibits would meet community interest, bring people into the library, and help build the library's local history collection. Paying attention to their audience's needs and desires paid off in a highly successful exhibit program.

Exhibits

The exhibits have concentrated on peoples from a variety of places including Lithuania, Mexico, Greece, and Africa. Although the ethnic groups differ, the format of the exhibits is standard. In each exhibit, materials portraying the life of one group in East Chicago are displayed and interpreted. Each exhibit opens with a reception and includes other programs that showcase the food, music, and dance of that culture. The exhibits last from four to six weeks and there is always one on display.

Many different kinds of items are displayed in the exhibits including photographs, letters, newspaper stories, art and jewelry, literature, costume, and crafts. The library has 18 cases in its exhibit gallery in which as many objects as possible are displayed. They include display units designed specifically to show photographs in an eye-catching manner and different sizes and heights of cases for displaying objects. Clothing is shown on mannequins. In addition to the main exhibit gallery, objects are often displayed in cases in other parts of the library, strategically placed to attract the attention of visitors and "wet their appetite."[1] Some exhibits also extend into the branch library across town. When an exhibit is not large enough to fill all the cases, related books from the library's regular col-

One of the East Chicago Public Library's many display units. This one shows photographs of local African-Americans to much better advantage than a flat case (courtesy East Chicago Public Library, East Chicago, Indiana).

lection are added to complement the objects on display and to increase patron interest in the collection.

The exhibit labels are informative, but don't take up a lot of room. One- to two-line captions are used to describe every photograph, identify every person, and interpret all objects except those that are self-explanatory. A history is written to explain the group's background, lifestyle, and contributions to life in the United States. This is sometimes printed in a pamphlet for distribution. A decorative title banner hangs over the door of the gallery. Often the flag of the group's native country influences the design of an exhibit, its colors used throughout.

Execution

The exhibit process begins by choosing a theme with the help of volunteers from the community. For example, the upcoming exhibit about African Americans titled "Impacting our community with education and experience" is about the contributions of local African American teachers. Once the theme is chosen, a committee of volunteers representing the ethnic group is assembled. The members of this committee take primary responsibility for collecting materials for the exhibit beyond what is already in the library's collection. They make decisions about what things are important to display and what stories need to be told. They also play an important advisory role, giving opinions about whether the exhibit labels and layout say things accurately, respectfully, and with sensitivity. The staff of the East Chicago History Room does the work of creating the exhibit including writing and making labels, putting the exhibit together, and planning events. The staff and committee meet every two weeks over the course of the two to three months it takes to plan and put up the exhibit.

In spite of the rigorous exhibit schedule, with a new exhibit going up as soon as the last comes down, the library works with a small exhibit budget. They do all printing of labels, fliers, and invitations in house. When possible, they try to get donated or discounted services such as food and entertainment for their events. Years of making community connections through the exhibits helps in their fund-raising efforts. Local businesses and community leaders often make donations to support the exhibits. For example, every year, a local Mexican candy company donates candy for the Mexican-American exhibit. In addition, recently, the library has received some grant money to fund the purchase of artifacts, exhibit materials and display cases, and other exhibit expenses.

Publicity for the exhibits follows a standard format as well. Each exhibit opens with a reception. The list of people to invite is put together by the exhibit committee. Fliers are posted around town at schools, banks, and businesses. School groups often come to tour the exhibit. Every exhibit is documented with photographs which are put in photo albums so people can revisit them years after the exhibit is taken down.

Evaluation

Gloria Dosen has been in charge of the community history exhibits at East Chicago Public Library for 13 years. During that time, the exhibit program has grown and adjust-

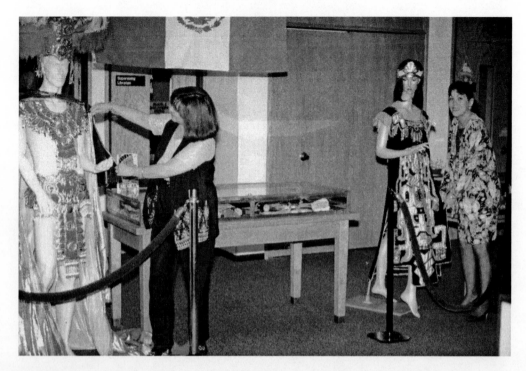

Two employees of the East Chicago Public Library put the finishing touches on the Mexican-American exhibit. Ceremonial dress is shown on mannequins and artifacts are displayed in a flat-topped case. A stanchion and velvet rope barrier is used to discourage visitors from touching the clothes (courtesy East Chicago Public Library, East Chicago, Indiana).

ments have been made to the exhibit process. One of the major changes grew from the library's commitment to its community. There is now increased input from community groups in the form of the exhibit committees mentioned earlier. The exhibits are considered "their display and not our display. We're helping them" make the exhibits.[2] The director of the library when the "Centennial History Project" began, Theodore T. Mason, described the change in exhibit philosophy as the desire for "each group to determine for themselves what was important to them so the exhibit would more truly depict their experience. The individuals involved can best decide what makes their group unique."[3]

The exhibits are also more advanced now than in the early years. Because of their success, more materials and volunteer labor are available allowing bigger exhibits. The library also pays attention to what parts of the exhibits are most successful. They show videotape of older community residents talking about what life was like when they were children "to add information and color" to the exhibits.[4] They've also found that clothing makes "such an imprint on people."[5] Focusing on items such as these helps their visitors connect with the exhibit, making it more enjoyable and more successful at getting its message across.

Community Impact

The evaluation of the exhibits leading to the addition of more community involvement in their creation paid off in community response. Mason said that the library did not initially "realize how much local interest the exhibits would generate. Every program has opened to a packed house, where old friends and neighbors, co-workers, and church members are reunited."[6] The opening of one exhibit about the African-American community opened with a "two-day celebration of their culture that featured music, dance, poetry, speakers, and traditional foods." So many visitors turned out that the originally planned venue was not large enough and "the show had to be moved from the meeting room to the library's central area to accommodate everyone."[7]

Success with an exhibit comes about through careful planning and flexibility. The East Chicago Public Library used some of the most basic but important parts of the exhibit process to their advantage. They had clear goals for their exhibits. They focused on their visitors, paying close attention to those things that are important them. They evaluated their work and adjusted their strategies to make each round of exhibits better than the last. They understood what makes a successful exhibit. Theodore T. Mason, the library director, summed up one of the most important aspects of a successful exhibit when describing the goal of one of their exhibits: "We especially wanted people to see themselves in this exhibit."[8]

"Go Figure!"

"Go Figure!" is a traveling exhibit about math based on children's books created in part by the American Library Association and hosted by a number of libraries.

The American Library Association regularly creates exhibits to be displayed in libraries around the country. One of its exhibits, "*Go Figure!,*" traveled to libraries and children's museums during the period of September 2000 to January 2003.[9] Here we discuss the process of creating the exhibit as well as the steps taken by the Kansas City Public Library to host the exhibit.

Planning and Evaluation

"Go Figure!" was produced through a collaboration between the American Library Association (ALA), the Minnesota Children's Museum, and the Association for Library Service to Children, a division of the ALA.[10] It was funded primarily by a $1.4 million grant from the National Science Foundation and received additional support from corporate sponsors Cargill ($300,000) and 3M ($100,000 worth of products.)[11]

The exhibit was designed to use familiar children's books to introduce the world of math to children ages 2 to 7. In the initial phases of development, staff from the ALA and ALSC "helped the museum select kids' books that use everyday math concepts, such as counting and sorting, in their stories."[12] The museum then created exhibit prototypes which were used in front-end studies to find out how parents and children interact with math-based exhibits and what parents understand about their children's learning. Twenty-six parent-child pairs were observed as they interacted with two exhibit prototypes, then the parents were interviewed.

Evaluators discovered that although parents described their children's play accurately, they did not necessarily understand the math-related implications of that play.[13] The museum decided the exhibit needed to "help parents of young children recognize that play activities, such as sorting and arranging, are important 'pre-math' processes" and that it should promote parent-child math play.[14] Another goal was to "let parents of older children know that math skills are not necessarily number-based and that getting the 'right' answer may not be the purpose of the activity."[15] Math, it seems, works similarly to exhibits-the informal play process can be just as important as the formal transmission of hard information. It turns out that everyone-parents and children-are comfortable with "pretend play" so "interactive scenarios that incorporate play with the practice of math-skills" was determined to be a potentially successful exhibit strategy.[16]

After further development of the exhibits using these initial goals, formative evaluation was conducted. Thirty family groups were observed interacting with one exhibit, then interviewed. The evaluators determined that adults understood the exhibit better when they read the labels and they were more likely to read a label when it posed a question such as "Where's the math in the kitchen?" that they could find the answer to by participating in the exhibit.[17] They also concluded that labels needed to explain to parents that young children can use math processes and that images in the exhibit should reflect diversity: women, men, girls, and boys should be shown doing the various activities.

The Exhibit

After the rigorous evaluation process, the design was finalized and the exhibit fabricated. It ended up being made up of "child-sized environments"[18] based on five children's books: *Arthur's Pet Business* by Marc Brown, *The Doorbell Rang* by Pat Hutchins, *The Quilt* by Ann Jonas, *Frog and Toad are Friends: A Lost Button* by Arnold Lobel, and *Goldilocks and the Three Bears* illustrated by James Marshall.[19] These environments provided hands-on activities and encouraged play centered on math concepts such as counting, sorting, arranging, estimating, and comparing. The exhibit was aimed particularly at helping parents and children play together using these concepts and showing parents how typical activities in child's play can often be important precursors to math skills.

One of the exhibit components, based on the book *The Doorbell Rang*, included activities based on the make-believe scenario of "making and baking pretend cookies and sharing them with different numbers of guests."[20] The exhibit was also designed with a specific area for parents and children to read together. The exhibit labels were written in both English and Spanish[21] and the exhibit included take-home materials to help parents and children play with math at home.

The Kansas City Public Library in Kansas City, Missouri hosted "Go Figure!" from December 5, 2002, through January 23, 2003. Margaret Clark, director of adult programs and exhibits, told us about their exhibit process.

Kids "play" with math in *Go Figure!* at the Kansas City Public Library. This component is based on the book *The Doorbell Rang* by Pat Hutchins (photograph provided by the Kansas City Public Library).

Planning

Since the Kansas City Public Library (KCPL) opened a new central library in 2004, its exhibit program has grown. It used to have only two to four exhibits a year throughout the system of ten libraries. Now it has about 24 each year, in part because the new library offers so much potential exhibit space including a dedicated gallery, a large mezzanine area, and a multistory, grand hall on the first floor. Although the number of exhibits has grown, the goals of the exhibit program remain the same: to bring people into the library, to call positive attention to the library, and to provide a central theme for adult programs. All the exhibits at KCPL focus on some aspect of the humanities as this is the dedicated goal of the money in the library's endowment that funds the exhibits. While this allows the library much scope, it does rule out certain exhibits. "Go Figure!," in addition to meeting all of these overarching goals, was hosted with the specific goal of celebrating the grand opening of one of the branch libraries.

Booking an exhibit from the American Library Association is a slightly different process than booking a typical traveling exhibit. Rather than being chosen on a first-come-first-served basis, venues are chosen through a formal application process. Libraries must meet certain requirements of space, planned programming to complement the exhibit, and ability to reach certain audiences. The requirements for "Go Figure!" included a commitment to providing an opening reception and at least one program, a focus on reaching low-income family audiences, and a collaboration with another community-based organization. These goals fit in well with KCPL's plan to display the exhibit in its new branch library, which is located in a low-income neighborhood whose residents have below-average education levels.[22]

Execution

The work for "Go Figure!," given that it was program rich and focused on collaboration, was conducted by committee. The team who worked on the exhibit included representatives from the marketing, youth services, adult programs, and outreach departments as well as the manager of the branch where the exhibit was displayed. Five staff members worked on the exhibit, each devoting ten percent of their full-time work week for eight weeks, a total of 160 hours of staff time.[23] This doesn't even take into account the time spent on promoting the exhibit by the library's partner organizations: Mattie Rhodes Counseling and Art Center, Head Start, Kansas City Parents as Teachers, and the Francis Child Development Institute.

In the case of this traveling exhibit, installation was a very small amount of work compared to planning the programs. Exhibits from the ALA are designed with libraries in mind. This one in particular was packaged in easily moved and managed fiberglass cases that open and shut with buckle fasteners rather than the customary heavier, wooden cases with screwed on lids. The exhibit was brought in by the movers and Margaret unpacked and installed with the help of two facilities staff. The library added its own book displays to the exhibit to showcase its collection of children's books relating to math.

But the hard work was the programming. While the exhibit was displayed in one branch, programs occurred throughout the system. There were seven kinds of programs: a grand opening reception; a lecture and discussion by a nationally-known speaker; a puppet show; a workshop for adults on how to teach math skills using literacy as a base; story times; Make 'n' Take craft activities; and school group visits. The library locations without the exhibit were served by regular story times using books that involved some aspect of math and Make 'n' Take craft tables where kids could participate in math-related activities similar to those in the exhibit. A collaboration with the Francis Child Development Institute produced the "More Than Just Counting" workshops which were offered to teachers, parents, and caregivers. The library donated copies of the books used in the exhibit to some local schools; teachers read the books to their classes, then brought them to see the exhibit.

The budget for the exhibit consisted primarily of staff time and the publicity and programming costs because there was no rental or shipping fees. (Exhibits of the ALA often do not have rental fees and sometimes do not have shipping fees. This is a great boon to the hosting libraries; not having to deal with shipping is always nice. Margaret told the story of a shipping mishap that occurred with another one of the library's traveling exhibits that was coming from a venue in the Philippines. That venue decided that shipping by air was too expensive, so it sent the exhibit by ship. By the time the library and the lending institution realized what had happened, it was too late: the exhibit was floating on the high seas. To comply with the contract and get the exhibit up in time at KCPL, the lending institution had to build another version of the exhibit.)

Just because rental fees were not a factor, however, doesn't mean the budget was small. The library spent a significant amount of money and staff time on publicity and programs; it spent over $11,000, received more than $1,000 of services in-kind, and devoted about $4,000 worth of staff time.[24] The cost of the programs alone was over $7,500 including refreshments and entertainment for the grand opening; the fee for the speaker; the puppet show; and in-kind donations of community center space and workshop leaders; over $4,000 was spent on publicity printings including bookmarks, brochures, and an invitation to the lecture.[25]

The bookmarks, brochures, and invitations were not the full extent of the library's publicity for the exhibit, however. Other publicity included a description of the exhibit and its programs on the library's website and cover articles for its calendar-of-events brochure in the opening month and the follow-up month. They added it to the events calendars of the local newspaper and the Convention and Visitor's Bureau. They sent a press release to all the print and electronic media which resulted in a TV feature and four newspaper articles about the exhibit and its programs. Because the local newspaper has such a wide distribution reaching users of a number of other public library systems, the library focused its publicity for the lecture with a nationally-known speaker by mailing invitations directly to over 2,000 people. In addition, they relied heavily on their partnerships with other community organizations to spread the word.

Even years after they hosted the exhibit, the library keeps a documentation file for this exhibit, as for all their others. This file includes a copy of the application to the ALA; a copy of the final report to the ALA; samples of the publicity brochures and invitations; clippings the four newspaper articles; printed materials used for the programs; the budget; and all other information pertaining to the exhibit.

Community Impact

Attendance at the library's programs was high. The opening reception, lecture/discussion, workshops, and puppet show brought in over 400 participants. Throughout the system, over 500 children attended story time and over 900 took advantage of the Make 'n' Take tables. Over 500 children visited the exhibit with their school classes.[26]

Undoubtedly, the collaborations between the library and other community groups was beneficial to the library, helping bring the library to the attention of new potential patrons. Hosting the exhibit in a branch in a typically underserved area surely had positive effects for both the community and the library. Not only did the exhibit programs benefit participants at the time, but they continued to have benefits after the exhibit closed. A local early childhood special education teacher felt that the "More Than Just Counting" workshop was "the most profitable workshop she has ever attended."[27] The leaders of that library workshop from the Francis Child Development Institute have since built on the workshop and presented at the annual conference of the National Association for the Education of Young Children.[28] Teachers, in particular, expressed their appreciation of a free educational resource to the branch manager and asked the library to "secure more exhibits like 'Go Figure!'"[29]

Together a parent and child read one of the books in *Go Figure!* The labels on the exhibits help parents use children's books to teach their kids about math in a fun and informal way. This label says, "Help your children understand size and measurement by:" and then provides suggestions (photograph provided by the Kansas City Public Library).

"Science in the Stacks"

"Science in the Stacks" is a series of hands-on exhibits created through a partnership between public libraries in Vermont and New Hampshire and the Montshire Museum of Science.

Libraries and museums are both forums for informal education. Partnerships between the two can take advantage of each other's strengths: museums can use a library's central place in the community to reach a wider audience and libraries can use a museum's expertise with informal educational methods to encourage "meaningful use of their collections and information resources."[30] To explore the world of possibilities in library-museum partnerships, the federal Institute of Museum and Library Services offers grants.[31] One of these grants (for almost $100,000) funded "Science in the Stacks," an exhibit collaboration between the Montshire Museum of Science in Norwich, Vermont, the Howe Library in Hanover, New Hampshire, and seven other area public libraries.[32]

Planning

In addition to pioneering a model for library-museum partnerships that might be replicated by others, the "Science in the Stacks" ("SITS") project had a number of goals. These included educational goals for the exhibits as well as an exploration of the role of libraries. The exhibit goals were to promote family interaction and to foster curiosity and invite further learning the exhibit topics. Recognizing the important role a parent plays in their child's educational success, the project aimed to create exhibits that emphasized collaborative learning and encouraged people to interact and talk with each other. The project participants also wanted to extend that learning beyond the time and space of the exhibit. The exhibits needed to encourage visitors to want to learn more about the topics presented and they should offer that "more" in the form of hand-outs, programs, and related library materials for circulation. Finally, the project would bring multiple exhibits to a typically underserved, rural community.

In an initial survey, the librarians participating in the project summed up the goal of exploring and expanding the library's role. One librarian was hopeful that the project would help libraries become places where people actually do something rather than simply quick stops on the to-do list. To this librarian the project had the possibility of "expanding the role the library plays in the community-making it more experience-oriented rather than a place to pick up what you need and go."[33] Another librarian, recognizing the importance of the public's perception of the role of libraries, felt that the project could "encourage all library patrons, of all ages, to come and see the library as a center for learning, as well as a place to get reading materials."[34] It was also hoped that the exhibits would offer a thematic hook the libraries could use to highlight their collections, thereby increasing circulation.[35]

Exhibits

Eight exhibits were created, one for each library in the partnership. They spent six weeks at each library, allowing all eight exhibits to be presented at each library over the course of one year. The exhibits touched on the science behind the topics of birds and flight, measuring units of time, color and light, carpentry tools, shapes used in construction, reaction times, and resonance. Every exhibit had hands-on components. These components included a bird's wing for touching, color filters and a light box, heartbeat monitors, special building blocks, materials with which to make measuring tools, an electronic drum machine with changeable rhythms, a computer program that tests reaction time, and a set of rods that resonate. Besides these components and other activities that formed the exhibit experience, each exhibit had additional materials to support it. These included a display of library materials related to the exhibit topic (fiction, nonfiction, and videos for children and adults); a bibliography of such materials and electronic resources; and a handout of further activities that could be conducted at home.

Some of the participating libraries were quite small (serving populations less than 2000) and located in old buildings. The exhibits not only had to be designed to fit in a small space, but they had to be able to be moved into that space. Each library's doors, hallways, and stairwells were measured, and the maximum dimensions of the exhibits were determined to be sure they could fit in all eight libraries. The exhibits also had to be designed to be easily transported between libraries. The exhibit designer settled on a final design of a metal table base with exchangeable table tops. The base remained in a library while the table tops and their exhibit components were moved. Next to each

Kids use the Science in the Stacks exhibit about tools. The boy is using a hands-on component to find out how levels work and the girl has used the materials provided to create her own plumb bob. The book display on the right includes three sides of books, videos, and kits for adults and childen (John Gilbert Fox).

exhibit table stood a three-sided book display unit on which the related library materials were placed. The related collection materials and bibliographies, programming activity print-outs, ideas, and instructions, and handouts for visitors to take home all traveled with the exhibits when they went to new libraries.

Execution

Bringing together eight libraries and a museum means bringing together a large number of staff. In addition to the two co-directors, this project required the work of one librarian from each library, an exhibit designer, a museum educator, and an exhibit evaluator. All of these people (and many more) gathered at a symposium on informal learning in community centers to start off the project.[36] Two workshops to begin the project planning followed. The first, held at the museum, included a discussion about what makes a successful exhibit and a brainstorming session for exhibit themes; at the second, held at the Howe Library, participants discussed what makes a good library program and how the libraries would share traveling collections.[37]

Following these workshops, museum staff determined which exhibit topics would be most feasible and worked with each of the eight librarians to develop their favorite exhibit idea. The exhibit designer then created and tested exhibit prototypes, with input from the librarians; the museum educator and librarians developed exhibit related activities for use in programs; and the librarians planned collections of related materials and specific programs for their libraries. When the libraries did not have appropriate materials in their collections, additional materials were purchased to travel with the exhibits. (A schedule for this project giving an idea of how much time was devoted to each part of the process is located in the Taking Stock section of Part I of Chapter 6.) Upon completion of the exhibits, a second workshop took place at which each exhibit was introduced and its use, maintenance, and accompanying activities and materials discussed.

The programming side of the project took a lot of time on the part of the librarians. Every library held programs in conjunction with each of the exhibits. Some special programs were planned specifically to complement the exhibits while others were typical library programs whose theme was adjusted. For instance, many libraries held their weekly story times using books that related to the exhibit and followed up with science-related activities and those libraries that offered after-school activities tried to choose ones that fit in with the current exhibit theme.[38] Special programs planned included a demonstration by cabinet makers to go with the exhibit about carpentry tools, a talk by the Audubon Society to go with the birds and flight exhibit, an afternoon of African drumming to go with the rhythm exhibit, and a juggling show to go with the exhibit on reaction times.[39] An especially innovative program was the "open houses" hosted by one librarian; during school vacations, she held all-day-long activity stations related to the exhibit which reached large numbers of patrons as they allowed for flexible scheduling for families.[40]

Evaluation

An outside evaluator assessed the project using written surveys and interviews. The evaluation turned up some interesting information about what kinds of exhibits were most successful at reaching an audience, what impact the exhibits had on the libraries, and how the library-museum collaboration worked.

The most successful exhibits turned out to be the ones with inherently interesting topics that were familiar to patrons or "related to something that they already had experienced."[41] Familiarity seemed to have two positive effects. It encouraged parents to interact with their children; when they already knew something about the topic, they felt confident. According to one librarian, "this confidence enabled adults to explain the exhibit to children without appearing to be 'stupid.'"[42] When an exhibit topic related in a special way to a community, as it did in one of the towns, the residents of that town took special notice. The town of one library in the collaboration has an industrial history of tool-making; the library took advantage of this when they got the tool exhibit and tied the programs to the town's history. Said the librarian, "the fact that we could tie in the local history of the town with patrons really held their interest" and this exhibit was particularly well-received.[43]

In this exhibit project, the collection materials did not circulate heavily, although they were used frequently inside the library. The librarians hypothesized a number of possible reasons for low levels of circulation that should be considered in future exhibits with displays of related library materials. One major problem was where to locate the materials. Often, the exhibits were in the children's section, however, this may have limited circulation of the books aimed at adults; conversely, when the exhibit was located in the adult section, children might not have known about the books for them.[44] One library found that displaying the exhibit near the circulation desk increased circulation.[45] Other factors influencing circulation might include patrons' reluctance to remove something they think is part of an exhibit; a limited one-week loan period; and the perception that science books are not for fun, but rather to be used only when researching specific topics.[46] These factors might be remedied by making signs encouraging removal of the books and designing programs and at-home activities that involve or refer to the books.[47]

Not surprisingly, the librarians all wished there was more time for them to plan and provide programs to go with the exhibits. An important aspect of this was the desire to have received training in conducting programs from the educators at the museum; some librarians, not feeling confident with the topics, tended to have outsiders come in to present programs.[48] There was clearly further opportunity for the libraries and museum to share knowledge in this collaboration.

The exhibit has been well-documented on the Montshire Museum of Science's website at www.montshire.net/stacks/. The information provided there remains indefinitely. It includes a transcription of the talk given at the symposium, "The Learning Landscapes of Museums and Libraries" by David Carr, associate professor in the School of Information and Library Science at the University of North Carolina at Chapel Hill; the original project proposal; photos and descriptions of each exhibit; bibliographies of the collection materials for each exhibit; press releases; the final project evaluation; and information on developing exhibits such as a "Checklist for Exhibit Topics" and guidelines for "What Makes a Good Interactive Exhibit?"

Two kids share control of the drum machine in the Science in the Stacks exhibit about rhythm. Library materials for circulation are displayed behind them (Jon Gilbert Fox).

Community and Library Impact

In the initial survey, a number of librarians had hoped that the exhibits would increase the visibility of the libraries and help them market themselves in a new way to patrons. The final interviews showed that this did happen. The exhibits opened the communities' eyes to new roles for the library and the librarians' eyes to new ways of conducting programs and activities.

The librarians felt that the libraries took on a new image to the children of the community because "working with the staff of the Museum has helped" the libraries "to teach children that the library is a fun place to be."[49] Through the exhibits, "the public was able to see the library as having additional roles than being a 'book place'" while at the same time it "connected learning and books in a positive fun way."[50] The public responded very positively to the exhibits as evidenced in the exhibit diary kept by one librarian; in the last week of an exhibit "people are asking again when will the next exhibit be here and what it will be!"[51]

The exhibits broadened the librarians' views of how successful programs in a library might work. Observation of patrons using the materials and participating in the activities of the exhibits has one librarian planning future summer reading programs in a new way. "My experience with SITS told me that it would be more effective (I would reach more people) if I put out and left out for a couple of weeks hands-on projects (craft-type stuff) and supporting materials than if I tried to run a one-time program."[52] Another library felt the exhibits were such a positive addition that they are planning to keep the "SITS" space reserved for changing hands-on activities.[53]

As does any collaboration, this one lead to the creation of a stronger network of local librarians. After getting to know the other participants throughout the project, one librarian was looking forward to "when our paths cross at meetings" because "we have something in common that connects us."[54] In addition, both the librarians and the museum staff indicated that they would like to work together on future projects or programs.[55] Not only might this kind of collaboration happen again in this community, it "could blossom in to something other institutions may consider doing in the future."[56]

12

Exhibits in Libraries: Three Course Syllabi

We believe the skills and knowledge introduced in this book will be more effectively and efficiently gained through a structured plan of study and practice. This chapter presents a set of syllabi to help guide the reader in their quest to becoming more knowledgeable about and skilled in mounting exhibits in libraries.

Three formats for a course in curating and creating exhibits in libraries are provided: one is appropriate for self-study (alone or in a small group), one is appropriate as a continuing education or professional development course, and one is appropriate for a graduate course such as in a master of library science (MLS) program. Each syllabus is presented as an extended course handbook and includes information and guidelines for creating a rich learning experience as well as assessing that experience.

In planning a continuing education, professional development, or graduate course based on this book, we suggest that guest speakers with a variety of experiences mounting exhibits in libraries or museums are invited to reinforce and enrich material provided in these chapters and to serve as resources during various phases of exhibit planning and creation. An end-of-course exhibition of exhibit prototypes and portfolios might be planned in association with a professional meeting or as an opportunity to receive critiques from guest exhibit personnel.

Syllabus 1: A Self-Study Course in Curating and Creating Exhibits in Libraries

Letter to the Student

Welcome to Exhibits in Libraries, a self-study course designed to complement this book and assist you in a hands-on learning experience.

During this course you will explore the following topics: kinds of exhibits, exhibit and education theory, audience and exhibit theme, budget and other administrative details, exhibit development and accessibility, exhibit design and conservation, exhibit labels, exhibit prototypes and formative evaluation, exhibit fabrication and installation, and publicity and programming. You will also plan and prototype and perhaps construct a library exhibit.

Readings, explorations, and assignments have been carefully spaced into units. It is suggested each unit be completed over one to two weeks.

We have tried to do two major things in the course: to introduce you to the mechanics of planning and preparing an exhibit in a library and a bit of the theory backing those mechanics, and to create a programmed study experience that will be enjoyable and result in significant improvements in your ability and/or confidence to mount successful exhibits in libraries.

To help you complete this hands-on self-study course we would like you to have the cooperation of a library director who agrees to sponsor your finished course project as a library exhibit. We would also like you to identify one to three library or museum personnel with at least some experience creating exhibits to serve as mentors during your course work. We will provide guidelines for approaching and maintaining relationships with mentors and sponsors. If you are unable to obtain a sponsor and mentors, you can create an exhibit for your own enjoyment and use friends and family in place of mentors.

We hope you enjoy this course. It should be a busy but fun experience. It requires you to read in this book and provides suggestions for additional readings. It also requires you to apply the readings to problems (such as identifying and planning an exhibit). It requires problem solving and, at times a bit of imagination. You will need to manage your time and resources closely. And you should to plan on spending time meeting with your mentor. We are very excited about this course and believe you will be proud of your accomplishments through the course activities.

Welcome!

Purpose of the Course

This course will prepare librarians and library staff to curate and create exhibits in their libraries by teaching about: the basic background and skills needed for exhibit work including exhibit and education theory; kinds, purposes, and themes of exhibits; exhibit budgets and other administrative aspects; exhibit design and development; exhibit prototyping and evaluation; exhibit accessibility; exhibit conservation; exhibit labels; exhibit fabrication; and publicity and programming for exhibits. Instruction will emphasize the practice of exhibit skills, relying on readings only for an introduction of topics. Students will follow the exhibit process to design and develop an exhibit. In some cases, the exhibit will be able to be fabricated and possibly displayed by the end of the course; in the case of large or costly exhibits, concentration should be on the design and prototyping only.

Course Description

Study of the techniques, management, and assessment of exhibit work, and theories supporting those techniques including exhibit and education theory.

Course Objectives

When you have completed this course, you should be able to:

- Define the goals of an exhibit
- Establish timelines and budgets for an exhibit
- Select appropriate exhibit materials, including labels, for various age groups
- Discuss exhibit and learning theory as it applies to planning exhibits
- Assess through formative and summative evaluations the exhibit process
- Demonstrate an ability to construct and document an exhibit prototype
- Evaluate an exhibit for physical and intellectual accessibility
- Write an exhibit conservation plan
- Write a publicity plan, exhibit press release and poster

Course Requirements

- Preparing a series of assignments that lead to an exhibit
- Reading material on techniques in exhibit work, available in this text
- Completing a series of assessments of the emerging exhibit prototype.

Resources

Required Text

Brown, Mary E., and Rebecca Power. *Exhibits in libraries: A practical guide* (Jefferson, NC: McFarland, 2005).

Recommended Texts

Serrell, Beverly. *Exhibits labels: An interpretive approach* (Walnut Creek, CA: Altamira Press, 1996).

Smithsonian Accessibility Program. *Smithsonian guidelines for accessible exhibition design* (2nd ed., 1996). Washington, DC: Smithsonian Institute Press. (Available free from www.si.edu/opa/accessibility/exdesign/ or by writing Smithsonian Accessibility Program, Smithsonian Institution, Arts and Industries Building, Arts and Industries Building, Room 1239 MRC 426, Washington, DC 20560; calling (202) 786-2942 or TTY (202) 786-2414 or emailing majewskj@si.edu).

Williams, Robin. *The non-designers design book: Design and typographic principles for the visual novice*, 2nd ed. (Berkeley, CA: Peachpitt Press, 2004).

Mentors and Mentoring

To assist you in creating a richer learning experience, we strongly suggest you establish a mentoring relationship with one to three library or museum staff with experience in exhibit work. To assist you in establishing these mentoring relationships, we highlight information based on Gordon F. Shea's 1997 book, *Mentoring* (rev. ed., 1997, Crisp Publications, Menlo Park, CA, ISBN 156052426X).

What Is Mentoring?

Mentoring is "a fundamental form of human development where one person invests time, energy, and personal know-how in assisting the growth and ability/development of another person" ('CSWT Papers / Empowerment of Mentees through Team Mentors / Ken Bryant www.workteams.unt.edu/reports/bryant.html'), helping that person to move toward fulfilling their potential. Mentoring is a way of encouraging human growth. Vogotsky called the gap between what one can accomplish on his own and what one can accomplish under the guidance of another the Zone of Proximal Development (ZPD). We could say that mentoring is the bridge across the ZPD.

Mentors styles may range from that of a persistent encourager who helps you build your self-confidence, to that of a stern taskmaster who teaches you to appreciate excellence in performance ('Mentoring Program / Defense Information Systems Agency http://jobopps.disa.mil/NewMentor/faq.html'). Mentoring relationships vary in two ways: formality (from highly structured to virtually no structure) and length of intervention (from long-term, including for life, to short-term and spontaneous).

Choosing a Mentor

Successful mentoring depends upon the knowledge that the mentor has to offer matching a gap in the mentee's own knowledge system — a gap which the mentee wishes to fill; and the willingness of the mentee to be mentored.

In choosing a mentor, look for someone who has knowledge you would like to gain (and is willing to put in the effort to help you learn). Try to be as specific as possible in setting up a mentoring relationship. For example, "I would like to learn about writing labels for exhibits for young children" and "I would like to learn what a typical day/week is like for a team "are specific mentoring goals while "Teach me everything you know about curating exhibits" is too broad and vague.

Setting Goals and Objectives

Any mentoring relationship should have common goals understood by both the mentor and mentee. It is important that the mentor and mentee share expectations of the benefits and opportunities that will be available in the relationship. Up to three key points or goals should be agreed upon (for example, to increase the mentee's awareness of and recognition in professional organizations). After the goals have been established, the mentor and mentee can then set a few objectives that will move them toward the goal (for example, attending a local professional meeting together and the mentor introducing the mentee to three colleagues). It is important not to take on too much at once. Three simultaneous goals are sufficient. One to three simultaneous objectives under each goal are sufficient. As objectives are meet, new objectives can be added.

We strongly suggest that you document your goals and objectives in a mentoring plan or agreement, thereby establishing expectations so that neither the mentor nor the mentee will be disappointed. The mentoring agreement should list three key points or goals that the mentor and mentee agree to work toward.

The mentoring agreement should list: initial goals and objectives of your mentoring plan; the date of meeting at which the goals and objectives were decided; a brief listings of topic(s) covered (brief key terms or phrases that best describe your discussion and/or skills to be practiced; and finally a narrative section that records any desired details.

Be sure to arrange with your mentor for reviews of the mentoring relationship. You will need to review and update goals as well as recommit to continuing the mentoring relationship (or discontinuing it) as the relationship progresses.

Evaluating the Mentoring Plan

Mentoring agreements need to be evaluated periodically and goals and objectives adjusted.

In long term mentoring situations, evaluation should take place after 30 days, after 90 days, and at six months. In short term mentoring situations, evaluation should take place monthly or weekly, depending on the intensity of the contact and the set goals and objectives. Assessment needs to consider the work toward each goal, the continued appropriateness of each goal, the match between mentee need and mentor resources, and the outcome of objectives. Any problem should be dealt with when it arises.

As a result of the assessments, goals may change or mentoring relationships may change. Mentoring requires investment of mentor resources and mentee need. There should be a match between the two. For example, if the mentee's need is high and the mentor' resources, time, skills, etc are low, perhaps the relationship would be better served if the current mentor help the mentee find another mentor with abundant resources.

Course Calendar

Unit	*Date**	*Topics / Reading assignments / Activity assignments*

*Set your own dates before to beginning this course. We suggest you allow one to two weeks for each unit.

1. TBA Introduction to and kinds of exhibits

Topics: Overview of the course and exhibit process. What is an exhibit? Why have exhibits in libraries? What are the goals of an exhibit? Kinds of exhibits. Which kinds of exhibits belong in libraries? Exhibit locations. Exhibit time frames.

Read: Chapters 1, 2, and 4

Assignment: Visit a library and analyze it for potential exhibit spaces. Record the details of these spaces including layout (description, dimensions, lighting, accessibility, etc.) in a document that a library could use for future reference when planning exhibits.

2. TBA Exhibit and education theories

Topics: How do people learn from exhibits? What makes a good exhibit? Creating successful objectives for exhibits.

Read: Chapter 3

Assignment: Visit three different kinds of museum or library exhibits and observe how visitors interact with them. Write a paper that discusses the positive and negative visitor behaviors at these exhibits and analyzes what about the exhibits seems to affect this behavior: what works, what doesn't work, what might be changed to improve them, etc. (Be sure to include one exhibit of the kind you want to make for this class.)

3. TBA Audience and exhibit theme

Topics: Researching the topic. Front-end evaluation and your audience. The big idea.

Read: Chapters 5 (Steps 1–2), and 6 (1.1–1.5)

Assignment: 1) Choose a theme for your exhibit. Research and think of some possible angles to approach this theme. 2) Analyze your audience. Create (and write down) front-end evaluation questions about your topic and interview library visitors. Write a brief synopsis of what you found during your evaluation. 3) Narrow your exhibit theme. Write down the "big idea" and the exhibit objectives.

4. TBA Budget and other administrative details

Topics: What costs are involved in exhibits? How much staff time is needed? Creating a budget. Finding the money. Contracts for borrowed items. Insurance and security.

Read: Chapters 5 (Step 3), 6 (1.5–1.8, 2.5–2.8, 3.4–3.7, 4.5–4.8), and 8

Assignment: Estimate staff time and create a budget for your exhibit. If you are unsure of what things cost, make some calls — to vendors, museum or library exhibit staff, etc.

5.	TBA	Exhibit development and accessibility

Topics: What story does an exhibit tell? Will items be on display? What will the visitor do or experience? How do we engage visitors and make them think? Accessibility: visitor backgrounds, kinds of disabilities, multisensory experiences. Displays of library materials related to the exhibit.

Read: Chapters 5 (Step 4), and 6 (1.2–1.3)

Also read: *Smithsonian Guidelines for Accessible Exhibition Design*

Assignment: 1) Brainstorm (and write down) a list of ways to present your exhibit theme in a multisensory manner. 2) Develop an initial written plan for what will "happen" in your exhibit. 3) If your exhibit is hands-on, make the fist prototype of the interactive parts.

6.	TBA	Exhibit design and conservation

Topics: Materials used in exhibits. Types of mounts and supports and installations methods. The principles and elements of design. How can design support the big idea? Physical accessibility of exhibits. Exhibit safety. Conservation considerations. Lighting. Location and traffic patterns.

Read: Chapters 5 (Step 5), and 6 (1.3)

Also read: Williams' *The Non-Designers Design Book*

Assignment: 1) If you are displaying items, research their conservation needs and write a conservation plan for your exhibit. 2) Sketch an initial design for your exhibit including layouts with room for labels, colors, materials, lighting, etc. and do a fast and dirty prototype to find major flaws.

7.	TBA	Labels

Topics: Kinds of labels. What makes a successful label? Writing and prototyping labels. Label design and accessibility. Label purpose and location. Images and copyright. Graphics applications and sending labels to outside printers.

Read: Chapters 5 (Step 6), 6 (2.1–2.2), and 7

Also read: Serrell's *Exhibit Labels*

Assignment: 1) Write the first draft label copy for your exhibit. Edit with help from others. 2) Design and create prototypes of the labels for your exhibit. (Use of a graphics application such as Adobe Photoshop for certain kinds of labels is encouraged.)

8.   TBA   Prototypes and formative evaluation

Topics: Creating a prototype: materials and methods. Testing the prototype. Successful interview questions for evaluation. Evaluation of exhibit accessibility, safety, conservation, and lighting.

Read: Chapters 5 (Step 7), and 6 (2.3–2.4)

Assignment: 1) Create a prototype of your exhibit and observe people using it. Make a written list of questions about the exhibit and interview people using it. Adjust prototype as necessary and start over until satisfied. Write a list of things you changed as a result of prototyping. 2) Create a scale drawing for the final layout/design of the exhibit.

9.   TBA   Exhibit fabrication and installation

Topics: Label fabrication. Installation techniques and materials. Exhibit maintenance.

Read: Chapters 5 (Step 8), and 6 (3.1–3.3)

Assignment: Practice fabricating labels. Practice fabricating and installing other exhibit parts.

10.   TBA   Publicity and programming

Topics: Kinds of publicity, events, and programming.

Read: Chapters 5 (Step 9), and 6 (1.9–1.10, 2.9–2.10, 3.9–3.10, 4.9–4.10)

Assignment: 1) Create a schedule of programs to go with your exhibit. Write a plan for each program detailing how it relates to the exhibit, its objectives, its timeframe, its audience, where it will take place, the staff required to conduct it, what supplies will be needed, the best places for it to be advertised, and the methods of evaluation. 2) Research and make a list of the best places in your community to advertise your exhibit and create a publicity plan that fits your budget. 3) Write a press release for your exhibit. Design a poster for your exhibit using a graphics application such as Adobe Illustrator.

11.   TBA   Summative evaluation and the overall Library Exhibits Program

Topics: Visitor interviews, surveys, and observation. Evaluating the right thing — your objectives. Documenting the exhibit. Evaluating the budget and staff time estimates. Has the exhibit impacted or benefited the library? Library exhibit policies and staff position descriptions. Should we let outside organizations create exhibits? Challenged exhibits. Museum-library partnerships. Cultivating outside resources: accessibility and conservation advisors, sponsors, volunteers, etc. Annual exhibit calendars.

Read: Chapters 5 (Step 10), 6 (4.1–4.4), 9, and 10

Assignment: 1) Create a list of questions for evaluative interviews that can show how successfully your exhibit has met its objectives. 2) Write a brief description of the documentation methods you will use for your exhibit.

Policies

As a student in this course, you will

- Assume responsibility for your learning
- Use the provided learning guides and resources; conduct information searches when necessary
- Manage your time effectively (plan a schedule and practice time management)
- Ask for assistance from your mentor when you need it; avoid unnecessary frustration and confusion
- Remain active in class and reading and practice activities
- Prepare all work at professional performance levels

Evaluation

Whether you are completing a program of study through an instructor-lead course or through self-study, you will want to evaluate the learning gained from your efforts.

You should evaluate four aspects of the course: your reactions to the course, the learning that took place through the course, job-related behavioral changes as a result of the course, and benefits your job may have derived from your continuing education studies. At the end of this chapter you will find Survey Concerning *Exhibits in Libraries* Course to help you in this evaluation.

We would love to hear about your experience learning with this book. If you are willing to share your experience, we would love to hear from you. You may send a copy of the completed survey to us at:

Mary E. Brown and Rebecca Power
(Exhibits in Libraries Survey)

Department of Information and Library Science
Southern Connecticut State University
501 Crescent St.
New Haven, CT 06515

How to Study for This Course

For each unit, you need to prepare in three ways: complete all assigned readings, write a brief summary or outline of key points or highlight key points directly in the text; and list questions which grow from the reading or from gaps in the reading's coverage; gather information and materials for the assignments; review notes and list any questions which grow from the assignment or from gaps in the reading's coverage and the tasks in the assignment.

For each hour you spend in the classroom, you should plan to spend a minimum of three hours in study outside the classroom. As each unit is planned to contain approximately two-and-a-half to three hours of reading and study time, you should spend a minimum of seven and a half hours in focused activities (work on assignments) for each unit of this course.

Success in self-study takes planning. Devise a study space where you can work uninterrupted. Gather materials you will need before you begin your study or assignment session. Schedule your study/work time, don't plan to fit it into spare moments or steal it out of time you have scheduled for other activities. Develop a network of family, friends, colleagues you can call upon for help.

Learning Tools

You, the student, are the center of the learning process. While your professor can provide you with the guidance and materials that you need to succeed, it is your responsibility to set goals, plan your work, make notes from readings, and schedule the time you will need to complete assignments.

Developing good study skills can not only save you time and energy, but can also help you learn better, independently, and with less guess work.

This section outlines the effective study skills that will promote learning.

- Self-management
- Set learning goals
- Plan and organize a schedule with ample time for reading, studying, reviewing, and preparing assignments
- Adjust your schedule as the course progresses
- Break down work into manageable units
- Pace the course workload evenly
- Use a study/work location free of distractions
- Review periodically
- Set incentives or rewards for the completion of a section

Reading to Learn

1. Determine the purpose for reading (general ideas, structure an argument, scrutiny of detail, inference, applications); adjust speed and process accordingly.

2. Preview for the text (titles, subheadings, maps, photos, summaries, intro) to help you understand and organize the concepts you will be reading.

3. Question the text (formulate questions about the text by changing headings into questions; after reading the section, answer the formulated question; what new questions are raised).

4. First reading: concentrate on major ideas, underline, highlight, or outline them; do not focus on details.

5. Reread to check understanding; summarize main ideas of each section by restating the concepts in your own words. If you are confused, go back and reread the part you don't fully understand. Make notes, margin notes, or underline key phrases. Visualize the information as you read it, relating it to something you already know; read out loud or think aloud, and discuss the reading with someone else.

6. Review the information in the text by rereading your notes, questions, and any exercises that have been assigned; use index cards to review key terms, recite the information out loud, and explain the information to someone else.

Making Useful Notes

1. Before class complete assigned readings and make an organized set of notes; include questions raised by the readings

2. During class take notes from the lecture selectively

3. After class rewrite notes to include new insights and questions raised

4. Periodically review and rewrite notes to clarify issues

Useful Notes

- Summarizing: after reading a section, it is helpful to summarize what you have just read in your own words. The act of writing this information helps you to remember it. Of course, the notes will be valuable later in reviewing for tests. Aside from writing paraphrased notes, you can also create graphic organizers like outlines, flowcharts, and trees (hierarchical and metaphorical).
- Concept maps: start by placing the central idea in the middle of a piece of paper. Add related ideas and draw lines to them from the central idea. Each idea can be further subdivided. The lines represent the relationships among the ideas, so you can draw any number of lines and the map can have any shape.
- Underlining: underline the main ideas; this is the process of deciding which information in the reading is worth underlining. Avoid the common pitfall of underlining everything and anything. Be selective and underline only relevant information in short segments.

This course syllabus is based on Judith Grunert's *The course syllabus: A learning-centered approach* (Anker Publishing Company, Bolton, MA, 1997, ISBN 1882982185), which includes samples for Learning Tools.

Continuing Education Syllabus

If a continuing education course is to be offered for a specific staff or library system, it is advisable to first conduct a needs assessment based on current knowledge and skills in the group compared to the topics suggested in the syllabus. To assist you in the needs assessment, we include the following sample questionnaire which seeks the attitude toward training (question 1), current knowledge and skills (question 2), preferred way to learn (question 3), willingness to learn (question 4), readiness to use technology (question 5), and preferred level of presentation (question 6). The responses to these questions will allow the course instructor to develop materials and explanations that better match background of participants.

Needs Assessment Survey

In preparation for the upcoming continuing education course *Exhibits in Libraries* we request that you complete the following questionnaire. The information gathered from completed surveys will be used to refine the course to better match the group's current knowledge and skills and methods of presenting material. Please do not write your name on the survey.

1. Please place a checkmark (⅜) next to each of the following skills and knowledge areas you feel are important to possess in order to create a successful exhibit in the library:

___ time management
___ money management
___ business considerations (added visibility, visitor needs, budget needs)
___ purpose and theme
___ exhibit theory
___ educational theory
___ exhibit and label design
___ spatial considerations
___ evaluation
___ accessibility
___ conservation
___ application of retail techniques
___ fabrication and installation techniques
___ exhibit programming and accompanying materials
___ methods of publicity

2. Please place a checkmark (✓) next to each of the following skills and knowledge areas you feel you already possess sufficiently to create a successful exhibit in the library:

___ time management
___ money management

__ business considerations (added visibility, visitor needs, budget needs)
__ purpose and theme
__ exhibit theory
__ educational theory
__ exhibit and label design
__ spatial considerations
__ evaluation
__ accessibility
__ conservation
__ application of retail techniques
__ fabrication and installation techniques
__ exhibit programming and accompanying materials
__ methods of publicity

3. When you need to gain new knowledge or learn a new skill, in which of the following ways would you prefer to learn:

__ read a book about the knowledge or skill
__ listen to someone talk explain the knowledge or skill
__ complete a project that demonstrates the knowledge or skill

4. Which of the following best describes the Exhibits in Libraries continuing education course?

__ attendance is voluntary
__ attendance is mandatory
__ attendance is mandatory but I attend voluntarily

5. Which of the following best describes your feelings toward using technology in preparing materials?

__ I do not use technology as I have few skills/experience with it
__ I would like to use technology but need instruction in its use
__ I use technology where ever possible and learn new technology easily

6. The highest level of education I completed or attended is:

__ high school __ undergraduate ___ graduate

Syllabus 2: A Continuing Education Course in Curating and Creating Exhibits in Libraries

Letter to the Student

Welcome to Exhibits in Libraries, a continuing education course designed to give you a hands-on learning experience in learning to plan and create exhibits in libraries.

During this course you will explore the following topics: kinds of exhibits, exhibit and education theory, audience and exhibit theme, budget and other administrative details, exhibit development and accessibility, exhibit design and conservation, exhibit labels, exhibit prototypes and formative evaluation, exhibit fabrication and installation, and publicity and programming.

We have tried to do two major things in the course: to introduce you to the mechanics of mounting an exhibit in a library and a bit of the theory backing those mechanics, and to create a study experience that will be enjoyable and result in significant improvements in your ability and/or confidence to mount successful exhibits in libraries.

We hope you enjoy this course. It should be a busy but fun experience. It requires you to read in this book and provides suggestions for additional readings. It also requires you to apply the readings to problem (such as identifying and planning an exhibit). It requires problem solving and, at times a bit of imagination. You will need to manage your time and resources closely. We are very excited about this course and look forward to hearing about your accomplishments.

Welcome!

Purpose of the Course

This four-week continuing education course will train librarians and library staff to curate and create exhibits in their libraries by teaching the basic background and skills needed for exhibit work including exhibit and education theory; kinds of purposes of, and theme of exhibits; exhibit budgets and other administrative aspects; exhibit design and development; exhibit prototyping and evaluation; accessibility; conservation; exhibit labels; exhibit fabrication; and publicity and programming for exhibits. Each of the four two hour sessions will emphasize the practice of exhibit skills. Students are requested to come to the first class with some ideas of exhibits they might like to do or are planning to do at their library. These ideas will be the basis for the our class assignments.

Course Description

Study of the techniques, management, and assessment of exhibit work; and exhibit and education theory.

Course Objectives

When you have completed this course, you should be able to:

- Define the goals of an exhibit
- Establish timelines and budgets for an exhibit
- Select appropriate exhibit materials, including labels, for various age groups
- Discuss exhibit and learning theory as it applies to planning exhibits
- Assess through formative and summative evaluations the exhibit process
- Demonstrate an ability to construct and document an exhibit prototype

- Evaluate an exhibit for physical and intellectual accessibility
- Write an exhibit conservation plan
- Write a publicity plan, exhibit press release and poster

Course Requirements

- Reading material on techniques in exhibit work, available in this text
- Preparing a series of assignments that lead to an exhibit
- Completing a series of assessments of the emerging exhibit prototype.

Resources

Required Text

Brown, Mary E., and Rebecca Power. *Exhibits in Libraries: A practical guide* (Jefferson, NC: McFarland, 2005).

Recommended Texts

Serrell, Beverly. *Exhibits labels: An interpretive approach* (Walnut Creek, CA: Altamira Press, 1996).

Smithsonian Accessibility Program. *Smithsonian guidelines for accessible exhibition design* (2nd ed., 1996). Washington, DC: Smithsonian Institute Press.

(Available free from *www.si.edu/opa/accessibility/exdesign/* or by writing Smithsonian Accessibility Program, Smithsonian Institution, Arts and Industries Building, Arts and Industries Building, Room 1239 MRC 426, Washington, DC 20560; calling (202) 786-2942 or TTY (202) 786-2414; or e-mailing majewskj@si.edu).)

Williams, Robin. *The non-designers design book: Design and typographic principles for the visual novice*, 2nd ed. (Berkeley, CA: Peachpitt Press, 2004).

Course Outline

Week 1

Topics

Introduction and kinds of exhibits: What is an exhibit? What are the goals of an exhibit? Kinds of exhibits. Exhibit locations.

Exhibit and education theory: How do people learn from exhibits? What makes a good exhibit? Creating successful objectives for exhibits.

Audience and exhibit theme: Front-end evaluation and your audience. The big idea.

Before Class

Read: Chapters 1–4, 5 (Steps 1–2), and 6 (1.1–1.5) in Brown and Power

In Class:

Discussion of participants' current experience with exhibits in their libraries.

Identify the goals of the exhibit you will create for this class. What kind of exhibit would you like to make/design?

Choose a theme for your exhibit.

Create front-end evaluation questions about your topic with which to analyze your audience

Assignments

Analyze your library for potential exhibit spaces. Record the details of these spaces including description, dimensions, lighting, accessibility, etc.

Interview library visitors using your front-end evaluation questions.

Narrow your exhibit theme. Write down the "big idea" and the exhibit objectives.

Week 2

Topics

Budget and other administrative details

Exhibit costs and staff time. Creating a budget. Contracts, insurance, and security.

Exhibit development and accessibility

What story does an exhibit tell? Will items be on display? What will the visitor do or experience? How do we engage visitors and make them think? Accessibility: visitor backgrounds, kinds of disabilities, multi-sensory experiences. Displays of library materials related to the exhibit.

Exhibit design and conservation

Materials used in exhibits. The principles and elements of design. How can design support the big idea? Physical accessibility of exhibits. Exhibit safety. Conservation considerations. Lighting.

Before Class

Read: Chapters 5 (Steps 3–5), 6 (1.2–1.8, 2.5–2.8, 3.4–3.7, 4.5–4.8), and 8 in Brown and Power

In Class

Brainstorm ways to present your exhibit theme in a multisensory manner.

Begin to develop an initial plan for what will "happen" in your exhibit.

Begin to sketch an initial design for your exhibit including layouts with room for label, colors, materials, lighting, etc.

Assignments

Estimate staff time and begin a budget for your exhibit.

Continue the design and development of your exhibit. Try to get far enough to begin writing labels next week.

Do a fast and dirty prototype in the exhibit's location to find major flaws.

To Bring Next Week

Materials you want to use in your exhibit. This can be items that will be interpreted (photos, artifacts, etc.), an interactive device, collection materials that will be displayed, and decorative props and materials.

Week 3

Topics
Labels: Kinds of labels. What makes a successful label? Writing and prototyping labels. Label design and accessibility. Label purpose and location.

Prototypes and formative evaluation: Creating and testing a prototype. Successful interview questions for evaluation. Evaluation of exhibit accessibility, safety, conservation, and lighting.

Before Class
Read: Chapters 5 (Steps 6–7), 6 (2.1–2.4), and 7 in Brown and Power

In Class
Begin writing label copy for your exhibit. Edit with help from others.
Create a basic label prototype.
Create a prototype of your exhibit (or a small part of your exhibit). Make a written list of questions about the exhibit and interview class members about it. Adjust prototype as necessary.

Assignments
Design and create prototypes of the labels for your exhibit.

Week 4

Topics
Exhibit fabrication and installation: Label fabrication. Installation techniques and materials. Exhibit maintenance.

Summative evaluation: Visitor interviews, surveys, and observations. Evaluating the right thing — your objectives. Documenting the exhibit.

Publicity and programming: Kinds of publicity, events, and programming.

Library exhibits program: Library exhibit policies and staff position descriptions. Museum-library partnerships. Cultivating outside resources: accessibility and conservation advisors, sponsors, volunteers, etc.

Before Class
Read: Chapters 5 (Steps 8–10), 6 (1.9–1.10, 2.9–2.10, 3.1–3.3, 3.8–3.10, 4.1–4.4, 4.9–4.10), 9, and 10 in Brown and Power

In Class
Practice fabricating labels.
Write summative evaluation questions that can show how successfully your exhibit has met its objectives.
Brainstorm a list of places in your community to advertise your exhibit (guided by the exhibit theme).

Policies

As a student in this continuing education course, you will

- assume responsibility for your learning
- use the provided learning guides and resources; conduct information searches when necessary
- manage your time effectively (plan a schedule and practice time management)
- ask for assistance from your course instructor when you need it; avoid unnecessary frustration and confusion
- remain active in class and reading and practice activities
- prepare all work at professional performance levels

Evaluation

Whether you are completing a program of study through a voluntary continuing education course offered outside your library or required professional development course offered within your library system, you will want to evaluate the learning gained from your efforts. If your library is financing the course, they may also want to evaluate the student learning and institutional benefit gained compared to the cost of attending or sponsoring the course. The following survey can be used by the student for a self-assessment or by the library for a cost-benefit assessment.

You should evaluate four different aspects of the course: your reactions to the course, the learning that took place through the course, job-related behavioral changes as a result of the course, and benefits your job may have derived from your continuing education studies. At the end of this chapter you will find Survey Concerning *Exhibits in Libraries* Course to help you in this evaluation.

We would love to hear about your group's experience learning in a workshop designed around this book. If you are willing to share your experience, we would love to hear from you. You may send a copy of the completed surveys or a compilation of the response of a whole class to us at:

> Mary E. Brown and Rebecca Power
> (Exhibits in Libraries Survey)
> Department of Information and Library Science
> Southern Connecticut State University
> 501 Crescent St.
> New Haven, CT 06515

How to Study for This Course

For each weekly unit, you need to prepare in three ways: complete all assigned readings, write a brief summary or outline of key points or highlight key points directly in the text; and list questions which grow from the reading or from gaps in the reading's coverage; gather information and materials for the assignments; review notes and list any questions which grow from the assignment or from gaps in the reading's coverage and the tasks in the assignment.

Each weekly unit is planned to contain approximately two hours of in-class time. In addition you will need to plan for reading and study time before each class (to read assigned chapters in this text) and you should plan to spend some time after each class reviewing needed sections of the text. You should spend a minimum of five to eight hours in focused activities (work on assignments) for each weekly unit of this course.

Success in continuing education courses takes planning. Devise a study space where you can work uninterrupted. Gather materials you will need before you begin your study or assignment session. Schedule your study/work time, don't plan to fit it into spare moments or steal it out of time you have scheduled for other activities. Develop a network of family, friends, colleagues you can call upon for help.

Learning Tools

You, the student, are the center of the learning process. While your instructor can provide you with the guidance and materials that you need to succeed, it is your responsibility to set goals, plan your work, make notes from readings, and schedule the time you will need to complete assignments.

Developing good study skills can not only save you time and energy, but can also help you learn better, independently, and with less guess work.

This section outlines the effective study skills that will promote learning.

Self-management

- Set learning goals
- Plan and organize a schedule with ample time for reading, studying, reviewing, and preparing assignments
- Adjust your schedule as the course progresses
- Break down work into manageable units
- Pace the course workload evenly
- Use a study/work location free of distractions
- Review periodically
- Set incentives or rewards for the completion of a section

Reading to Learn

1. Determine the purpose for reading (general ideas, structure an argument, scrutiny of detail, inference, applications); adjust speed and process accordingly.

2. Preview for the text (titles, subheadings, maps, photos, summaries, intro) to help you understand and organize the concepts you will be reading.

3. Question the text (formulate questions about the text by changing headings into questions; after reading the section, answer the formulated question; what new questions are raised).

4. First reading: concentrate on major ideas, underline, highlight, or outline them; do not focus on details.

5. Reread to check understanding; summarize main ideas of each section by restating the concepts in your own words. If you are confused, go back and reread the part you don't fully understand. Make notes, margin notes, or underline key phrases. Visualize the information as you read it, relating it to something you already know; read out loud or think aloud, and discuss the reading with someone else.

6. Review the information in the text by rereading your notes, questions, and any exercises that have been assigned; use index cards to review key terms, recite the information out loud, and explain the information to someone else.

Making Useful Notes

1. Prior to class complete assigned readings and make an organized set of notes; include questions raised by the readings

2. During class take notes from the lecture selectively

3. After class rewrite notes to include new insights and questions raised

4. Periodically review and rewrite notes to clarify issues

Useful Notes

- Summarizing: after reading a section, it is helpful to summarize what you have just read in your own words. The act of writing this information helps you to remember it. Of course, the notes will be valuable later in reviewing for tests. Aside from writing paraphrased notes, you can also create graphic organizers like outlines, flowcharts, and trees (hierarchical and metaphorical).

- Concept maps: start by placing the central idea in the middle of a piece of paper. Add related ideas and draw lines to them from the central idea. Each idea can be further subdivided. The lines represent the relationships among each of the ideas, so you can draw any number of lines and the map can have any shape.

- Underlining: underline the main ideas; this is the process of deciding which information in the reading is worth underlining. Avoid the common pitfall of underlining everything and anything. Be selective and underline only relevant information in short segments.

This course syllabus is based on Judith Grunert's *The course syllabus: A learning-centered approach* (Anker Publishing, Bolton, MA, 1997, ISBN 1882982185), which includes samples for Learning Tools.

Syllabus 3: A Graduate Course in Curating and Creating Exhibits in Libraries

Letter to the Student

Welcome to Exhibits in Libraries, a graduate course designed to give you a background in some theories that support exhibit work and a hands-on learning experience in the exhibit process.

During this course you will explore the following topics: kinds of exhibits, exhibit and education theory, audience and exhibit theme, budget and other administrative details, exhibit development and accessibility, exhibit design and conservation, exhibit labels, exhibit prototypes and formative evaluation, exhibit fabrication and installation, and publicity and programming.

Readings, explorations, and assignments have been carefully spaced and timed over the term. It is important that you keep up with the schedule and not fall behind.

We have tried to do two major things in the course: to introduce you to the mechanics of mounting an exhibit in a library and a bit of the theory backing those mechanics, and to create a programmed study experience that will be enjoyable and result in significant improvements in your ability and/or confidence to mount successful exhibits in libraries.

At times this course may feel a bit more challenging than you had anticipated. For those times when frustration should take over, stop and ask yourself these questions: What exactly am I feeling right now? Why am I feeling this way? What do I need to appease this feeling? Once you get to the third answer, devise an action plan.

We hope you enjoy this course. It should be a busy but fun experience. It requires you to read in this book and provides suggestions for additional readings. It also requires you to apply the readings to problem (such as identifying and planning an exhibit). It requires problem solving and, at times a bit of imagination. You will need to manage your time and resources closely. We are very excited about this course and look forward to hearing about your accomplishments.

Welcome!

Purpose of the Course

This course will prepare librarians to curate and create exhibits in their libraries by teaching the basic background and skills needed for exhibit work including exhibit and education theory; kinds of purposes of, and theme of exhibits; exhibit budgets and other administrative aspects; exhibit design and development; exhibit prototyping and evaluation; accessibility; conservation; exhibit labels; exhibit fabrication; and publicity and programming for exhibits. Instruction will emphasize the practice of exhibit skills, relying on lectures only for a brief introduction of topics. Students will follow the exhibit process to design and develop an exhibit. In some cases, the exhibit will be able to be fabricated and possibly displayed by the end of the semester; in the case of large or costly exhibits, concentration will be on the design and prototyping only. (There is a great deal of flexibility in the kinds of exhibits that students can make.)

Course Description

Study of the techniques, management, and assessment of exhibit work, and theories supporting those techniques including exhibit and education theory.

Course Objectives

When you have completed this course, you should be able to:

- Define the goals of an exhibit
- Establish timelines and budgets for an exhibit
- Select appropriate exhibit materials, including labels, for various age groups
- Discuss exhibit and learning theory as it applies to planning exhibits
- Assess through formative and summative evaluations the exhibit process
- Demonstrate an ability to construct and document an exhibit prototype
- Evaluate an exhibit for physical and intellectual accessibility
- Write an exhibit conservation plan
- Write a publicity plan, exhibit press release and poster

Course Requirements

- Reading material on techniques in exhibit work
- Preparing a series of assignments that lead to an exhibit or exhibit prototype
- Completing a series of assessments of the emerging exhibit prototype.

Resources

Required Texts

Brown, Mary E., and Rebecca Power. *Exhibits in libraries: A practical guide* (Jefferson, NC: McFarland, 2005).

Serrell, Beverly. *Exhibits labels: An interpretive approach* (Walnut Creek, CA: Altamira Press, 1996).

Smithsonian Accessibility Program. *Smithsonian guidelines for accessible exhibition design* (2nd ed.), (1996) Washington, DC: Smithsonian Institute Press. (Available free from www.si.edu/opa/accessibility/exdesign/ or by writing Smithsonian Accessibility Program, Smithsonian Institution, Arts and Industries Building, Arts and Industries Building, Room 1239 MRC 426, Washington, DC 20560; calling (202) 786-2942 or TTY (202) 786-2414; or e-mailing majewskj@si.edu).)

Recommended Text

Williams, Robin. *The non-designers design book: Design and typographic principles for the visual novice*, 2nd ed. (Berkeley, CA: Peachpitt Press, 2004).

Course Calendar

Unit	Date	Topics / Reading assignments / Activity assignments

1. TBA Introduction to and kinds of exhibits

Topics: Overview of the course and exhibit process. What is an exhibit? Why have exhibits in libraries? What are the goals of an exhibit? Kinds of exhibits. Which kinds of exhibits belong in libraries? Exhibit locations. Exhibit timeframes.

Read: Chapters 1, 2, and 4

Assignment: Visit a library and analyze it for potential exhibit spaces. Record the details of these spaces including layout (description, dimensions, lighting, accessibility, etc.) in a document that a library could use for future reference when planning exhibits.

2. TBA Exhibit and education theories

Topics: How do people learn from exhibits? What makes a good exhibit? Creating successful objectives for exhibits.

Read: Chapter 3

Assignment: Visit three kinds of museum or library exhibits and observe how visitors interact with them. Write a paper that discusses the positive and negative visitor behaviors at these exhibits and analyzes what about the exhibits seems to affect this behavior: what works, what doesn't work, what might be changed to improve them, etc. (Be sure to include one exhibit of the kind you want to make for this class.)

3. TBA Audience and exhibit theme

Topics: Researching the topic. Front-end evaluation and your audience. The big idea.

Read: Chapters 5 (Steps 1–2), and 6 (1.1–1.5)

Assignment: 1) Choose a theme for your exhibit. Research and think of some possible angles to approach this theme. 2) Analyze your audience. Create (and write down) front-end evaluation questions about your topic and interview library visitors. Write a brief synopsis of what you found during your evaluation. 3) Narrow your exhibit theme. Write down the "big idea" and the exhibit objectives.

4. TBA Budget and other administrative details

Topics: What costs are involved in exhibits? How much staff time is needed? Creating a budget. Finding the money. Contracts for borrowed items. Insurance and security.

Read: Chapters 5 (Step 3), 6 (1.5–1.8, 2.5–2.8, 3.4–3.7, 4.5–4.8), and 8

Assignment: Estimate staff time and create a budget for your exhibit. If you are unsure of what things cost, make some calls — to vendors, museum or library exhibit staff, etc.

5.   TBA   Exhibit development and accessibility

Topics: What story does an exhibit tell? Will items be on display? What will the visitor do or experience? How do we engage visitors and make them think? Accessibility: visitor backgrounds, kinds of disabilities, multisensory experiences. Displays of library materials related to the exhibit.

Read: Chapters 5 (Step 4), and 6 (1.2–1.3)

Also read: *Smithsonian Guidelines for Accessible Exhibition Design*

Assignment: 1) Brainstorm (and write down) a list of ways to present your exhibit theme in a multisensory manner. 2) Develop an initial written plan for what will "happen" in your exhibit. 3) If your exhibit is hands-on, make the fist prototype of the interactive parts.

6.   TBA   Exhibit design and conservation

Topics: Materials used in exhibits. Types of mounts and supports and installations methods. The principles and elements of design. How can design support the big idea? Physical accessibility of exhibits. Exhibit safety. Conservation considerations. Lighting. Location and traffic patterns.

Read: Chapters 5 (Step 5), and 6 (1.3)

Also read: Williams' *The Non-Designers Design Book*

Assignment: 1) If you are displaying items, research their conservation needs and write a conservation plan for your exhibit. 2) Sketch an initial design for your exhibit including layouts with room for labels, colors, materials, lighting, etc. and do a fast and dirty prototype to find major flaws.

7.   TBA   Labels

Topics: Kinds of labels. What makes a successful label? Writing and prototyping labels. Label design and accessibility. Label purpose and location. Images and copyright. Graphics applications and sending labels to outside printers.

Read: Chapters 5 (Step 6), 6 (2.1–2.2), and 7

Also read: Serrell's *Exhibit Labels*

Assignment: 1) Write the first draft label copy for your exhibit. Edit with help from others. 2) Design and create prototypes of the labels for your exhibit. (Use of a graphics application such as Adobe Photoshop for certain kinds of labels is encouraged.)

8.   TBA   Prototypes and formative evaluation

Topics: Creating a prototype: materials and methods. Testing the prototype. Successful interview questions for evaluation. Evaluation of exhibit accessibility, safety, conservation, and lighting.

Read: Chapters 5 (Step 7), and 6 (2.3–2.4)

Assignment: 1) Create a prototype of your exhibit and observe people using it. Make a written list of questions about the exhibit and interview people using it. Adjust prototype as necessary and start over until satisfied. Write a list of things you changed as a result of prototyping. 2) Create a scale drawing for the final layout/design of the exhibit.

9.   TBA   Exhibit fabrication and installation

Topics: Label fabrication. Installation techniques and materials. Exhibit maintenance.

Read: Chapters 5 (Step 8), and 6 (3.1–3.3)

Assignment: Practice fabricating labels. Practice fabricating and installing other exhibit parts.

10.   TBA   Publicity and programming

Topics: Kinds of publicity, events, and programming.

Read: Chapters 5 (Step 9), and 6 (1.9–1.10, 2.9–2.10, 3.9–3.10, 4.9–4.10)

Assignment: 1) Create a schedule of programs to go with your exhibit. Write a plan for each program detailing how it relates to the exhibit, its objectives, its timeframe, its audience, where it will take place, the staff required to conduct it, what supplies will be needed, the best places for it to be advertised, and the methods of evaluation. 2) Research and make a list of the best places in your community to advertise your exhibit and create a publicity plan that fits your budget. 3) Write a press release for your exhibit. Design a poster for your exhibit using a graphics application such as Adobe Illustrator.

11.   TBA   Summative evaluation and the overall Library Exhibits Program

Topics: Visitor interviews, surveys, and observation. Evaluating the right thing — your objectives. Documenting the exhibit. Evaluating the budget and staff time estimates. Has the exhibit impacted or benefited the library? Library exhibit policies and staff position descriptions. Should we let outside organizations create exhibits? Challenged exhibits. Museum-library partnerships. Cultivating outside resources: accessibility and conservation advisors, sponsors, volunteers, etc. Annual exhibit calendars.

Read: Chapters 5 (Step 10), 6 (4.1–4.4), 9, and 10

Assignment: 1) Create a list of questions for evaluative interviews that can show how successfully your exhibit has met its objectives. 2) Write a brief description of the documentation methods you will use for your exhibit.

Policies

As a student in this course, you will

- assume responsibility for your learning
- use the provided learning guides and resources; conduct information searches when necessary
- manage your time effectively (plan a schedule and practice time management)
- ask for assistance when you need it; avoid unnecessary frustration and confusion
- remain active in class and reading and practice activities
- prepare all work at professional performance levels

Evaluation

The final grade for this course will be based on the following assignments:
Attendance and class participation (10 percent)
Assignment on exhibit spaces (5 percent)
Paper on exhibits and visitor behavior (10 percent)
Exhibit portfolio (75 percent)

The exhibit portfolio will include the following

- Exhibit goals
- Exhibit timeline
- Front-end evaluation questions and synopsis of front-end evaluation
- *The big idea and objectives of the exhibit
- *Exhibit budget
- *Ideas for multisensory methods of presenting theme
- Plan for what will "happen" in exhibit (initial)
- Conservation plan or photo of first hands-on prototype
- Exhibit design sketch (initial) and photo of fast prototype
- *Label copy (first draft, revised draft, and any in between drafts)

- *Label designs/prototypes (first design, revised designs, final design)
- *Photos of accurate exhibit prototype, formative evaluation questions, and list of things changed during prototyping
- Exhibit design/layout scale drawing (final)
- Program plans
- Publicity plan and exhibit press release and poster
- *Summative evaluation questions
- Documentation plan

In grading, overall presentation of the portfolio will also be considered.

The seven starred items in the portfolio will be given more weight (approximately twice the weight) than the ten nonstarred items and overall presentation of the portfolio. Some of these items will be used in class on the day they are due, although they will not be turned in until the end of the semester.

Note: A digital camera will be available for loan for photos if needed.

Course Evaluation

Your professor or university may have standard course evaluation forms that are used to evaluate each course. You may also want to evaluate your learning, through this course, about exhibits. The following survey can be used by the student for a self-assessment.

You should evaluate four different aspects of the course: your reactions to the course, the learning that took place through the course, job-related behavioral changes as a result of the course, and benefits your job may have derived from your continuing education studies. At the end of this chapter you will find Survey Concerning *Exhibits in Libraries* Course to help you in this evaluation.

We would love to hear about your experience learning in a class designed around this book. If you are willing to share your experience, we would love to hear from you. You may send a copy of the completed surveys or a compilation of the response of a whole class to us at:

> Mary E. Brown and Rebecca Power
> (Exhibits in Libraries Survey)
> Department of Information and Library Science
> Southern Connecticut State University
> 501 Crescent St.
> New Haven, CT 06515

Grading Procedures

All assignments will be graded on a 6-point scale where 6=Outstanding, 5=Strong, 4=Adequate, 3=Limited, 2=Seriously flawed, 1= Fundamentally deficient, and 0=Unable to evaluate. This scoring convention is after the GRE Scoring Guide. Adapted and in more detail this is:

6, Outstanding: Presents a cogent, well-presented response to the assignment and demonstrates mastery of the elements of effective presentation. The work typically: develops the assignment with insightfulness, sustains a well-focused, well-organized presentation, and expresses ideas clearly and precisely.

5, Strong: Presents a well-developed assignment and demonstrates a strong control of the elements of effective presentation. The work typically: develops the assignment with well-chosen examples, is focused and generally well organized, expresses ideas clearly and well.

4, Adequate: Presents a competent rendering of the assignment. The work typically: develops the assignment with relevant examples, is adequately organized, expresses ideas clearly.

3, Limited: Demonstrates some competence in fulfilling the assignment but is clearly flawed. Exhibits one or more of the following: vague or limited development of the assignment, weak in the use of examples, poorly focused and/or poorly organized, has problems expressing ideas clearly.

2, Seriously flawed: Demonstrates serious weakness in fulfilling the assignment. Exhibits one or more of the following: is unclear or seriously limited in developing the assignment, provides few relevant examples, is unfocused and/or disorganized, contains numerous errors that severely interferes with meaning.

1, Fundamentally deficient: Exhibits one or more of the following: contains numerous errors in content, either of omission or accuracy or both; provides little evidence of the ability to develop or organize a coherent response to the assignment; pervasive pattern of errors that severely interferes with meaning.

0, Unable to be evaluated: Not submitted on time or off assignment or merely copies the assignment.

Class Organization

Each class meets weekly for three hours. Generally, each class will be divided into three sections: professor's lecture and/or discussion of assigned readings; application of lecture and readings to specific existing or emerging exhibits; and peer consulting/critiquing of student assignments.

Special Needs

As a student with a disability, before you may receive accommodations in this class, you will need to make an appointment with the Disability Resource Center, located [instructor fill in]. To speak with me about accommodations, or other concerns, such as medical emergencies or arrangements in case the building must be evacuated, please make an appointment as soon as possible. My office location and hours are: [instructor fill in].

How to Study for This Course

For each unit, you need to prepare in three ways: complete all assigned readings, write a brief summary or outline of key points or highlight key points directly in the text; and list questions which grow from the reading or from gaps in the reading's coverage; gather information and materials for the assignments; review notes and list any questions which grow from the assignment or from gaps in the reading's coverage and the tasks in the assignment.

For each hour you spend in the classroom, you should plan to spend a minimum of three hours in study outside the classroom. This means each week you should spend a minimum of nine hours in focused study for this course. The exhibit project you choose to create for this course may require additional time.

Success in graduate courses takes planning. Devise a study space where you can work uninterrupted. Gather materials you will need before you begin your study or assignment session. Schedule your study/work time, don't plan to fit it into spare moments or steal it out of time you have scheduled for other activities. Develop a network of classmates, family, friends, and colleagues you can call upon for help.

Learning Tools

You, the student, are the center of the learning process. While your professor can provide you with the guidance and materials that you need to succeed, it is your responsibility to set goals, plan your work, make notes from readings, lectures and discussions, and schedule the time you will need to complete assignments.

Developing good study skills can not only save you time and energy, but can also help you learn better, independently, and with less guess work.

This section outlines the effective study skills that will promote learning.

Self-management

- Set learning goals
- Plan and organize a schedule with ample time for reading, studying, reviewing, and preparing (studying) for tests
- Adjust your schedule as the course progresses
- Break down work into manageable units
- Pace the course workload evenly
- Use a study location free of distractions
- Review periodically
- Set incentives or rewards for the completion of a section

Reading to Learn

1. Determine the purpose for reading (general ideas, structure an argument, scrutiny of detail, inference, applications); adjust speed and process accordingly.

2. Preview for the text (titles, subheadings, maps, photos, summaries, intro) to help you understand and organize the concepts you will be reading.

3. Question the text (formulate questions about the text by changing headings into questions; after reading the section, answer the formulated question; what new questions are raised).

4. First reading: concentrate on major ideas, underline, highlight, or outline them; do not focus on details.

5. Reread to check understanding; summarize main ideas of each section by restating the concepts in your own words. If you are confused, go back and reread the part you don't fully understand. Make notes, margin notes, or underline key phrases. Visualize the information as you read it, relating it to something you already know; read out loud or think aloud, and discuss the reading with someone else.

6. Review the information in the text by rereading your notes, questions, and any exercises that have been assigned; use index cards to review key terms, recite the information out loud, and explain the information to someone else.

Making Useful Notes

1. Prior to class complete assigned readings and make an organized set of notes; include questions raised by the readings
2. During class take notes from the lecture selectively
3. After class rewrite notes to include new insights and questions raised
4. Periodically review and rewrite notes to clarify issues

Useful Notes

- Summarizing: after reading a section, it is helpful to summarize what you have just read in your own words. The act of writing this information helps you to remember it. Of course, the notes will be valuable later in reviewing for tests. Aside from writing paraphrased notes, you can also create graphic organizers like outlines, flowcharts, and trees (hierarchical and metaphorical).
- Concept maps: start by placing the central idea in the middle of a piece of paper. Add related ideas and draw lines to them from the central idea. Each idea can be further subdivided. The lines represent the relationships among each of the ideas, so you can draw any number of lines and the map can have any shape.
- Underlining: underline the main ideas; this is the process of deciding which information in the reading is worth underlining. Avoid the common pitfall of underlining everything and anything. Be selective and underline only relevant information in short segments.

Studying with Others

One of the best ways of learning is to study with someone else. Get to know one or more students enrolled in this course and work together. After a reading assignment, review the answers to any questions you have been given and discuss what you believe were the major points. Test each other on specific knowledge. Or try explaining what you are trying to learn to a friend who has never studied the subject. Your understanding of the material is clarified when you must present ideas so that others can understand them. Studying with others has been shown to be one of the most effective ways to study and learn.

This course syllabus is based on Judith Grunert's *The course syllabus: A learning-centered approach* (Anker Publishing Company, Bolton, MA, 1997, ISBN 1882982185), which includes samples for Learning Tools.

Survey Concerning Exhibits in Libraries Course

Directions: Please indicate your agreement with each of the following statements.

1. Course Satisfaction

1.1 The authors seem knowledgeable about the subject matter.

__ Strongly agree __ Agree __ Don't know __ Disagree __ Strongly disagree

1.2 The material in the book and exercises in the course were relevant to my information needs about mounting exhibits in libraries.

__ Strongly agree __ Agree __ Don't know __ Disagree __ Strongly disagree

1.3 The skills and knowledge I gained through this course will assist me in planning and creating exhibits in the library.

__ Strongly agree __ Agree __ Don't know __ Disagree __ Strongly disagree

Please include any additional comments on satisfaction with the course.

2. Learning Appraisal

2.1 Compared to my beliefs before beginning this course, I now feel more strongly that exhibits are within the scope of library services/programs and can support the library's mission.

__ Strongly agree __ Agree __ Don't know __ Disagree __ Strongly disagree

2.2 Compared to my knowledge before beginning this course, I now feel more familiar with the history of exhibits and theories supporting exhibit techniques.

__ Strongly agree __ Agree __ Don't know __ Disagree __ Strongly disagree

2.3 Compared to my knowledge before beginning this course, I now feel more familiar with the skills of exhibits planning and creation.

__ Strongly agree __ Agree __ Don't know __ Disagree __ Strongly disagree

Please include any additional comments on learning that took place through the course.

3. Behavioral Changes

3.1 Compared to my motivation before beginning this course, I now feel more inclined to plan and create exhibits for the library.

__ Strongly agree __ Agree __ Don't know __ Disagree __ Strongly disagree

3.2 Compared to my knowledge and skills before beginning this course, I now feel I know what to do and how to do it in planning and creating exhibits for the library.

__ Strongly agree __ Agree __ Don't know __ Disagree __ Strongly disagree

3.3 Compared to the climate in my library before I begin this course, I now feel library staff are more supportive of planning and creating exhibits for the library.

__ Strongly agree __ Agree __ Don't know __ Disagree __ Strongly disagree

3.4 Compared to the recognition in my library before I begin this course, I now feel library staff view me as capable planner and creator for exhibits for the library.

__ Strongly agree __ Agree __ Don't know __ Disagree __ Strongly disagree

Please include any additional comments on behavioral changes that took place through the course.

4. Final Results

4.1 Compared to the exhibits in my library before I begin this course, I now feel visitors view exhibits in the library as more attractive and more informative.

__ Strongly agree __ Agree __ Don't know __ Disagree __ Strongly disagree

4.2 Compared to the costs of completing this course (books, materials, time of those involved), I believe my library has received greater benefit in my new skills and knowledge in planning and creating exhibits in my library.

__ Strongly agree __ Agree __ Don't know __ Disagree __ Strongly disagree

Please include any additional comments on improved performance of your library that took place through the course.

What did you like best about learning with this book about exhibits in libraries?

How can future self-study with Exhibits in Libraries be improved, in particular was anything lacking?

Chapter Notes

1. Exhibits from Beginnings to Libraries

1. Norman Douglas, *London Street Games* (Folcroft, PA: Folcroft Library Editions, 1931). *Project Gutenberg of Australia* <http://gutenberg.net.au/ebooks03/0300281.txt> (28 November 2004).

2. Kenneth W. Luckhurst, *The Story of Exhibitions* (New York: Studio Publications, 1951), p. 9.

3. Douglas.

4. Luckhurst, p. 9.

5. "Cabinets of Curiosity: Sites of Knowledge." *Microcosms: Objects of Knowledge (A University Collection)* <http://microcosms.ihc.ucsb.edu/essays/002.html> (2 June 2004).

6. Susan F. Saidenberg, "Displaying Our Wealth: Exhibitions Make an Auspicious Comeback," *American Libraries* 22, no. 2 (1991): pp. 128–131.

7. Erma Loveland, "Library Exhibits," 28 October 1993, <exlibris@library.berkeley.edu> (15 December 2002).

8. Tom Beck, "Library Exhibits," 2 November 1993, <exlibris@library.berkeley.edu> (15 December 2002).

9. Saidenberg, p. 128.

10. Saidenberg.

11. Saidenberg.

12. Sarah Funke, "Who's That Curator? The Role of Exhibitions in Shaping Curators and Their Collections," unpublished manuscript, Palmer School, Long Island University, 2000.

13. Funke.

14. Funke, p. 10.

15. Funke, p. 10.

16. Funke, p. 9.

17. Judith Dobrzynski, "Glory Days for the Art Museum," *New York Times*, 5 October 1997, sec. 2. quoted in Roger Kimball, "The New Museum: Entertainment or Political Theater?" *New Criterion* 16, no. 3 (1997): pp. 77–80.

18. Cathleen Towey, "We Need to Recommit to Readers' Advisory Services," *American Libraries* 28, no. 11 (1997): p. 31.

19. Sandy Whiteley, "What do I read next?" *American Libraries* 24, no. 10 (1993): 954.

20. Funke, p. 10.

21. Wayne A. Wiegand, "What American Studies Can Teach the Library and Information Studies Community about the Library in the Life of the User," *American Studies Association Newsletter* 26, no. 1 (2003): pp. 2–3.

22. Wiegand.

23. Tony Bennett, *The Birth of the Museum: History, Theory, Politics* (New York: Routledge, 1995).

24. Erma Loveland, "Library Exhibits," 28 October 1993, <exlibris@library.berkeley.edu> (15 December 2002).

25. George M. Eberhart, "Gay-pride Exhibit Recalled, Reinstalled at Anchorage PL, *American Libraries* 32, no. 7 (2001): p. 14.

26. Alden Todd, "Exhibiting Censorship in the City of Lights and Flowers," *American Libraries* 33, no. 7 (2002): p. 47.

27. Enid Schidkrout. (1999). "Challenging Exhibitions," *African Arts* 32, no. 3 (1999): 1.

28. Schidkrout, p. 2.

29. "Go Figure!," <www.boulder.lib.co.us/calendar/gofigure/> (28 May 2004).

30. "Make It Move" (A Hands-on Exhibit), <www.boulder.lib.co.us/calendar/gofigure/makeitmove.html> (28 May 2004).

31. Kathryn Graves, "Lost in the Library? Stop Floundering — Follow the Fish," *College & Research Libraries News* 54, no. 7 (1993): pp. 384–385.

32. Rosanna Miller, "Sherlock Detected," *College & Research Libraries News* 52, no. 1 (1991): pp. 12–14.

33. Martha Wilson and Marilyn Flachman. "Help Yourself, It's Free," *School Library Journal* 31, no. 2 (1984): p. 115.

34. "Microcosms: Objects of Knowledge (A University Collects)," <http://microcosms.ihc.ucsb.edu/index.html> (28 May 2004).

2. Exhibit Theory

1. G. Ellis Burcaw, *Introduction to Museum Work*, 3rd ed. (Walnut Creek CA: AltaMira Press, 1997), p. 24.

2. Michael H. Harris, *History of Libraries in the Western World*, compact textbook ed. (Metuchen NJ: Scarecrow Press, 1984), p. 12.

3. "Ancient Greek and Roman Libraries," Internet Encyclopedia of Philosophy, 2001 <www.utm.edu/research/iep/l/library.htm>.

4. Kevin Flude, "The Origins & Development of Museums," prepared for Central Saint Martin's College of Art & Design <www.chr.org.uk/Museums/museumindex.htm>.

5. Burcaw. *Also see* Harris.

6. Burcaw, p. 56

7. "Library," Britannica Concise Encyclopedia <*www.britannica.com/ebc/article?eu=395477*> (11 May 2004).

8. "Museum," Britannica Concise Encyclopedia. <*www.britannica.com/ebc/article?eu=395477*> (11 May 2004).

9. John Veverka, "Using interpretive themes and objectives will make your program planning easier and more effective" <www.heritageinterp.com/developing_theme_and_objectives.htm> (10 April 2004).

10. John Veverka, "Tips and concepts for planning truly 'interpretive' exhibits" Retrieved April 10, 2004 <www.geographie.uni-freiburg.de/ipg/forschung/ap6/interpret-europe/Downloads/publications/exhibits.pdf> (10 April 2004).

11. Burcaw.

12. Burcaw, pp. 58–59.

13. F.W.C., "Review," *Lowell Courier Citizen*, Saturday, May 10, 1924 <www.concordart.org/oldnews/1924.html>.

14. Beverly Serrell, *Exhibit labels: An interpretive approach* (Walnut Creek, CA: AltaMira Press 1996), p. 1.

15. Serrell.

16. Althea Dotzour, Capree Houston, Grace Manubay, Jenifer Smith, and Kathy Schultz, "Can a exhibit cause environmentally responsible behavior? Three methods of evaluating a behavior change exhibit" (University of Michigan 2002) <www.snre.umich.edu/eplab/research/brookfield/VSA_poster_2002.pdf

17. Veverka, "Tips and Concepts."

18. Veverka, "Tips and Concepts."

19. Veverka, "Using Interpretive Themes."

20. Veverka, "Using Interpretive Themes."

21. Veverka, "Tips and Concepts."

22. Veverka, "Tips and Concepts."

23. Veverka, "Tips and Concepts."

24. Veverka, "Tips and Concepts."

25. Center for Universal Design, "The Principles of Universal Design," NC State University, 1997 <www.design.ncsu.edu:8120/cud/univ_design/princ_overview.htm

26. Michael J. Crosbie and Peter A. Stratton, "Designing for Accessibility Doesn't Have To Be Expensive or Complex," *Architectural Record*, 187, no. 3 (1999), p. 22.

27. Center for Universal Design.

28. National Center for Chronic Disease Prevention and Health Promotion, "Data and Statistics" <www.cdc.gov/nccdphp/dnpa/surveill.htm>.

29. Museum of Science, Boston, "A juggling act" <www.mos.org/exhibitdevelopment/access/consider.html>.

30. Museum of Science, Boston, "Universal Design (Accessibility)" 2001 <www.mos.org/exhibitdevelopment/access/index.html>.

31. Museum of Science, Boston, "General Consideration — for everyone" <www.mos.org/exhibitdevelopment/access/consider.html>.

32. Burcaw.

33. Robert Gardner, *Make an Interactive Science Museum: Hands-On Exhibits* (New York: TAB Books 1996), p. 3.

34. Gardner, viii–ix.

35. Museum of Science and Industry, "Exhibits" <www.msichicago.org/exhibit/exhome.html> (21 January 2005).

36. Gardner.

37. Gardner, p. 9.

38. Idaho Museum of Natural History, "Exhibits" <http://imnh.isu.edu/Main/Exhibits.htm> (21 January 2005).

39. Gardner, p. 43.

40. St. Louis Children's Museum, "For Baby and Me" <www.magichouse.com/HTML/handson.htm>.

41. Gardner, p. 77.

42. Montshire Museum of Science, "Crime Lab Detectives Exhibit" .

43. UNESCO, *Temporary and Travelling Exhibitions* (Paris: United Nations Educational, Scientific and Cultural Organization, 1963), p. 9.

44. Northeast Louisiana Children's Museum, "The Kids' Café" <www.nelcm.org/perm.htm>.

45. UNESCO, p. 9.

46. Otter Tail County Historical Society, "To Your Health: Otter Tail County's Public Hospitals" <www.otchs.org/index.html>.

47. UNESCO, p. 10.

48. Red Hill Studio and the Science Museum of Minnesota, "Playing with Time" <www.playingwithtime.org/>.

49. Oregon Museum of Science and Industry, "Amazing Feats of Aging" <www.omsi.edu/visit/life/aging/index.cfm>.

50. San Francisco State University, "Exhibits Policy," *Library Administrative Manual* (San Francisco, CA: J. Paul Leonard Library, 1998) <www.library.sfsu.edu/general/lam/lam3.10.html#nature>.

3. Learning Theory

1. George E. Hein, *Learning in the Museum* (New York: Routledge, 1998).

2. Paul J. Francis and Aidan P. Byrne, "The Use of Role-Playing Exercises in Teaching Undergraduate Astronomy and Physics," *Electronic Publications of the Astronomical Society of Australia*, 16 (2): p. 206, 1999. Available from www.atnf.csiro.au/pasa/16_2/francis/paper/ (11 May 2004).

3. Hein, p. 7.

4. "A Brief Overview of Progressive Education," John Dewey Project on Progressive Education, College of Education and Social Services, The University of Vermont (30 January 2002) <http://www.uvm.edu/~dewey/articles/proged.html>.

5. Hein, p. 136.

6. Hein, p. 143.

7. Hein, p. 144.

8. Hein, p. 2.

9. "When Kids Show Up Hungry," *NEA Today* 18, no. 8 (May 2000): p. 39.

10. Rochel Gelman and Renée Baillargeon, "A Review of Some Piagetian Concepts," In John H. Flavell and Ellen M. Markman (eds.), *Handbook of Child Psychology: Vol. 3. Cognitive Development (4th ed.)* (New York: John Wiley, 1983). *See also* William G. Huitt and John H. Hummel, "Piaget's Theory of Cognitive Development, *Educational Psychology Interactive.* (Valdosta, GA: Valdosta State University, 2003) <http://chiron.valdosta.edu/whuitt/col/cogsys/piaget.html>.

11. David A. Kolb, *Experiential Learning: Experience as the Source of Learning and Development* (Englewood Cliffs, NJ: Prentice-Hall, 1983).

12. Barrie Brennan, "Adults as learners in museum visitor studies," Paper Presented at *Power and Empowerment*, Museums Australia Annual Conference, Sydney (1996) <http://amol.org.au/evrsig/lib_papers/brennan96.pdf> (10 May 2004).

13. Philip C. Candy, *Self-direction for lifelong learning: A Comprehensive Guide to Theory and Practice* (San Francisco: Jossey-Bass, 1991).

14. Hein.

15. Minda Borun, Ann Cleghorn, and Caren Garfield, "Family Learning in Museums: A Bibliographic Review," *Curator*, 38 no. 4 (1995): pp. 262–270.

16. Lynn D. Dierking, and John H. Falk, "Family Behavior and Learning in Informal Science Settings: A Review of the Research," *Science Education*, 78, no. 1 (1994): pp. 57–72.

17. Hope J. Leichter, K. Hensel, and E. Larsen, "Families and Museums: Issues and Perspectives," *Marriage and Family Review*, 13 no. 4 (1989): pp. 15–50.

18. Jeremy Roschelle, "Learning in Interactive Environments: Prior Knowledge and New Experience," *Public Institutions for Personal Learning: Establishing a Research Agenda* (American Association of Museums, 1995) www.exploratorium.edu/IFI/resources/museumeducation/priorknowledge.html.

19. Jane Reynolds, "Older Adults and Family Learning," *Adults Learning*, 8, no. 7 (1997): pp. 182–183.

20. Reynolds.

21. Hein, p. 150.

4. Status of Exhibits in Libraries

1. ALA, description of *Creating a Winning Online Exhibition: A Guide for Libraries, Archives, and Museums* by Martin R. Kalfatovic <www.alastore.ala.org/>.

2. American Library Association, "Policy 53.1.8," *Policy Manual* (ALA, 1991) <www.ala.org/ala/ourassociation/governingdocs/policy-manual/intellectual.htm>.

3. American Library Association Council, "Exhibit Spaces and Bulletin Boards: An Interpretation of the Library Bill of Rights" (American Library Association, 2004) <http://www.ala.org/>.

4. ALA Council, "Exhibit Spaces."

5. *Competencies for Librarians Serving Children in Public Libraries*, Rev. Ed. (1999). <www.ala.org/ala/alsc/alscresources/forlibrarians/professionaldev/competencies.htm>.

6. *Competencies for Librarians Serving Young Adults* (2003) <http://www.ala.org/ala/yalsa/professsionaldev/yacompetencies/competencies.htm>.

7. *Professional Competencies for Reference and User Services Librarians* (2003) <www.ala.org/ala/rusa/rusaprotools/referenceguide/professional.htm>.

8. *ALA/AASL Standards for Initial Program for School Library Media Specialist Preparation* (2003) <www.ala.org/ala/aasl/aasleducation/schoollibrarymed/ala-aasl_slms2003.pdf>.

9. *Competencies for Reference and User Services Librarians.*

10. *Competencies for Librarians Serving Children.*

11. *Competencies for Librarians Serving Young Adults.*

12. *ALA/AASL Standards*, p. 23.

13. Smithsonian Center for Education and Museum Studies, "ICOM Curricula Guidelines for Museum Professional Development" (2000) <http://museumstudies.si.edu/ICOM-ICTOP/comp.htm>.

14. Paul J. Francis and Aidan P. Byrne, "The Use of Role-Playing Exercises in Teaching Undergraduate Astronomy and Physics," *Electronic Publications of the Astronomical Society of Australia*, 16, no. 2 (1999): p. 206 <www.atnf.csiro.au/pasa/16_2/francis/paper/> (11 May 2004).

15. University of Texas, *TILT* (Texas Information Literacy Tutorial) <http://tilt.lib.utsystem.edu/>.

16. *The Big 6: Information Literacy for the Information Age.* <www.big6.com>

17. Mike Eisenberg, "Introducing the Super3: Working with the Very Youngest" <www.big6.com/showarticle.php?id=109>.

18. Jamieson McKenzie, "BeforeNet and Afternet." *Multimedia Schools*, 2, no. 3 (May-June, 1995): 6–8. See also Jamie McKenzie, "Making Web Meaning," *Educational Leadership* 54, no. 3 (November 1996): pp. 30–32.

6. The Comprehensive Exhibit Process

1. Susan Brazer and Andrea Wyman, "Display Cases for Academic Libraries: Ten Tips for Display Case Persons," *College & Research Libraries News* 62, no. 9 (2001): 904-908.

2. Kate Coplan, *Effective Library Exhibits: How to Prepare and Promote Good Displays, 2nd Edition* (Dobbs Ferry, NY: Oceana Publications, 1974), p. 7.

3. "Fertilize Your Mind," *Library Journal* 108, no. 17 (1983): 1832.

4. Mark Schaeffer, *Library Displays Handbook* (New York: H. W. Wilson, 1991), p. 3.

5. Brazer and Wyman.

6. Barry Lord and Gail Dexter Lord (ed.), *The Manual of Museum Exhibitions* (Walnut Creek, CA: Altamira Press, 2002), pp. 48–49.

7. Beverly Serrell, *Exhibit Labels: An Interpretive Approach* (Walnut Creek, CA: Altamira Press, 1996), p. 41.

8. Serrell, p. 137.

9. Serrell, p. 41, p. 138.

10. Serrell, p. 1.

11. Serrell.

12. Bob Raiselis, *What Makes a Good Interactive Exhibit?* (Montshire Museum of Science) <www.montshire.net/stacks/exhibits/goodexhibits.html> (25 September 2003).

13. Raiselis.

14. Raiselis.

15. Raiselis.

16. Serrell, p. 46.

17. Lord and Lord, p. 116.

18. Anne C. Tedeschi, *Book Displays: A Library Exhibits Handbook* (Fort Atkinson, WI: Highsmith Press, 1997), p. 29.

19. Lord and Lord, p. 116.

20. Tedeschi, p. 30.

21. Lord and Lord, p. 119.

22. Tedeschi, p. 29.

23. Mary Todd Glaser, "Protecting Paper and Book Collections During Exhibition," *Preservation of Library and Archival Materials: A Manual* (Section 2, Leaflet 5) <www.nedcc.org/plam3/tleaf25.htm> (24 January 2005).

24. Cynthia A. Char, *Evaluation of the "Science in the Stacks": A Museum-Library Collaboration to Create Traveling Science Exhibits for Libraries* (A report prepared for the Montshire Museum of Science) (Char Associates, February 2002), p. 22. <www.montshire.net/stacks/final_evaluation.html> (25 September 2003).

25. Andrew Dutka, Sherman Hayes, and Jerry Parnell, "The Surprise Part of a Librarian's Life:

Exhibition Design and Preparation Course," *College & Research Libraries News* 63, no. 1 (2002): pp. 19–22.

26. Trudy Ralston and Eric Foster, *How To Display It: A Practical Guide to Professional Merchandise Display,* (New York: Art Direction Book Company, 1984), p. 21.

27. Lothar P. Witteborg, *Good Show!: A Practical Guide for Temporary Exhibitions,* (Washington, DC: Smithsonian Institution Traveling Exhibition Service, 1981), p. 9.

28. Schaeffer, pp. 8–9.

29. Schaeffer, p. 12.

30. Schaeffer, p. 14.

31. Schaeffer, pp. 15–19.

32. Arminta Neal, *Help for the Small Museum: Handbook of Exhibit Ideas and Methods, second edition,* (Boulder, CO: Pruett, 1987), p. 66.

33. Mona Garvey, *Library Displays: Their Purpose, Construction, and Use,* (New York: The H. W. Wilson, 1969) p. 31.

34. Witteborg, p. 9.

35. Coplan, p. 4, p. 7.

36. "Frequently Asked Questions" (American Association of State and Local History, 2003). <www.aaslh.org/faqs.htm> (22 January 2004).

37. Lord and Lord, p. 132.

38. Tedeschi, p. 21.

39. Lord and Lord, p. 131.

40. Char, p. 22.

41. Lisa A. Wolfe, *Library Public Relations, Promotions, and Communications,* (New York: Neal-Schuman, 1997), p. 151.

42. Wolfe, p. 95.

43. Wolfe, p. 95.

44. Serrell.

45. Serrell, p. 25.

46. Serrell, p. 89.

47. Serrell.

48. *Smithsonian Guidelines for Accessible Exhibition Design* (Washington, DC: Smithsonian Institution Press, 1996). <www.si.edu/opa/accessibility/exdesign/> (27 January 2004).

49. *Smithsonian Guidelines for Accessible Exhibition Design.*

50. Serrell, p. 84.

51. Serrell, p. 98.

52. Serrell, p. 86.

53. Serrell, pp. 105–106.

54. Serrell, p. 127.

55. *Smithsonian Guidelines for Accessible Exhibition Design.*

56. *Smithsonian Guidelines for Accessible Exhibition Design.*

57. *Smithsonian Guidelines for Accessible Exhibition Design.*

58. Witteborg, p. 117.

59. Inverness Research Associates, "Annotated Question List for Visitors Using Exhibit Prototypes," unpublished document, TEAMS 2 project, Montshire Museum of Science, Norwich, VT, 2001.

60. *Smithsonian Guidelines for Accessible Exhibition Design.*

61. *Smithsonian Guidelines for Accessible Exhibition Design.*

62. Wolfe, p. 162.

63. Wolfe, p. 80.

64. Wolfe, p. 90.

65. Glaser.

66. Wolfe, p. 95.

67. Tedeschi, p. 39.

68. "Borrowing and Lending Books for Exhibition" (Association for Library Service to Children National Planning of Special Collections Committee, 2002). <www.ala.org/ala/alsc/alscresources/forlibrarians/borrowing/borrowforms/forms.htm> (26 January 2005).

69. Joan Waltermire, personal communication, 2004.

70. Lord and Lord, p. 52.

71. Serrell, p. 224.

72. Neal, p. 171.

73. Wolfe, pp. 190–192.

8. Hands-on Exhibits

1. John Veverka, "Tips and concepts for planning truly 'interpretive' exhibits" <www.geographie.uni-freiburg.de/ipg/forschung/ap6/interpret-europe/Downloads/publications/exhibits.pdf> (6 February 2005).

2. Bob Raiselis, *What Makes a Good Interactive Exhibit?* <www.montshire.net/stacks/exhibits/goodexhibits.html> (25 September 2003).

3. Raiselis.

4. Beverly Serrell, *Exhibit Labels: An Interpretive Approach* (Walnut Creek, CA: Altamira Press, 1996), p. 170.

5. Serrell, p. 169.

6. Serrell, p. 169.

7. Inverness Research Associates, "Annotated Question List for Visitors Using Exhibit Prototypes," unpublished document, TEAMS 2 project, Montshire Museum of Science, Norwich, VT, 2001.

9. The Exhibit Program

1. Susan Brazer and Andrea Wyman, "Display Cases for Academic Libraries: Ten Tips for

Display Case Persons," *College & Research Libraries News* 62, no. 9 (2001): 904-908.

2. Brazer and Wyman.

3. "Exhibit Spaces and Bulletin Boards," (American Library Association, 2004). <www.ala.org/ala/oif/statementspols/statementsif/interpretations/exhibitspaces.htm> (2 February 2005).

4. Anne C. Tedeschi, *Book Displays: A Library Exhibits Handbook* (Fort Atkinson, WI: Highsmith Press, 1997), p. 29.

5. Brazer and Wyman.

6. "Accessible Practices: Access Advisors," (Association of Science-Technology Centers). <www.astc.org/resource/access/advdisab.htm> (27 January 2004).

7. "Accessible Practices: Access Advisors."

8. Gloria Dosen, personal communication, January 21, 2005.

9. Brazer and Wyman.

10. Brazer and Wyman.

11. "Exhibit Spaces and Bulletin Boards."

10. Cataloging Library Exhibits and Exhibit Objects

1. Visual Resources Association, *Cataloguing Cultural Objects: A Guide to Describing Cultural Works and Their Images—Draft* (5 May 2004) <www.vraweb.org/CCOweb/>.

2. Learning Technology Standards Committee, *Learning Object Metadata (LOM)* <P1484.12 (12 June 2002) http://ltsc.ieee.org/wg12/>.

3. Wisconsin Technical College System, *What are Learning Objects?* (Wisconsin Online Resource Center) <www.wisc-online.com/Info/FIPSE%20-%20What%20is%20a%20Learning%20Object.htm>.

4. Wisconsin Technical College System <www.wisc-online.com/index.htm>/

5. Wisconsin Technical College System <www.wisc-online.com/index.htm>.

11. Examples of Exhibits in Libraries

1. Gloria Dosen, personal communication, January 21, 2005.

2. Dosen.

3. Ginger Rodriguez, "Forging Civic Pride in the Rust Belt: East Chicago's History Project," *American Libraries* 22, no. 11 (1991): pp. 1026–1028.

4. Rodriguez.

5. Dosen.

6. Rodriguez.

7. Rodriguez.

8. Rodriguez.

9. "Go Figure!" (American Library Association, 2004). <www.ala.org/ala/ppo/progresources/gofigure.htm> (30 January 2005).

10. "Go Figure!"

11. Rick Margolis, "Oh, the Joys of Math," *School Library Journal* 46, no. 7 (2000): p. 22.

12. Margolis.

13. Randi Korn and Johanna Jones, "*Go Figure!* Evaluating a Math Exhibition," *ASTC Dimensions* March/April 2001. <www.astc.org/pubs/dimensions/2001/mar-apr/go_figure.htm> (25 February 2004).

14. Korn and Jones.

15. Korn and Jones.

16. Korn and Jones.

17. Korn and Jones.

18. Korn and Jones.

19. "Go Figure!"

20. Korn and Jones.

21. "Go Figure!"

22. Helma Hawkins and Margaret Clark, "'Go Figure' Traveling Library Exhibition Application," (Kansas City, MO: Kansas City Public Library, 1999).

23. Margaret Clark, "Final Report—Go Figure! Exhibit," (Kansas City, MO: Kansas City Public Library, 2003).

24. Clark.

25. Clark.

26. Clark.

27. Clark.

28. Clark.

29. Clark.

30. "Original IMLS Project Proposal," <www.montshire.org/stacks/proposal.html> (12 September 2003).

31. "National Leadership Grants for Library-Museum Collaborations," <www.imls.gov/grants/l-m/l-m_lead.asp> (16 September 2003).

32. "Science in the Stacks," <www.montshire.net/stacks/> (31 January 2005).

33. Cynthia A. Char, *Evaluation of the "Science in the Stacks": A Museum-Library Collaboration to Create Traveling Science Exhibits for Libraries,* (Norwich, VT: Montshire Museum of Science, 2002), p. 5. <www.montshire.net/stacks/final_evaluation.html> (25 September 2003).

34. Char, p. 5.

35. Char, p. 12.

36. "Original IMLS Project Proposal."

37. "Science in the Stacks."

38. Char, p. 10.
39. Char, p. 10.
40. Char, p. 10.
41. Char, p. 9.
42. Char, p. 9.
43. Char, p. 9.
44. Char, p. 13.
45. Char, p. 13.
46. Char, p. 13.
47. Char, p. 22.

48. Char, pp. 11–12, 18.
49. Char, p. 17.
50. Char, p. 14.
51. Char, p. 11.
52. Char, p. 15.
53. Char, p. 15.
54. Char, p. 17.
55. Char, p. 19.
56. Char, p. 20.

Bibliography

This bibliography is offered for readers who would like a few supplementary readings in areas covered in this book.

Learning

Barra, Dianna. *What Learning Type Is Your Child? Keys to Unlocking Your Child's Potential.* Dewey, AZ: Idea Designs, 2006.

Driscoll, Marcy P. *Psychology of Learning for Instruction,* 3rd ed. Upper Saddle River, NJ: Allyn & Bacon, 2004.

Maynard, Ashley and Mary I. Martini. *Learning in Cultural Context: Family, Peers, and School.* New York: Kluwer Academic, 2005.

Mazur, James E. *Learning and Behavior,* 6th ed. Upper Saddle River, NJ: Prentice Hall, 2005.

Learning and Exhibits

Hein, George E. *Learning in Museums.* New York: Routledge, 1998.

Larrabee, Eric (ed.). *Museums and Education.* Washington, D.C.: Smithsonian Institution Press, 1968.

Moffatt, Hazal, and Vicky Woollard (eds.). *Museum Gallery Education: A Manual of Good Practice.* Lanham, MD: Rowman & Littlefield, 2000.

Sachatello-Sawyer, Bonnie, Robert A. Fellenz, Hanly Burton, Laura Gittings-Carlson, Janet Lewis-Mahony and Walter Woolbaugh. *Adult Museum Programs: Designing Meaningful Experiences.* Walnut Creek, CA: AltaMira Press, 2002.

Cataloguing Exhibit Objects

Blackaby, James R., Patricia Greeno, The Nomenclature Committee. *The Revised Nomenclature for Museum Cataloging: A Revised and Expanded Version of Robert G. Chenhall's System for Classifying Man-Made Objects.* Walnut Creek, CA: Altamira Press, 1995.

Stuckert, Caroline M. *Cataloging from Scratch: A Manual for Cataloging Undocumented Collections in Small Museums,* 2nd ed. Havertown, PA: MACC Associates, 1991.

Swidler, Nina, Daniel B. Reibel, Kurt Dongoske, Roger Anyon, and Alan Downer. *Registration Methods for the Small Museum*, 3rd ed. Walnut Creek, CA: Altamira Press, 1997.

Exhibit Techniques

Balloffet, Nelly, and Jenny Hille. *Preservation and Conservation for Libraries and Archives*. Chicago: American Library Association, 2004.
Daifuku, Hiroshi, et al. *Temporary and Travelling Exhibitions* (Paris: UNESCO, 1963).
McAlpine, Alistair, and Cathy Giangrande. *Collecting and Display*. London: Conran Octopus, 1998.
Neal, Arminta. *Help for the Small Museum: Handbook of Exhibit Ideas and Methods*. Boulder, CO: Pruett, 1987.
Serrell, Beverly. *Exhibit Labels: An Interpretive Approach*. Walnut Creek, CA: AltaMira, 1996.
Witteborg, Lothar P., *Good Show!: A Practical Guide for Temporary Exhibitions*, Washington, D.C.: Smithsonian Institution Press, 1990.

Exhibits

Dean, David K. *Museum Exhibition*. New York: Routledge, 1996.
Luckhurst, Kenneth W. *The Story of Exhibitions* (New York: Studio Publications, 1951).
Walford, Cornelius. *Fairs, Past & Present: A Chapter in the History of Commerce* (New York: Augustus M. Kelley, 1968 reprint of 1883).

Museum Work

Burcaw, Ellis G. *Introduction to Museum Work*. Walnut Creek, CA: AltaMira , 1997.
Carbonell, Bettina Messias (ed.). *Museum Studies in Context: An Anthology*. Oxford: Blackwell Publishing, 2003.
Edson, Gary, and David K. Dean. *Handbook for Museums*. New York: Routledge, 1997.
Hooper-Greenhill, Eilean (ed.). *Museum, Media, Message*. New York: Routledge, 1999.
Nichols, Susan K. (ed.). *Organizing Your Museum: The Essentials*. Washington, D.C.: American Association of Museums, 1989.

Index

Bold italics indicate an exhibit planning form, aid, or checklist